CAREERS
Working with Animals

A Publication of
THE HUMANE SOCIETY OF THE UNITED STATES

Patrick B. Parkes, Contributing Editor
Vice-President, HSUS

CAREERS
Working with Animals

An Introduction to Occupational Opportunities
in Animal Welfare, Conservation,
Environmental Protection and Allied Professions

By

Guy R. Hodge
Director, Research and Data
The Humane Society of the United States

ACROPOLIS BOOKS Ltd.
Washington D.C. 20009

The Humane Society of the United States
Washington, D.C. 20037

Reprinted June 1980

© 1979 by The Humane Society of the United States

ACROPOLIS BOOKS LTD.
Colortone Building, 2400 17th St., N.W., Washington, D.C. 20009

Printed in the United States of America by
COLORTONE PRESS Creative Graphics, Inc.
Washington, D.C. 20009

Library of Congress Cataloging in Publication Data
Main entry under title:

CAREERS: WORKING WITH ANIMALS

L.C. No. 78-51883
ISBN: 0-87491-259-8

ACKNOWLEDGEMENT

The author wishes to express his gratitude to those individuals, organizations, and government agencies whose assistance was invaluable in the preparation of this career guidance manual. A special note of acknowledgement is owed to Dr. F. Barbara Orlans of the National Institute of Health, Dr. George B. Rabb of the Brookfield Zoo, the United States Department of the Interior, the United States Department of Labor, and The American Veterinary Medical Association.

I also want to express my appreciation for the invaluable guidance and assistance provided by my co-workers on the staff of The Humane Society of the United States, in particular:

Charles F. Herrmann . . . . Book Designer
Ellen S. Arneson . . . . Researcher & Proofreader
R. Dale Hylton . . . . Consultant
John J. Dommers . . . . Consultant
Sherra B. McLeod . . . . Researcher & Proofreader
Patrice Mohr . . . . Researcher & Typist
Mary Carol Malcolm . . . . Typist

CAREERS
Working with Animals

TABLE OF CONTENTS

FOREWORD

During the past two decades occupational opportunities have dramatically expanded in the fields of animal welfare and environmental protection and conservation. Increased awareness and concern for the welfare of animals and protection of the environment has opened the door to a new era in animal protection and conservation programs. Many children dream about turning their love of animals into a full-time profession. Today that vision is no longer an unachievable aspiration. There are jobs within animal welfare, environmental protection, and conservation agencies for persons with widely varying skills, interests, and temperaments.

More persons than ever before are seeking occupations which will bring them into contact with wildlife or domestic animals. *Careers: Working With Animals* has been specifically developed to provide guidance to that person who is intent upon the pursuit of a career as a conservationist or animal welfare worker. This publication explores a variety of professions requiring diverse educational backgrounds and skills, and analyzes the prospects for young professionals in selected major career fields.

For concerned individuals there are few more exciting careers than those which afford an opportunity to improve the quality of life for other creatures. Conservation and animal welfare professions are truly careers with their own intrinsic rewards.

On behalf of The Humane Society of the United States I wish you success and fulfillment in the pursuit of a career working with animals.

John A. Hoyt
President
The Humane Society of the United States

It is the first of all problems for individuals to find out what kind of work they are to do in this universe . . . .

. . . . Carlyle

1
THE JOB MARKET: AN INTRODUCTION AND ANALYSIS

Career opportunities involving work with animals are commonly stereotyped as comprising a narrow field of employment which is confined to jobs in zoos, veterinary hospitals and shelters. In reality, there exists a complex job market offering a diversity of positions within the basic career fields of animal welfare, pet sales and service, veterinary medicine, environmental protection, animal science, conservation, wildlife management, zoological park management, and biological science. Within each of these specialities there are numerous occupational options featuring varied opportunities for self-fulfillment, divergent work situations, differing degrees of independence and responsibility, and distinctly varied rates of financial compensation.

Not every job in animal welfare or allied professions holds the promise of direct contact with animals. Persons assigned administrative, clerical, or related duties may have limited opportunity for interaction with animals. Nor does every occupation guarantee continuing stimulation and challenge. Yet, there is the compensating reward of contributing meaningfully to the welfare and protection of animals.

Careers in animal welfare and allied professions involve all manner of working conditions and job settings from the business office of an administrative executive to the tent home of the field biologist who resides on a remote island. Unconventional work schedules are encountered by many persons who are employed working with animals.

Employers of persons who work in animal welfare and allied professions include charitable organizations, educational institutions, commercial businesses, associations, foundations, and municipal, state and federal agencies.

An estimated 200,000 persons are currently employed in jobs with humane societies, zoological parks, veterinary hospitals, nature centers, pet stores, kennels, wildlife refuges, and other institutions directly involved with the welfare, protection, and husbandry of animals. Allied occupations in environmental protection, conservation, and biological science account for approximately 1,700,000 additional workers.

During the past nineteen years there has been a dramatic growth in the number of employment positions in animal welfare and allied professions. For example, during the previous decade, the staff of the U.S. Fish and Wildlife Service expanded by forty-seven percent. During the same period, The Humane Society of the United States experienced a phenomenal fourfold growth in the size of its staff. However, these statistics are not fully representative of the current employment situation. At most levels of employment there is intensive competition for available jobs. Often, positions are quickly filled without ever being advertised or announced. This situation exists because the number of qualified persons entering the job market is expanding at a significantly more rapid pace than job openings arise. Thus, despite the growth in the size of the labor force, there are more job seekers than are needed to fill new positions and vacancies created through promotions, retirements, and resignations.

To successfully enter the job market requires preparation. No matter the field or specialty, prospective workers must build a solid academic foundation while acquiring the basic skills and early experience which will qualify them for employment in careers working with animals. The Bureau of Labor Statistics of the United States Department of Labor estimates that one-quarter of all job openings require a college degree. In 1985, according to the Department of Labor, an estimated one of every five workers will possess a college diploma. A wider choice of career options await college graduates than persons who terminate their educations following high school, technical

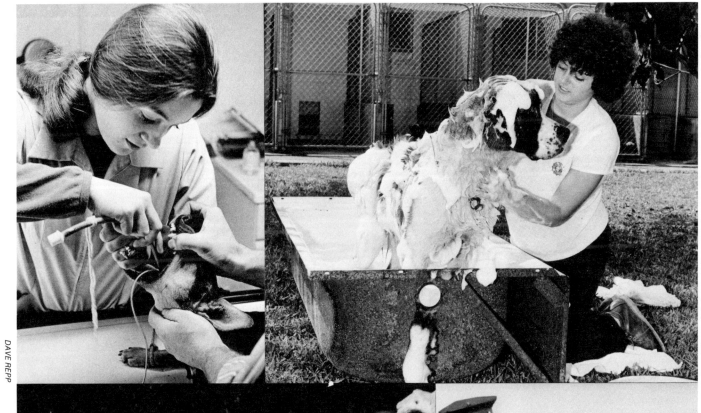

Occupational Specialties

Anatomy: A field of study relating to the form and structure of animal bodies.

Animal Science: A field of study, also known as animal husbandry, relating to the production of food animals especially pertaining to their breeding, feeding, and health.

Anthropology: A field of study relating to the evolution of life in human history including the correlation between primate behavior and human behavior as exemplified by recent attempts to teach human language to chimpanzees and gorillas.

Apiculture: An activity relating to the keeping of bees especially on a large scale basis.

Aquatic Biology: A division of biological science relating to the study of interactions of plants and animals living in water. Aquatic biologists are concerned with protecting and maintaining the balance of the aquatic environment.

Bacteriology: A field of study relating to bacteria including the relationship of bacteria to animals.

Biochemistry: A division of biological science which applies the theories and principles of chemistry to the study of life forms — both plants and animals. Biochemists are concerned with the chemical substances which influence the functions and processes of living organisms. They may study the effects of chemicals upon reproduction, growth, development, heredity, nourishment, metabolism, digestion, and responses to environmental changes.

Biology: A field of study relating to living organisms, their relationships and life functions. Biologists may study the evolutionary development, structure, and behavior of living organisms.

Biological Systematics: A division of biological science relating to living organisms, their relationships, life processes, and evolutionary history. Of particular concern is the impact of human activity upon ecological systems.

Biophysics: A division of biological science which applies the theories and principles of physics to the study of the living cells and organisms and their response to physical forces such as heat, light, and radiation.

Botany: The study of plants including algae, fungi, trees, and flowers. Botany is applied to the analysis of environmental pollution and management of wildlife habitat. Botanists may be concerned with the conservation and yield of wildlife foods, or may participate in the management of parks and wilderness areas.

Cytology: A branch of anatomy relating to the study of cell structure.

Dendrology: The study of trees including their relationship to animals.

Ecology: A field of study relating to the interrelationships of living organisms — plants and animals — with each other and their interaction with the physical environment.

Embryology: A field of study relating to the development of organisms from fertilization of the egg until growth of the mature animal.

Entomology: A division of zoology relating to the study of insects including their identification, classification, physiology, behavior, evolution, development, and natural history. Entomologists may be concerned with the relationship between insects and other forms of animal life especially with regard to the role of insects in disease transmission and damage to wildlife foods.

Environmental Engineering: A field of study which applies the principles, practices, and methods of engineering to environmental problems such as the degradation of natural resources.

Epidemiology: A field of study relating to the control of diseases including those affecting animals.

Ethology: A field of study relating to animal behavior.

Forestry: A field of study, also known as forest science, relating to the study of forest communities including animal life which inhabits forest land.

Genetics: A field of study which explores the origins, transmission, and development of hereditary characteristics with emphasis upon plants and animal breeds of economic importance, especially livestock and poultry.

Geography: A field of study concerned with the earth and its life forms including the distribution of animal organisms.

Geology: A field of study relating to the earth's history, composition, and process especially as it pertains to surface features and structure. Geologists may be concerned with natural occurrences and features which influence animal habitat.

Herpetology: A branch of zoology relating to the study of reptiles and amphibians including their identification, classification, physiology, behavior, and natural history.

Histology: A branch of anatomy relating to the structure of tissues and organs.

Horticulture: A field of study relating to the development of new and improved strains of fruits, nuts, ornamental plants, and other flora which may serve as food or shelter for wildlife.

Ichthyology: A branch of zoology relating to the study of fish including their identification, classification, physiology, behavior, and natural history.

Immunology: A field of study relating to the phenomena and causes of immunity including the prevention of diseases in animals.

Mammalogy: A branch of zoology relating to the study of mammals including their identification, classification, physiology, behavior, and natural history.

Meteorology: A field of study concerned with the phenomena of an atmosphere and application of scientific knowledge to the analysis, prediction and control of atmospheric conditions including those which affect wild-life and wildlife habitat. Meteorologists may be concerned with forest fire control.

Microbiology: A field of study relating to microscopic plants and animals including algae, bacteria, fungi, protozoa, and viruses. Microbiologists may be concerned with the control of microscopic organisms affecting the food, water, environment, or health of animals.

Morphology: A division of biological science relating to the form and structure of animals and plants.

Mycology: A division of botany primarily relating to the beneficial and harmful characteristics of fungi including their medical application as antibiotics and their use as edible wild foods.

Nematology: A field of study relating to nematodes which is an animal grouping including hookworms and round-worms. Nematologists may investigate the vulnerability of animals (especially sheep, dogs, and cats) to infection by nematodes.

Nutrition: A field of study which examines the processes through which food is utilized by living organisms. Nutritionists study the kinds and quantities of food elements and the composition of ingredients in animal diets, especially with regard to farm and zoo animals.

Oceanography: A field of study relating to oceans including their contents, movements, physical properties, characteristics, plant life, and animal life.

Oology: A branch of zoology relating to the study of eggs, especially the coloration and shape of birds' eggs.

Ornithology: A branch of zoology relating to the study of birds including their identification, classification, physiology, behavior, and natural history.

Paleontology: A field of study relating to the fossilized remains of animals, plants, and protista.

Parasitology: A field of study relating to the life processes of parasites, the effects of parasites upon host organisms, and the reaction of host organisms to the presence of parasites.

Pharmacology: A field of study relating to the actions of drugs and chemicals on living organisms. Pharmacologists may study the possible harmful effects of chemical substances in the environment and may evaluate or develop veterinary drugs used in the medical treatment of animal maladies.

Photobiology: A field of study relating to the effects of light upon living organisms including animals. Photo-biologists may investigate the effects of light upon the biological rhythm of animals, the photosensitivity of animals to environmental pollution, or photoallergic reactions in animals.

Physiology: A field of study relating to the function of animal organs, tissues, and cells. Physiologists may study the effects of life processes as they relate to environmental factors.

Plant Pathology: A field of study relating to the causes, development, prevention, and control of plant diseases including those which affect wildlife foods and wildlife habitat.

Primatology: A branch of zoology relating to the study of primates including their identification, classification, physiology, behavior, and natural history.

Protozoology: A field of study relating to one-celled animals and certain plants. Protozoologists are concerned with the detection, prevention, and control of diseases, such as animal toxoplasmosis, caused by protozoa.

Psychology: A field of study relating to the effects of environment on human and animal behavior, human attitudes toward animals, and the natural behavior of animals.

Range Science: A field of study relating to the effects of interaction between plants, soils, animals, and climate conditions in biological communities known as rangelands.

Soil Science: A field of study relating to the conservation and management of soil including the protection of watersheds.

Taxonomy: A field of study relating to the description, classification, and titling of living organisms and investigation of processes which maintain or change them.

Toxicology: A field of study relating to the adverse effects of chemicals, including drugs, on living systems. Toxicologists may be concerned with incidents of poisoning in animals.

Urban Planning: A field of study relating to the design and development of urban communities including park planning.

Vertebrate Paleonotology: A branch of paleonotology concerned with the fossilized remains of mammals, reptiles, birds, fish, and amphibians.

Veterinary Pathology: A branch of veterinary medicine concerned with the causes, development, and effects of diseases which affect animals and the application of scientific knowledge to the diagnosis and treatment of diseases in animal organisms.

Veterinary Science: A field of study, also known as veterinary medicine, relating to the prevention and treatment of diseases and injuries to animals.

Virology: A field of study relating to viruses and their effects upon living organisms including animals.

Wildlife Biology: A field of study, also known as wildlife science, relating to the study of wild animals including their physiology, behavior, natural history, and habitat.

Zoology: A field of study relating to animal life including their origins, classification, identification, behavior, life processes, environmental influences, and natural history.

school, or community college. Several occupations require postgraduate study or internship.

Generally, those jobs which offer the greatest stimulation and reward also demand the highest degree of training and skill. Thus, prospective animal welfare workers must be willing to work toward their job objectives. Proper credentials and qualifications are an increasingly important factor in the hiring of employees.

Job opportunities are not necessarily limited to those persons possessing the backgrounds and qualifications specified by employers. Job requirements may be more flexible than indicated in announcements of position openings. Hiring decisions are not made exclusively according to applicants' years of education or previous work experience. Skills and expertise developed through independent study or self-training are not unmarketable. However, there are limits to the value of special talents, aptitudes, commitment, and personal characteristics as a substitute for academic training and work experience.

Financial compensation varies widely within the animal welfare profession and allied career fields. In general, the greater the degree of skill and expertise required of workers the greater will be their earnings. Within an individual profession, a person's rate of financial compensation will be based upon such considerations as geographic location, work experience, education, training, reputation, and professional accomplishments.

In addition to the jobs which are profiled in this book there are unconventional routes to jobs in animal welfare, conservation, and allied professions. Accountants, computer technicians, architects, printers, carpenters and other specialists are also employed by those institutions responsible for the protection and conservation of animals.

The basic fields of specialization involving work with animals include:

Animal Welfare: Institutions specializing in this field are concerned with the prevention and alleviation of animal suffering. Animal welfare involves programs of cruelty investigation, humane education, animal rescue and animal control. The principal institutions working in this field are community humane societies and municipal animal control agencies.

Zoological Park Management: Zoos are, by definition, facilities which exhibit collections of living animals. The activities of zoos include species propagation, public education, and zoological research. The principal institutions working in this field are municipal parks and recreation departments and commercial amusement businesses.

Conservation: This field is concerned with the planned protection of flora and fauna to prevent their exploitation, destruction, or neglect. Conservation involves programs of habitat preservation, species propagation, and field research. The principal institutions working in this field include state and national non-profit organizations chartered for the protection or study of wild animals.

Wildlife Management: This field is concerned with the management of wildlife as a natural resource. Wildlife management is concerned with the planned use and exploitation of wild animals in a manner which minimizes waste and assures that wildlife populations are not depleted. Wildlife management programs involve law enforcement, game management, and field research. The principal institutions working in this field are the state and federal natural resources departments of government agencies.

Veterinary Medicine: This field is concerned with the prevention and treatment of animal health problems. Veterinary medicine involves animal care and research. The principal institutions involved in this work are private veterinary hospitals.

Pet Sales and Service: This field includes the breeding, kenneling, and sales of pet animals and the supplying of pet accessories. Pet sales and service involves animal care, animal husbandry, product design, and salesmanship. The primary institutions in this work include pet stores and kennels.

Biological Science: This field includes interrelated scientific disciplines which are concerned with the study of living organisms. Programs involve research and teaching. The principal institutions working in this field include universities and biomedical laboratories.

Environmental Protection: This field is concerned with the planned protection of ecological communities including air, water, flora, fauna, and land. Programs include urban planning, pollution control, and habitat preservation. The principal institutions working in this field include state and national non-profit organizations and government environmental protection agencies.

Animal Science: This field is concerned with the product of domestic animals, especially livestock and poultry. Activities include animal breeding, animal husbandry, and salesmanship.

2
A HISTORICAL PROFILE OF THE ANIMAL WELFARE AND CONSERVATION MOVEMENTS

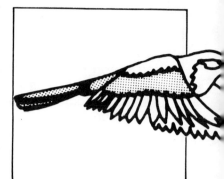

Career decisions can be drastically influenced by the programs and policies of the primary employers in individual career fields. Only through an understanding of the structure and history of animal protection and conservation agencies can a prospective employee determine if anticipated job opportunities are consistent with his interests and preferences. The job applicant's failure to investigate the program priorities of employers may lead a person to pursue a profession which will not offer personal job satisfaction. Similarly, misunderstandings as to the services and philosophies associated with a profession may cause a job applicant to dismiss consideration of a potentially rewarding career option.

This chapter will provide the reader with insight into the structure and focus of organizations which are concerned with animal protection and conservation.

A SHORT HISTORY OF THE ANIMAL WELFARE MOVEMENT

In 1641 the Puritans of the Massachusetts Bay Colony enacted the first statutory measure protecting domestic animals from mistreatment and overwork. Entitled "Liberties of Brute Creatures," the Puritan rules were not in the form of laws, but were a voluntary code of conduct. Two centuries were to pass before a structured animal welfare movement was established.

It is difficult to comprehend the abuses to which living creatures were subjected in 18th and 19th century America. Many citizens were indifferent to or unaware of the cruelties routinely inflicted upon animals. The most visible animal in the 1800's was the horse, the backbone of commerce and an important mode of transportation. Horse-drawn street-cars were regularly overloaded with passengers. Exhausted horses, unable to pull the cars, were frequently beaten to death on the streets and received not a murmur of sympathy from their passengers. In New York City an estimated 25,000 horses suffered from poor care, overwork, and abuse during a single year.

Working horses and other animals found a champion in Henry Bergh, a New York socialite and career diplomat. While on assignment in Russia, Bergh became alarmed at the mistreatment of animals. Vowing to help animals everywhere, Bergh left the diplomatic corps and resolved to dedicate his life to the prevention of cruelty to animals. On February 8, 1866 Bergh gave a moving public speech in which he resolved that "the blood red hand of cruelty shall no longer torture dumb animals with impunity." At that meeting in New York's Clinton Hall, the first animal welfare organization in the United States was established. It was named the American Society for the Prevention of Cruelty to Animals (ASPCA).

The first electric horse ambulance, circa 1910.

PENNSYLVANIA SPCA

Bergh enlisted the support of a small group of civic leaders, and within weeks he convinced the New York State Legislature to issue a statewide charter to the ASPCA. He also maneuvered a bill through the Legislature, the Animal Welfare Act of 1866, which provided "every person who shall, by his act or neglect, maliciously kill, maim, wound, injure, torture, or cruelly beat any horse, mule, cow, cattle, sheep, or other animal belonging to himself or another shall, upon conviction, be adjudged guilty of a misdemeanor." This Act, the first enforceable statute containing specific criminal penalties for animal abuse, was to be the forerunner of contemporary state animal welfare laws which even today remain remarkably similar in wording to Bergh's original draft.

On April 25, 1866, only six days after enactment of the Animal Welfare Act, a Brooklyn butcher was convicted in court and fined $10 for piling tied calves and sheep into a cart. In the first twelve months of operation Henry Bergh and the ASPCA were to

A contemporary horse ambulance.

prosecute 119 persons and obtain 66 convictions for the mistreatment of animals.

Henry Bergh originally envisioned the ASPCA as a national organization. However, realizing the Society's charter and jurisdiction were confined to New York state and faced with a shortage of funds, Bergh abandoned his plan for a national animal welfare program.

But Henry Bergh's efforts were to have a lasting impact on the American humane movement. Drawing on Bergh's experiences in New York, animal welfare organizations were independently established in Massachusetts, Pennsylvania, New Jersey, and California. By the time Bergh died in March 1888, there were 33 animal welfare agencies in the United States and his own ASPCA had 15 state branches employing 230 workers.

Despite its laudable beginnings, many obstacles remained before the American humane movement. Plagued by a perpetual shortage of funds and dominated by strong willed, aggressive moralists, humane societies were faced with internal disputes that led to the division and dissolution of several animal welfare agencies. In 1877 a national federation of animal welfare agencies was formed in an effort to bring unity and cohesiveness to animal welfare programs. In 1954 that federation itself was to experience a division which resulted in the formation of The Humane Society of the United States (HSUS).

The founders of The HSUS sought a means of attacking national animal welfare problems that were beyond the capabilities of local societies or state federations. Assuming the role of the national animal welfare agency originally envisioned by Bergh, The HSUS spearheaded campaigns that led to federal humane slaughter and laboratory animal welfare legislation.

While the animal welfare movement experienced

a rebirth during the 1950's, there has been no significant alteration in the relationship between humane organizations; community animal welfare agencies have necessarily remained separate from The Humane Society of the United States. Each group is individually chartered and governed by its own board of directors. As non-governmental, charitable organizations, animal welfare groups continue to be financed almost exclusively through contributions and bequests.

Today there are almost 2,000 local, state, and national animal welfare organizations in the United States. These groups are known by several generic names such as humane society, SPCA, or animal welfare league. Some agencies operate shelters and employ professional staff. Others operate out of private homes and continue to exist only because of the persistent efforts of dedicated volunteers.

Some societies are concerned primarily with the operation of shelters, others with cruelty investigations, and several concentrate on humane education programs. Although different in programs and structure these groups are bound by a common goal—the prevention of animal suffering.

As the American humane movement reflects upon its first century of service to animals we are still witness to many of the cruelties Henry Bergh labored to halt. Nevertheless, humane societies have come to be recognized as forceful, effective voices for the welfare of animals. The humane movement is heralding a new era for animal welfare aided by far-reaching new legislation such as the Marine Mammal Protection Act, substantially improved community support, and the enlistment of young professionals into animal welfare careers.

The animal shelter is the most visible element of humane society and animal control agency programs.

A SHORT HISTORY OF THE CONSERVATION MOVEMENT

The 17th Century is commonly regarded as the period during which natural history began to develop as a science. During that time naturalists first began to record, in detail, data on the size, numbers, coloration, and habitat of wild species. Coincidentally, the 17th Century also marked the beginning of the civilized world's assault upon nature.

Under the American system of democracy wildlife was considered to be the joint property of all citizens. Animals could be taken without restriction from state and federal governments which controlled wildlife usage. Wilderness was regarded as a hostile environment to be replaced with a landscape of spired towns or cultivated into agricultural crops.

To early Americans the abundance of woodland and wildlife seemed a limitless resource. This attitude, combined with a commercial demand for meat, fur, and feathers, stimulated the exploitation of wild animals. A chronic shortage of labor, capital, and machinery fostered the utilization of wildlife and land as a principal trading commodity.

Contemporary historian Susan L. Flader wrote that the attitudes and institutions which prompted environmental manipulation and degradation in 18th Century America were even more enthusiastic and reckless in their actions during the next 100 years. The United States was experiencing an industrial revolution. A premium was placed upon productivity. Policymakers were governed by the belief that rapid growth in material production was socially beneficial. It was thought that individual enterprise in pursuit of economic gain must necessarily be conducive to the public good.

During the 19th Century constant and indiscriminate hunting and trapping caused serious declines in wildlife populations. Two hundred years of ceaselessly slaughtering wildlife took a heavy toll. Once there were more than 60 million bison, but by 1880 less than 1,000 animals remained on the plains. The passenger pigeon was an awesomely abundant species with individual roosts numbering more than 100 million birds. Flocks in flight were reported to stretch more than 200 miles in length. The last wild passenger pigeon was shot in 1899 and the species became extinct in 1914. Also exploited to extinction were the Steller's sea cow, great auk, Labrador duck, Carolina parakeet, and several other species of wildlife. The beaver was spared from a similar fate by an arbitrary shift in fashion from men's beaver skin hats to silk headwear. As a group, the furbearers — beaver, otter, mink, marten, fisher, and muskrat — were subjected to one of the most concentrated, unyielding, and enduring attacks known to man.

Fortunately, an interest in nature and conservation was to persist and develop through the writings and paintings of men such as Henry Thoreau, John Burroughs, John Muir, and James Audubon. As individuals, these early naturalists were disturbed by the evidence of conflict between nature and civilization.

An increased concern for the environment was in evidence following the civil war. The first citizens' groups were organized and began to press for action. Citizen pressure was used to stimulate government fish culture and timber culture programs. But the very term "culture" (meaning cultivation or rearing) signifies that these efforts harmonized with the prevailing attitude. Early conservation programs emphasized production and replenishing of natural resources rather than discouraging the exploitation of wildlife or wilderness. Such programs enjoyed the enthusiastic support of industry because they did not pose any threat or hindrance to private development while promising economic benefit.

The late 19th Century was a golden age for citizen conservation organizations. In a single generation Americans were to witness the near demise of plume birds, shore birds, furbearers, and large terrestrial mammals. Provoked by the wholesale destruction of wildlife, citizens formed more than 400 community, regional, and national conservation-oriented organizations during the final three decades of the 19th Century. Included in this group were the Sierra Club (1892), American Ornithologists Union (1883), and the New York Zoological Society (1895) which claims the distinction of being the first organization in the United States to be specifically formed for the avowed purpose of conservation. Most noticeable in number among 19th Century wildlife organizations were hunting clubs.

The ceaseless slaughter of wildlife took a heavy toll during the 19th Century.

HISTORICAL PICTURE SERVICE

Hunters recognized the encroachment of civilization and unregulated slaughter of wildlife as a threat to their pastime and mobilized into local clubs which were dedicated to the propagation of wildlife and perpetuation of sport hunting.

Early conservation efforts were only a small element of a broad protest which was a product of the industrial revolution. Following the Civil War, demands for reform were perceived as a general protest against the concentration of power and wealth among a few private citizens and corporations. Yet, by 1880 it had become apparent that society could no longer afford to extoll a production-oriented approach toward wildlife. Citizens were intent upon protecting the remaining wild animals and woodlands from exploitation by market hunters, the millinery trade, and lumber interests. For the first time, the public indicated a willingness to circumscribe individual freedom and entrepreneurial activity through restrictive state laws. Critical support of conservation efforts was provided by the Congress which enacted the Lacey Act of 1900 prohibiting the interstate shipment of birds taken illegally for the market or millinery trade.

Nineteenth Century conservation organizations provided the impetus for reserving national forests, parks, and wildlife refuges. Conservation programs were to make significant strides during the presidency of Theodore Roosevelt. Although an ardent big game hunter, Roosevelt was also an advocate of a conservation policy which has been described as promoting ''fuller and wiser use of the nation's resources.'' Roosevelt was willing to establish public lands and preserve them as a part of the national heritage. In 1903 President Roosevelt established the first national wildlife refuge at Pelican Island on the east coast of Florida. The practice of retaining certain lands in public ownership for conservation purposes marked a significant departure from past policy.

At the turn of the century, advocates of the controlled exploitation of natural resources capitalized upon the pre-existing moral fervor for the protection of wildlife and preservation of wilderness. Between 1908 and 1940 public interest in wildlife was channeled into the establishment of state and federal wildlife agencies. The objective of government programs was to develop a rational management plan for the productive use of natural resources in manners consistent with the public interest.

By the early 1920's Aldo Leopold, a professional forester, had initiated a gradual transformation toward the concept of scientific resource management. Leopold applied forestry techniques and biological information into principles for managing game species — wild animals which are hunted

LEONARD LEE RUE III

Conservationists have been particularly concerned about furbearing animals such as the fisher which, as a group, have been intensively hunted and trapped.

and trapped for sport, food, or profit. The fundamental orientation of scientific game management did not markedly differ from earlier attitudes toward the utilization of wild animals. The emphasis of game management was upon the production of a harvestable crop of game animals. However, Leopold did apply a new concept in attempting to manipulate and propagate game species. The immediate objectives of early wildlife managers were to restore deer and turkey to huntable populations. Only incidentially were wildlife managers concerned with the protection of less commercially valuable species. In fact, wildlife management programs included provision for the elimination of predatory animals and undesirable species which were in competition with game animals.

Evolutionary and ecological theory began to blend in the 1930's. Leopold himself was to recognize a new concept — the existence of complex ecosystems. His later writings were to question the validity of wildlife management plans designed to provide a competitive advantage to those species deemed favorable by man.

Not all biologists and resource managers were to adopt Leopold's attitude of humility with regard to man's ability to understand and control natural systems. Wartime technological innovations were to reinforce an attitude of arrogance and optimism toward the management of natural resources. The development of DDT for the chemical control of insects and introduction of new methodologies for harvesting forests were to convince many biologists and resource managers that problems from increasing demands for and pressures upon natural resources could be resolved through technological changes. An effective challenge to this concept was to be stimulated by the 1962 publication of Rachel Carson's book on the environmental consequences of human activity titled *Silent Spring.* The contemporary citizens' environmental/conservation movement spawned by Carson was to prompt the Wilderness Act, formation of the Environmental Protection Agency and President's Council on Environmental Quality, Endangered Species Act, National Environmental Policy Act, as well as anti-pollution and energy conservation measures.

To date, the thrust of government wildlife management and conservation programs has been anthropocentric, operating as it does on the assumption that so-termed ''wildlife resources'' exist for the use and benefit of man. Wildlife management programs, as currently administered by state and federal governments, retain a commodity-oriented philosophy which tends to focus upon the productive use of individual species. A disproportionate share of budgets for wildlife management agencies is reserved for the propagation of game animals. Yet we are undergoing a period of conceptual reorientation which increasingly is stressing the esthetic dimension of man's relationship with the natural world. The consumptive use of flora and fauna will continue to be a part of wildlife management and conservation programs; however, we are slowly moving toward the day when exploitation will no longer be the dominant theme of public conservation efforts.

Perhaps to a greater extent than at any time since the founding of the nation, American citizens today are questioning the economic, social, and environmental values of our civilization. There is emerging a new order of naturalism which de-emphasizes man's mastery over nature and devalues economic growth at the expense of lands and wildlife. Mankind cannot survive without exploiting natural resources; yet, we are beginning to recognize the need for striking a better balance between our expectations of material growth, the need for preservation of natural resources, and our ethical relationship with other living creatures.

The United States is moving toward a society which recognizes the fundamental doctrine of animal rights. Americans are increasingly reluctant to kill or displace wildlife except out of necessity. Our society is confronting a complex question of human values and biological alternatives. Today, consideration is given to satisfying economic needs and human recreational energies in a manner which will not place a continuous drain upon natural systems or corrupt man's relationship with other life forms.

Wildlife policies, unfortunately, continue to be subject to political whims and pressures from special interests. Nonetheless, government, industry, and the general public have come to recognize the critical relationship between nature and the survival of mankind. It is apparent that professional conservationists are to play an important role in the future development of our nation as a society and as an ecosystem.

3
SELF ASSESSMENT: ATTITUDES, EMOTIONS, AND PHILOSOPHIES

Author Bruce Buchenholz writing in *Doctor in the Zoo* noted that man's relationship with other animals encompasses the full range of human emotions. Since man is an animal, we share basic biological characteristics with other living creatures. Most humans have a conscious sense of relatedness to other animals, an ability to identify with them, and a tendency to project into animals certain of their own emotional responses.

Mankind is capable of intimate personal relationships with other creatures. Americans own 48 million dogs, 25 million cats, 8 million saddle horses, 340 million fish, 23 million birds, and 12 million exotic pets. These statistics offer testimony to a primal relationship between animals and man. Even if animals play no direct part in a person's daily life, they influence our existence in a very real sense. In contemporary society animals have symbolic, religious, social, cultural and utilitarian significance.

Each person has within him or her the germ of complex emotional relationships with animals. Every individual, depending upon our personal experiences and life circumstances, reacts in some manner to these inner emotional feelings. For more than one-half of all U.S. households, the need to interact with animals has been satisfied by adopting a pet into the family and home. Yet, there are some persons among us whose empathy for animals is so acutely developed that these individuals are compelled to reserve a major role in their lives for other living creatures. These people may be classified by a singular denominator — they care about animals. It is this group of individuals who are inclined to pursue a career working with animals. Some persons simply appreciate the beauty and unique character of animals and desire the opportunity to observe and study other living creatures. Other persons have a keenly developed social consciousness and are anxious to tangibly contribute to the welfare and protection of animals. Regardless of personal motivation the depth and range of human feelings engendered by animals will significantly influence a person's career goals and occupational options.

Self-assessment is a critical step in career exploration. A person's values, priorities, goals, interests, skills, abilities, and feelings should play an important role in defining his or her career objectives. It is deceptively simple to identify an attractive career and learn the job skills which are a prerequisite for employment. Job satisfaction, however, has proven to be surprisingly elusive. Disenchantment and failure on the part of persons working with animals is often attributable to three factors: attitude, emotion, and philosophy. No amount of enthusiasm or dedication will overcome fundamental conflicts in moral or ethical issues which alienate a careerist from his or her profession. Thus, as an initial step in career exploration, a person must identify and inventory his or her aptitudes, temperament, and values and analyze their relationship to career options.

EMOTIONS

Man shares with other animals the basic experience of birth, life, and death. Any experience of helplessness, whether personal or indirect, brings with it a subtle reminder of our vulnerability and perishability. Reptiles, birds, and mammals are capable of exhibiting clear signs of stress, pain, and pleasure. Evidence of animal suffering evokes powerful emotional responses on the part of humans. Most persons cannot remain indifferent in the presence of animal suffering.

A human response to an animal's helplessness is a compound reaction of guilt, compassion, and the fundamental awareness of frailty and dependency which we share with all other creatures. Individuals exhibit varied responses when confronted with an

animal that is suffering or abused. The intensity of an emotional response may be so powerful as to immobilize the observer or elicit a frantic, undirected attempt at assistance. Some persons feel vengeful toward the individual responsible for the plight of an animal and may be tempted to use their authority as a mechanism for retribution.

Empathy and respect for living creatures is essential for a person contemplating a career working with animals. However, it is also necessary to exercise discipline, restraint, and control. Emotional instability can hinder a person's response during a crisis involving the welfare or safety of an animal and could unintentionally cause harm to an animal or jeopardize a criminal investigation by reason of the person's inability to perform in a professional manner during a critical situation. Individuals incapable of controlled sensitivity would better serve both themselves and the cause of animal welfare by confining consideration of career options to occupations which do not require direct contact with animals.

PHILOSOPHIES

Philosophical opinions regarding man's relationship with other animals are based upon moral, social, religious, and ethical considerations which have evolved from a complex series of value systems and abstract concepts. Neither government agencies, private institutions, nor commercial enterprises are monolithic in their policies or in their views on the man-animal relationship. Philosophical differences focus primarily upon varied interpretations of the utilitarian function of animals. At issue are the moral and ethical implications of utilizing and manipulating animals in order to achieve human goals or satisfy human wants. The philosophical dispute arising from this issue is termed ''animal rights.''

AMERICAN PETROLEUM INSTITUTE/KEITH HAY

The tragic death of an oil-covered bird is among the emotional heartbreaks of working with animals.

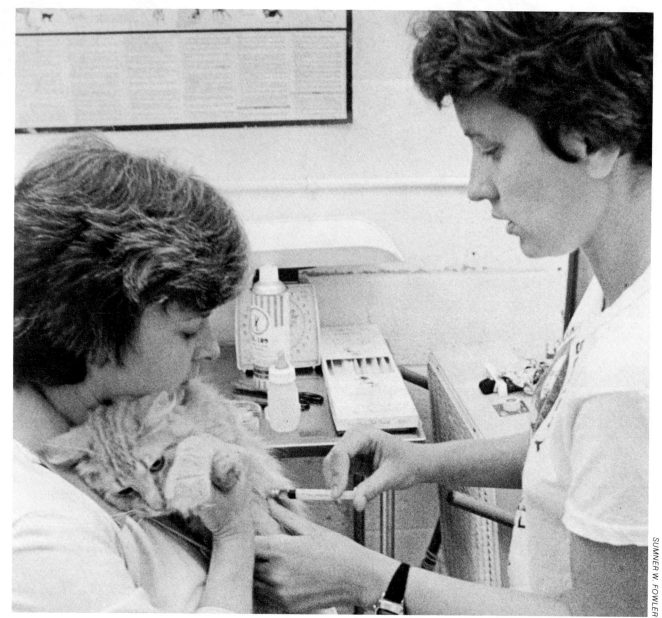

The euthanasia of unwanted pets entrusted to their care creates a moral dilemma for animal shelter workers.

Within both animal welfare and conservation there are distinct philosophical factions. The major areas of philosophical conflict are vivisection, euthanasia, consumptive use, and exploitation.

Euthanasia — Animal shelters have been reluctantly transformed into exterminating facilities where 13.5 million homeless dogs and cats must be put to death each year. Shelter employees must assume the burden for selecting the displaced, unwanted animals to be killed and must themselves perform the distasteful act of euthanasia.

Vivisection — Many undergraduate and graduate scholastic programs require that students perform experiments upon live animals as well as dissecting the carcasses of creatures which were killed specifically for classroom use. Vivisection is a particularly common element within programs of study leading to degrees in the biological sciences or veterinary medicine. The performance of vivisection may also be required of professional biologists and veterinarians engaged in drug testing and development, animal behavior studies, nutrition studies, or biomedical research.

Exploitation — Animals are marketed as a commodity. Breeding kennels, pet stores, animal dealer facilities, and livestock farms produce and sell animals on a profit-making basis. Zoological parks, aquariums, and circuses use animals as a medium of public entertainment and recreation.

Consumptive Use — Animals are used as a natural resource in the production of food, clothing, cosmetics, drugs, as well as a variety of supplies and equipment. Animals also perish in connection with the principal activities associated with wildlife management - sport hunting and commercial trapping.

Personal outlook is important in reviewing educational requirements, job duties, and employer policies. As a facet of career exploration, the person interested in an occupation working with animals should narrow his or her list of occupational positions to those which are compatible with personal beliefs and philosophies.

ATTITUDES

Occupations involving work with animals currently enjoy a position of glamour and prestige among both youth and adults. Nature-oriented television programs and popular literature have helped to foster the popularity of careers in animal welfare, conservation, and environmental quality. Many of the people contemplating careers working with animals visualize themselves as a future Marlin Perkins, Jane Goodall, or Jacques Cousteau. They envision a job involving daring adventures in exotic or remote locations or imagine the fun of rearing orphaned animals. Such portraits of careers working with animals are unrealistic for all but an elite few who are the beneficiaries of exceptionally good fortune.

Persons who equate job satisfaction with their rate of financial compensation, minimal workloads, regular business hours, or public recognition are unlikely to find fulfillment in the career opportunities available in animal welfare, conservation, or environmental quality. Career options do offer varied opportunities for self-fulfillment. Every job may not offer

A person's outlook and values are an important consideration in the selection of an occupation.

an opportunity for continuing stimulation and challenge. Yet, there is the reward of meaningfully contributing to the welfare and protection of animals.

The person considering a career working with animals should be familiar with the demands and dimensions of his or her chosen occupation. Popular career guidance literature is often designed to avoid unpleasant or controversial aspects of an occupation which detract from the image or reputation of that career field. The student or job seeker who does not carefully investigate an occupation may not be afforded an opportunity for employment in a role which is consistent with his or her views and interests. Professional success is not measured solely by performance; personal enjoyment and self-pride must also be considered. Thus, an individual's outlook and values should be a fundamental factor in exploring and evaluating career options and job opportunities.

4
ANIMAL CAREER PROFILES

HUMANE SOCIETY
EXECUTIVE DIRECTOR
DIRECTOR OF ANIMAL CONTROL
SHELTER MANAGER

A shelter manager and a veterinary technician discuss the care of unusual shelter animals.

Animal welfare organizations operate approximately 550 shelters while municipal animal control agencies operate an estimated 2,000 facilities created for the kenneling of impounded dogs and cats. An additional 1,500 shelterless community animal welfare organizations sponsor programs of cruelty investigation and humane education.

The humane society executive director is responsible for overall administration of an animal welfare agency's programs. As the chief administrator of the humane society, the executive director oversees the operation of all organizational departments including humane education, shelter management, cruelty investigation, and community relations. The executive director is concerned with all facets of the humane society's operation including fund raising, membership recruitment, personnel management, and program planning. As the chief salaried official of the humane society, the executive director serves as the principal spokesperson of the organization. The executive director may testify at municipal hearings, address civic groups, and appear on community radio and television shows. The executive director is, commonly, accountable to a governing body known as the board of directors. The board of directors is appointed by an election of the humane society's general membership. Often, the executive director is appointed to an *ex officio* seat on the governing board.

The director of animal control is the municipal equivalent of the humane society executive director. The director of animal control administers the community animal control program. While animal welfare organizations are primarily concerned with the prevention and alleviation of animal suffering, muncipal animal control agencies are concerned with the prevention and elimination of conflicts between animals and community residents. It is the responsibility of the animal control agency to patrol for, and impound, animals running at large in violation of the local ordinance. The animal control agency investigates complaints regarding barking dogs, animal attacks upon humans, and damage caused to personal property by a neighbor's pet.

The shelter manager is responsible for the operation and maintenance of a kennel facility providing for the impoundment of dogs, cats, and other animals. Shelter managers are employed by both community animal welfare organizations and municipal animal control agencies. The duties of a shelter manager change in accordance with the staff structure of the employing institution. The basic responsibilities of the shelter manager include the hiring and supervision of shelter personnel, purchase of shelter supplies and equipment, and the development of operational procedures for the shelter.

The shelter manager is directly accountable to the humane society executive director or director of animal control. However, the shelter manager employed by a small budget institution may serve as the chief administrator of the organization or agency. Several shelters do not employ managers but, rather, assign the duties associated with this position to the humane society executive director or director of animal control.

A director of animal control or humane society executive director must be experienced in both animal shelter management and business administration. Practical experience is a prerequisite for employment as an executive director or director of animal control. There is no standard method for advancing to the position of humane society executive director or director of animal control. Persons currently employed as chief administrators for humane societies and animal control agencies include promoted employees, veterinarians, ex-military officers, and former commercial kennel managers.

The humane society executive director and director of animal control earn an average of $12,000 to $20,000 in annual salary. Income is proportionate to an institution's budget and size. The chief administrators of humane societies and animal control agencies located within major metropolitan centers such as New York City and Philadelphia can earn in excess of $40,000 per year.

Increasingly, shelter managers are being recruited from the ranks of assistant shelter managers with formal education in veterinary technology or animal science. Persons with extensive practical experience in commerical kennel management or animal husbandry also account for a significant portion of the current labor force of shelter managers. Occasionally, a kennel worker may advance to a supervisory position and then be promoted to shelter manager.

A humane society executive director discusses plans for the remodeling of the animal shelter.

A shelter manager will earn a minimum annual salary of $12,000. A manager who serves as the chief administrator of a humane society or animal control agency can earn as much as $30,000. In some instances, shelter managers are provided with free or low rent housing as an employment benefit.

There are a limited number of annual job openings for shelter managers, humane society executive directors, and municipal directors of animal control. The person aspiring to a career as an executive with a humane society or animal welfare agency must be prepared to relocate wherever job opportunities are to be found.

HUMANE EDUCATION SPECIALIST

A humane education specialist instructs volunteers in the technique of teaching animal care to school children.

The earliest humane education program dates to the founding of the American Humane Education Society (A.H.E.S.) in 1889. The A.H.E.S. was responsible for the formation of the American Bands of Mercy — youth clubs organized and promoted through schools and by individuals. The Bands of Mercy had an estimated peak enrollment of 2,000,000 members each of whom pledged ''I will try to be kind to all harmless living creatures and try to protect them from cruel usage.'' The A.H.E.S. also sponsored the publication and distribution in the United States of an early humane education book, *Black Beauty*, which today remains among the most popular of children's literary classics.

While humane education has long been recognized as an integral part of humane society programs, it has only been within the past twenty years that this discipline has evolved into a specialized field of education. Thus, the position of humane education specialist has only recently been incorporated into the staffs of animal welfare organizations, animal control agencies, and school systems.

Humane education deals with humane attitudes and behavior. Contemporary humane education programs apply trends, philosophies, methods, and new developments in general education to the teaching of kindness towards animals. The humane education specialist seeks to educate the public to animal problems; to establish in man a fundamental attitude of reverence for life; to encourage natural curiosity and motivate further study of animals; to provide a learning experience regarding the treatment of animals; to instill in man the habits of courtesy, consideration, and responsibility toward other living creatures; to provide information about animals and to provide contact with animals.

Twenty-one states have enacted statutes which provide for the compulsory teaching of humane education in the classroom. The humane education specialist collaborates with teachers in fulfilling this legally imposed scholastic requirement. The humane educator develops and structures both written and audio-visual materials for integration into general classroom curricula. The humane education specialist also designs shelter exhibits and community displays, drafts animal care literature, lectures adult groups, makes classroom presentations, guides shelter tours and field trips, conducts workshops, leads study groups, teaches pet care courses, coordinates community humane education projects, instructs obedience classes, provides career guidance counseling, and transports animals on visits to hospitals and nursing homes.

Community animal welfare organizations are the primary employer of humane education specialists. Approximately 300 humane educators currently hold permanent positions with local humane societies and SPCA's. A limited number of humane education specialists are employed by animal control agencies, national humane organizations, and local school systems. An indeterminate number of part-time and seasonal personnel are also employed in the field of humane education.

In general, animal welfare organizations and animal control agencies can afford only one humane education specialist per institution. However, in some instances humane education programs are administered by a special humane education department which is headed by a Director of Education. The Director of Education is responsible for coordinating the overall community humane education program. Every aspect of animal welfare in some sense involves humane education.

Therefore, the Director of Education has diverse duties encompassing every aspect of humane society operations. In particular, the Director of Education may assume responsibility for an animal welfare organization's public relations projects.

Persons planning careers as humane education specialists are advised to obtain a baccalaureate degree in elementary education or a closely related educational field. A degree minor in animal science or biology is recommended. Also considered beneficial are courses in journalism, parks and recreation, advertising, and public relations. In past years, Tulsa University in Tulsa, Oklahoma, has offered a graduate independent study program with a major in humane education. Stephen F. Austin University in Nacogdoches, Texas, has offered, for credit, a summer workshop in humane education. Several universities offer curricula in the closely related fields of outdoor education and environmental education. A continuing series of regional workshops in humane education is sponsored by the National Association for the Advancement of Humane Education which is a division of The Humane Society of the United States.

Job opportunities for humane education specialist are clustered around major metropolitan communities. In some communities the expense of a salary for a humane education specialist is jointly shared between the local humane society and the school system. The majority of job opportunities for humane educators occur among large, established animal welfare organizations. Salaries for humane educators vary in accordance with the experience and qualifications of personnel, geographic region, and the size of the employing organization. The general salary range for humane education specialists is $8,000 to $16,000. Within individual communities, beginning salaries for humane education specialist tend to be commensurate with starting salaries for elementary and secondary school teachers.

There has been a gradual but steady expansion in positions for humane education specialists. A majority of the nation's animal welfare organizations and animal control agencies recognize the importance of humane education and are anxious to expand their programs. Fiscal limitations are the only impediment to a more rapid expansion in job opportunities for humane education specialists.

DOCTOR OF VETERINARY MEDICINE

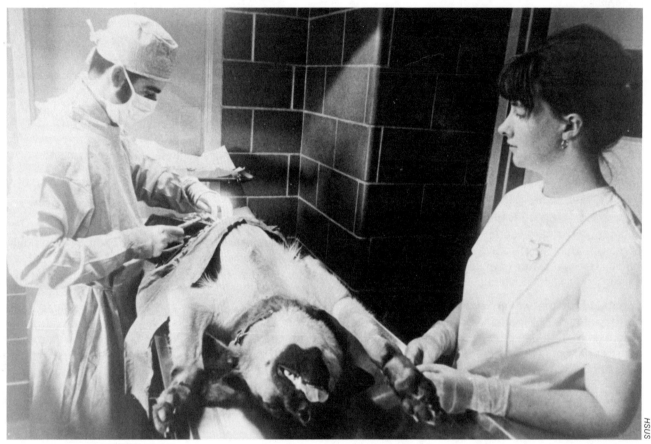

A veterinarian, assisted by a veterinary technician, performs surgery on a dog.

HSUS

A veterinarian is a medical specialist who is skilled in the prevention, diagnosis, and treatment of animal health problems.

There are currently 30,000 veterinarians in the United States working in approximately thirty fields of interest. The major areas of concentration are private practice, community health, and research. Other veterinary occupations include food inspection, teaching, environmental health, animal shelter management, pet products marketing and zoological park management.

Approximately seventy-two percent of all veterinarians are engaged in private practice. One third of all doctors of veterinary medicine are in mixed practice administering to both livestock and domestic pets. An equal number of veterinary practitioners are engaged in small animal practice and confine their work to the treatment of dogs, cats, and other small household pets. Another seven percent of all veterinarians specialize in the treatment of horses and livestock. The newest specialty among practicing veterinarians is exotic animal medicine. Veterinarians usually concentrate their practices in areas with large livestock or domestic pet populations. In fact, two fifths of all veterinarians in the United States are located in the states of California, New York, Texas, Illinois, Iowa, Ohio, and Pennsylvania.

To become a veterinarian, a person must earn a Doctor of Veterinary Medicine (D.V.M.) degree or its equivalent. There are currently 22 colleges of veterinary medicine in North America, including three in Canada. These institutions enroll approximately 1500 new students annually. To qualify for admission to a veterinary school, an applicant must complete at least two years of college study; however, over one third of the students enrolled in veterinary colleges in 1973 held bachelor degrees. Although requirements for admission are not uniform, veterinary colleges typically demand that an applicant have completed undergraduate courses in mathematics, language arts, social sciences, humanities, and the biological and physical sciences. Several universities offer a pre-veterinary curriculum.

Successful completion of a pre-veterinary undergraduate program does not assure admittance to a college of veterinary medicine. Because educational facilities are limited, many capable persons are denied an opportunity to study veterinary medicine. Nationwide, veterinary institutions accept for enrollment only 15% of qualified applicants. The number of applications for admittance to veterinary schools more than doubled between the 1977-1978 school years. Seventeen schools of veterinary medicine are located at state supported universities, and they generally must give first preference for enrollment to applicants who are state residents. Women also have an advantage in the selection process as a result of past discriminatory selection practices. In recent years the number of women attending colleges of veterinary medicine has doubled; however, female veterinary students remain in the minority and currently account for less than 20% of enrollments. In 1976 the School of Veterinary Medicine at the University of Illinois received 500 applications for 76 vacancies in its fall freshman class. Even more persons might have applied, however, the school actively discouraged prospective students from submitting applications. The school also refused to consider applications from persons who were out-of-state residents. Moreover, the University of Illinois discontinued its pre-veterinary curriculum for undergraduate

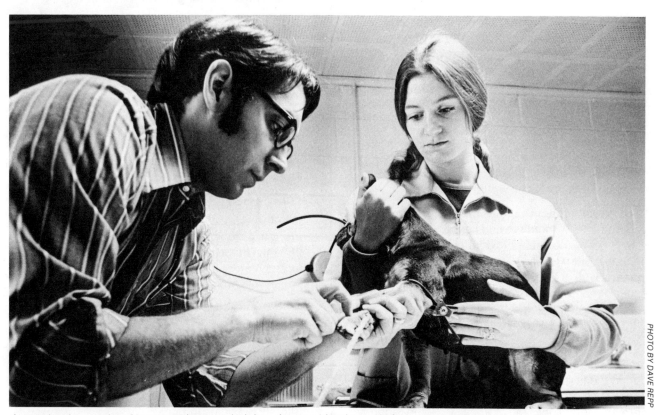

PHOTO BY DAVE REPP

A veterinarian, assisted by a veterinary technician, draws a blood sample from the vein of an injured puppy.

students. Educators predict a growing trend toward the elimination of pre-veterinary programs attributable to the inability of colleges to place qualified graduates in a school of veterinary medicine.

Most veterinary schools require four years of study; however, at least two institutions, Texas A&M and Michigan State University, offer three year programs of instruction. Fewer than 10% of the students enrolling in veterinary colleges fail to obtain their diploma as a Doctor of Veterinary Medicine.

Programs of study at veterinary colleges are divided into a pre-clinical phase involving classroom and laboratory study and a clinical phase involving work with animal patients. The curriculum at a college of veterinary medicine includes courses on infectious and non-infectious diseases, advanced pathology, applied anatomy, obstetrics, radiology, clinical medicine, and surgery. Students also study public health, preventive medicine, toxicology, nutrition, professional ethics, and business practices.

The trend toward specialization in the animal health field has led many veterinarians to pursue graduate study programs. A Master of Science or Ph.D. degree is particularly important to the veterinarian considering a career in teaching, research, public health, or specialized practice. The nine specialties the American Veterinary Medicine Association now recognizes include: public health, radiology, toxicology, laboratory animal medicine, microbiology, pathology, surgery opthamology, and theriogenology (reproduction).

Veterinarians must be licensed by a state examination board before they may practice veterinary medicine. To qualify for a license the veterinarian must pass rigid oral and written examinations.

Starting government salaries for newly graduated veterinarians without previous experience are currently established at approximately $17,000 annually. Entry level government salaries for veterinarians with previous experience or demonstrated superior ability may exceed $20,000. Senior staff veterinarians working with the Federal Government earn $24,000 to $31,000 a year.

Veterinary school graduates establishing a private practice usually manage to cover their expenses during the first year, and they may earn $13,000 to $15,000. Graduates joining an established practice earn an average income of $17,500. Some recently

GLADYS PORTER ZOO

Exotic animal medicine is among the nine areas of specialization in which a veterinarian may practice.

graduated doctors of veterinary medicine supplement the income derived from private practice by working part-time for government agencies.

As veterinarians become established and gain experience, their incomes increase substantially. The income of the private practitioner is generally higher than the salary of the government veterinarian. In 1971 the United States Department of Health, Education and Welfare reported the average annual income of the private veterinary practitioner at more than $30,000. Some veterinarians with large practices located in major metropolitan communities earned as much as $200,000 a year after expenses.

Prior to 1978 the general employment outlook for the veterinarian appeared excellent. The American Veterinary Medical Association estimated that by 1980 the United States would require 44,000 veterinarians. Veterinary colleges are expanding in order to meet this projected demand, and several new institutions are in the planning stage. However, there is growing concern that the continuing expansion of veterinary colleges may produce a surplus of practitioners. At present, the high admittance standards of veterinary schools are prompting fewer students to apply for admission. Thus, graduating veterinarians continue to encounter little difficulty in finding jobs.

ZOO DIRECTOR
CURATOR

A zoo director and zoo veterinarian discuss the specialized diet of the zoo's koala bears.

The zoo director is a member of an exclusive fraternity of administrators who operate the two hundred recognized zoological parks in the United States. The chief administrator of a zoo may also be known as a Manager or Superintendent. Directorships require a solid background in animal management and an understanding of contemporary concepts in natural-habitat exhibits. Directors usually possess degrees in zoology or related fields. Some zoological institutions are managed by persons with backgrounds in business administration. Zoos are also administered by veterinarians. There is no standard route of advancement to a zoo directorship. Individuals with experience outside of the zoological park management profession are often appointed to directorships. On occasion, keepers or curators with extensive practical experience may become directors of zoological institutions.

Second in the line of authority within a zoological park is the Assistant Director, Deputy Director, Foreman or Assistant Superintendent. Both job titles and job duties vary significantly among zoos. Assistant directors may manage personnel, supervise animal care staff, or be assigned other administrative duties.

A zoo curator is a department chief who has responsibility for one of the major sections of the animal collection: birds, reptiles, or mammals. In some zoological facilitles there may be a general curator or zoologist who oversees the entire animal collection. The curator has responsibility for the general supervision of the caretaker work force and for the care of animals. In addition to these duties, curators plan the design and alteration of animal exhibits. Curators are responsible for selecting the species of animals to be exhibited and for acquiring the animal stock.

Curators are commonly appointed from among applicants with advanced degrees in zoology or a related field who have previous experience in zoological park management. Senior and head keepers may be appointed to a curatorial position, but this is a difficult and risky method of advancement.

Undergraduate and graduate degrees in zoology, herpetology, ornithology and related fields of study are offered at more than one hundred universities. Several major zoos now offer internship programs

A curator cautiously examines a rhinoceros newly added to the zoo's animal collection.

to candidates for an advanced degree in zoology. The intern is hired as a salaried staff member and works as an assistant to the curator in the department of the intern's preference. Intern programs are adapted to the individual's experience. Most zoological parks require that interns commit themselves for a minimum period of one year's employment.

Remuneration for curators and zoo directors varies according to the size and prestige of the zoological park. Salaries for curators range from $9,000 to $30,000 with general curators and zoologists earning the highest incomes. The salary range for zoo directors is equally broad. Directors may earn from $10,000 to $40,000. Assistant directors may earn from $9,000 to $30,000 and assistant curators may receive salaries of $9,000 to $25,000. Salaries for top administrative positions in zoological parks are based in large part upon an individual's background, professional stature, and experience.

As might be expected, it is extremely difficult to gain consideration as a curator or director because of the high wages and attractive working conditions offered by major zoological parks.

Natural-habitat zoological park exhibitions are rapidly gaining in popularity and public acceptance. The number of persons visiting zoos during a typical year exceeds the total attendance at all professional sport events. There is a nationwide trend toward new construction and renovation in zoos. The related demand for zoological park management personnel is creating new opportunities for persons with the required technical backgrounds.

A curator is responsible for the care of the animals in his or her section of the zoo and must regularly visit animal exhibit areas.

ANIMAL TRAINER
ANIMAL HANDLER

A customs agent and detector dog working at an airport check parcels for narcotics.

U.S. CUSTOMS SERVICE

Animal training is a technical skill which uses knowledge of an animal's habits and learning ability. The trainer teaches an animal to perform certain feats upon command.

Approximately 125 persons earn a living as trainers of performing animals, both domestic and wild, which work within the entertainment industry. Performing animals appear in circuses and carnivals. Among the species of animals commonly associated with this segment of the performing animal industry are lions, tigers, horses, elephants, and dogs. An estimated 25 professional trainers work within the motion picture and television industries.

The trainer works under contract to the producer. The animal trainer working within the film industry may be required to teach an animal a specific trick demanded by the script. He or she may be hired to provide animals to decorate film sets, or may receive a contract to provide a specific performing animal which is noted for a special trick. Other trainers of performing animals specialize in animal acts which appear at fairs, trade shows, shopping malls, and civic events. Animal trainers are also employed by zoological parks which feature performing animal shows.

The trainer of a performing animal may receive a fee as low as $75 for an appearance at a child's birthday party. A fee of $5,000 or more may be paid for a trick performed for a television program or motion picture. Higher fees may be paid to the trainers of animals which have starring roles in feature films or are featured characters on television programs. Animal trainers employed by circuses and zoos are paid an annual salary.

Dog obedience instructors account for the greatest number of animal trainers who are professionally employed. The objective of obedience training is to produce a manageable pet dog which is responsive to direction. Advanced obedience training is used for show dogs and to teach working dogs to perform tasks upon command. It is estimated that five thousand handlers and instructors are employed by military and law enforcement agencies. The number of personnel working within the commercial dog obedience industry has not been determined.

Trainers working within the commercial dog obedience industry conduct classes for dog owners as well as providing training for individual animals both at the owners' residences and on the premises of dog training academies. Trainers may be employees of dog obedience academies or may be self-employed. Many trainers earn a portion of their income conducting classes in association with adult education centers, community animal welfare agencies, pet shops and kennels. Trainers receive only nominal payments for classes sponsored by community service organizations.

For many dog obedience instructors animal training is an avocation or part-time vocation rather than a profession. Self-employed dog obedience instructors commonly earn from $2,000 to $10,000 per year. Those trainers who obtain employment with an academy may earn $10,000 to $16,000 in annual income.

There are at least nine institutions in the United States which train guide dogs for the blind. Each year 8,500 sightless persons are taught to function with the assistance of a guide dog. Approximately sixty persons are employed nationwide as trainers of guide dogs for the blind. Several trainers are currently employed in a related field teaching deaf persons to function with the assistance of hearing dogs. An apprentice with a guide dog school will earn $9,000 to $10,000 in annual salary while a senior trainer averages $22,000 in annual income.

The animal handler works in partnership with an individual animal. Approximately 150 handlers are employed within the United States Customs Service while 4,000 handlers are employed by military branches and perhaps another 2,000 handlers are employed by municipal and state law enforcement agencies. Novice handlers earn $10,000 to $20,000 with the upper salary range reserved for experienced police officers who join the departmental K-9 Corps. Within the military service, handlers are assigned the rank of Specialist 5th Class and may advance to the rank of Master Sergeant.

The show handler exhibits animals for a fee at dog shows. To become a professional show handler a person must own and exhibit purebred dogs for a period of approximately six years. Those individuals of demonstrated ability may be given the opportunity to apprentice with a professional handler. Many professional handlers continue to operate breeding kennels in addition to handling dogs on behalf of persons who are too busy or too inexperienced to show their own animals. There is a wide variation in the fees earned by show handlers. A top caliber handler with an exceptionally good record can earn $75,000 or more in annual income.

Animal trainers work irregular hours. Frequently, dog obedience classes are conducted during evening hours. The work day, which averages ten hours, fluctuates between periods of activity and inactivity.

There is no standard method of training for a career as an animal trainer or handler. Many trainers are self-taught. They may combine a scholastic background in animal science with work experience in kennels and independent study. Traditionally, military service has been the accepted method of entering the dog training profession. The owners of dog training academies continue to give preference in hiring to trainers with a formal background obtained through military service.

Vocational programs are offered by at least eleven dog training academies. The fee for enrollment in a vocational program averages $2,000 to $5,000. The length of the course of instruction varies in duration from seven weeks to six months. The principal duties of the trainee are to exercise and feed kenneled animals. The trainee is given an opportunity to observe the professional trainer at work and is given instruction in the rudimentary aspects of obedience training. Trainees are given some opportunity for supervised practice in basic obedience work. Authorities within the animal training profession are generally critical of vocational schooling. Programs are too brief in duration to provide adequate experience or to permit the trainee to develop required skills. Often, vocational programs are unstructured and make no allowance for classroom instruction.

Apprenticeship is recommended as a practical alternative to enrollment in a vocational program. The apprentice may begin as a salaried kennel worker and gradually progress to assisting a professional trainer, and ultimately to training animals under the instruction and supervision of the professional trainer. An apprenticeship commonly requires two to five years of work depending upon previous experience in showing and handling dogs. Amateur experience can be obtained through association with a community dog training club or 4-H program.

An instructor trains a guide dog to aid its blind owner in passing through fence gates.

The U.S. Customs Service, law enforcement agencies, and military branches develop their own trainers and handlers. A person need not complete a vocational program or apprenticeship prior to seeking employment with these agencies. However, the U.S. Customs Service and municipal law enforcement agencies accept applications only from their own officers and agents. In making application for employment, there is no guarantee that the prospective employee will be selected to participate in the Detector Dog or K-9 Corps programs.

It can be difficult to obtain admittance into an apprenticeship program. The Seeing Eye, a guide

dogs for the blind facility located in New Jersey, each month receives several hundred unsolicited applications for employment from persons wishing to apprentice as animal trainers. Dog training academies advertising openings for experienced trainers commonly receive more than 200 applications from unqualified persons requesting an opportunity to apprentice.

The Seeing Eye demands the following qualifications of persons applying for a position as an apprentice animal trainer: the strength and stamina to handle animals; previous experience in working with animals; scholastic training in veterinary technology, animal science, or equivalent experience working in a veterinary hospital, kennel, or farm; and maturity.

Increasingly, a college education is regarded as a desirable qualification of applicants for a position as an apprentice animal trainer. Some authorities advocate a scholastic background in psychology or animal behavior while other experts recommend animal science or veterinary technology as a useful program of study.

The prospective apprentice must use caution in selecting a professional trainer with whom to work. Professional trainers vary significantly in competence and ability. The job applicant should obtain information on the techniques used by a trainer, as well as the trainer's background, experience, and professional reputation. Some trainers emphasize punishment training and physically or verbally reprimand an animal when it fails to act in a desired manner. Other trainers prefer to offer positive reinforcement through praise and reward when an animal correctly follows commands. Trainers also have differing approaches to particular problems such as barking, biting, and housebreaking.

The type of instruction received by an apprentice is critical to his or her future success. There are few employment opportunities for apprentices who are instructed in obsolete techniques or who study under trainers lacking in reputation.

At the present time there are limited opportunities for placement within the animal trainer and dog handler professions. In the absence of permit or license requirements for trainers, there are no standards to be met before a person may claim to be an animal trainer. Thus the ranks of persons seeking employment are inflated by self-appointed animal trainers who are seriously lacking in schooling or competence.

WILLDLIFE BIOLOGIST

A wildlife biologist releases a rehabilitated golden eagle which had been illegally shot.

Wildlife management, wildlife science, and wildlife biology are interrelated terms which refer to the study and regulation of wild animals.

Wildlife management involves the practical application of biological data in combination with ecological principles and techniques to preserve and control wild animal populations. The professional wildlife biologist may specialize in the planning and administration of programs for the protection, maintenance, and economic and recreational utilization of wildlife. A wildlife management biologist whose primary duties relate to the consumptive exploitation of animals is known as a game biologist. The wildlife management biologist who manages wildlife populations for non-consumptive uses is known as a non-game biologist.

Game biologists are concerned with the abundance and utilization of wildlife having economic value. The game biologist establishes the abundance and distribution of wildlife populations through censusing, analysis of harvest data, and other sampling techniques. The game biologist engages in habitat alteration, selective planting of preferred wildlife foods, control of predatory species, the captive breeding of game animals, and the study of animals killed by hunters and trappers. The game biologist is also responsible for recommending seasonal game regulations relative to the length of hunting and trapping seasons, bag limits and game quotas.

Non-game biologists are new to the wildlife management profession. The non-game biologist is concerned with those species of animals, such as song birds, which are not exploited by man. The non-game biologist applies the same skills and techniques of wildlife management as the game biologist. The non-game biologist also studies the abundance and distribution of animal species. The non-game biologist may engage in habitat alteration or the selective planting of preferred wildlife foods.

Some wildlife management biologists specialize in the control of wildlife species which have reached destructive abundance. These biologists, known as animal damage control specialists, apply deterrents to control wild animals which are harmful to agricultural crops or compete with or are injurious to livestock.

Wildlife management clearly involves a utilitarian approach to the conservation of wild animals. State agencies which administer wildlife programs are often titled "Fish and Game Departments." Fully 90% of state fish and game department annual budgets are expended on the management of game species — wild animals which are hunted and trapped for sport, food, and commercial gain. The wildlife management biologist is concerned with the productive utilization of animals as a natural resource. To some extent the wildlife management biologist is a technician who applies scientific knowledge so as to manipulate wildlife populations for the use and benefit of man. The work of the biologist, although of a scientific nature, is oriented toward a practical application in accordance with both political and pragmatic considerations.

A second area of concentration among wildlife biologists is concerned with research. The wildlife research biologist studies all forms of vertebrate animal life including birds, reptiles, mammals, and amphibians. The research biologist conducts both basic and applied research in wildlife taxonomy, physiology, genetics, ethology, ecology, species distribution, species abundance, disease, nutrition, population dynamics, mortality, field identification, food preferences, and virtually every other facet of the biological sciences. The wildlife research biologist collects, analyzes, and interprets data and factual biological information relating to wild animals.

The position of wildlife research biologist might be termed the glamour profession of the decade for prospective conservation workers. This position enjoys wide appeal as a result of nature-oriented television programs featuring researchers such as Jane Goodall. In reality, there are few employment opportunities in field research. A majority of the available positions are reserved for biologists with graduate degrees. Many researchers work under grants and contracts and must frequently seek refinancing of their research programs.

Wildlife biologists work in laboratories, universities, wildlife refuges, parks, game preserves, and offices. The primary employers of wildlife biologists are the U.S. Fish and Wildlife Service and state fish and game departments. Wildlife biologists also may be employed by zoological parks, private conservation organizations and foundations. Approximately 65% of all wildlife biologists work for state wildlife agencies while another 20% are employed by the federal government.

The annual salaries paid to wildlife biologists employed by state wildlife agencies vary in accordance with seniority, professional training, and job duties. The wildlife area manager may earn $8,000 to $12,000; a junior biologist can earn $8,500 to $12,000; a senior biologist will earn $10,500 to $15,000; while a wildlife management division chief may earn $15,000 to $19,000. Research biologists employed by the federal government receive entry level salaries of $14,000 to $23,000 with persons possessing Ph.D.'s earning the highest rates of compensation. A newly hired biologist with a master's degree will earn from $10,000 to $13,000 while a biologist not possessing a graduate degree can expect to receive an annual salary of $8,500 to $11,000.

OUTDOOR RECREATION PLANNER
PARK NATURALIST

A park naturalist discusses methods of attracting songbirds to the backyards of homes.

GUY HODGE

Outdoor recreation is a broad term encompassing a variety of social, cultural, physical, and educational programs. Outdoor recreation planners are concerned with land acquisition and the development of recreational facilities.

Municipal governments are the largest employers of trained personnel in the recreation field. However, the agency which most commonly utilizes outdoor recreational planners in conservation pro grams is the Bureau of Outdoor Recreation of the United States Department of Interior. The Bureau's primary responsibility is the coordination of

government and non-government projects involving the outdoors. Planners assist states in examining potential outdoor recreation areas, acquiring land and developing outdoor recreation facilities and programs.

Applicants for outdoor recreation planner positions with the Bureau of Outdoor Recreation must have a bachelor degree in either biological science, natural resource management, conservation, or earth science. In addition, the Bureau requires at least three years professional, managerial, or technical experience in recreational planning, conservation, or natural resources management.

Entry level appointments to positions as outdoor recreation planners offer an annual salary of approximately $8,500. Middle range planner positions pay from $10,000 to $15,000 per year. Senior planners working in metropolitan areas may earn $30,000 or more.

The park naturalist, professionally known as an *interpretive naturalist*, organizes, coordinates, and directs recreational programs relating to the environment. Park naturalists guide nature walks, lecture on natural history, design visitor center exhibits, and manage park lands. Naturalists also study, manage, and protect the wildlife inhabitants of park lands. The mission of the park naturalist is to assist the public in appreciating and understanding the natural world. The naturalist seeks to inspire public participation in, and support for, conservation and wildlife protection programs.

Naturalists are employed in municipal, state, and national parks, forests, refuges, and other public recreation areas. Naturalists are also employed in privately operated amusement parks which feature wildlife exhibits. Municipal parks and recreation departments are the primary employers of park naturalists.

Applicants for the position of park naturalist commonly are required to possess a baccalaureate degree in parks and recreation or a related discipline such as outdoor education, wildlife science, herpetology, or ornithology.

Beginning positions for park naturalists pay $8,000 to $10,000 while senior naturalists may earn $16,000 or more. The natualist has an excellent opportunity to advance into a position as a nature center director or parks and recreation department administrator. In fact, to qualify for salary increases naturalists may be compelled to accept administrative or supervisory positions.

At present, there is keen competition for job openings among park naturalists. It is not unusual for 200 or 300 applicants to respond to a job announcement. During the past ten years there has been a continual rise in the number of jobs for park naturalists. However, the rolls of qualified job applicants have expanded at a much greater rate. Newly imposed budgetary restraints are severely curtailing the inception of additional interpretive programs. Increasingly, naturalists are looking to the private sector for employment as field trip leaders. It is estimated that as few as one in twenty trained naturalists are currently employed within their profession.

HSUS/JOHN DOMMERS

A park naturalist discusses turtle behavior with visitors to a nature center.

PROFESSIONAL WRITER

Roger Caras, author of more than twenty books on animals, also works as a television commentator and radio reporter.

Careers opportunities for professional writers exist within the fields of animal welfare and conservation. Career options for persons with writing ability may be delineated by seven job titles: dog writer, outdoor writer, photojournalist, environmental writer, columnist, publicist, and staff writer/editor.

Many professional writers have diversified interests. Few persons within the animal welfare or conservation professions rely exclusively upon their writing talents as a basis of income. Writers commonly combine their writing activity with a related

occupation which provides a regular salary and financial security. Significant numbers of writers earn their principal income as veterinary practioners, interpretive naturalists, wildlife biologists, and humane society administrators. Even those persons who specialize in the written word may intermix a syndicated column, book writing, and feature article writing.

It is doubtful that any writer specializing in animal welfare or conservation topics can earn a satisfactory income solely from books, feature articles, or a syndicated column. Each week 2,000 books are published in the United States. Natural history and pet care titles enjoy popularity with the reading public. However, there is a limited sales market for animal books. Author royalties on animal books vary from $2,000 to $30,000. Earnings on a book title are spread over a period of years and probably will not exceed $5,000 in the peak sales year. Similarly, syndicated animal columns only return to the writer $5 to $30 monthly per newspaper carrying the column. Authorship of books and articles does constructively contribute to an individual's professional reputation. Publication of books and feature articles may increase the speaker's fee or honorarium commanded by the writer and can contribute to a promotion or pay raise.

The professional writer may be a specialist with a demonstrated aptitude for writing or, alternatively, a skilled writer with a scholastic background in journalism. The principal employers of writers include newspaper publishers, magazine publishers, and institutions which publish literature that is concerned with animal welfare, conservation, and environmental quality. Many writers work on a freelance basis. The freelance writer independently researches and writes manuscripts either on

The job of San Diego zoo public relations representative Joan Embery includes television appearances with animals.

SAN DIEGO ZOOLOGICAL SOCIETY

assignment for a publisher or on speculation for unsolicited submission to potential publishers. Freelance writing is synonymous with self-employment. Freelance writing is a difficult method of earning a living. There is intense competition for publication space and many periodicals do not accept unsolicited manuscripts.

Dog writers are concerned with all facets of knowledge relating to the domestic canine including care, lore, grooming, nutrition, breeds, show, training, and behavior. It has been estimated that more than 100 periodicals are concerned with some phase of dog ownership. There are seventy magazines devoted to specific breeds of dog. There are in excess of 400 titles in print which relate to domestic canines. In fact, there are three publishing firms which specialize in books on dogs: Howell Book House, Incorporated; Delinger's; and Arco Publishing Company, Incorporated.

It is presumed that 2,000 persons currently qualify as dog writers less than 50 of whom rely upon writing as the only or primary source of income. One hundred and eight persons hold professional membership in The Dog Writers' Association of America.

Columnists author weekly or daily columns using a personal byline. A columnist may be employed as a salaried staff member of a newspaper or magazine, write under contract to a newspaper or magazine, or freelance a syndicated series. Two of the most popular pet care columns currently in print are authored by veterinarians: ''Understanding Your Pet'' by Dr. Michael Fox appears monthly in *McCall's Magazine* while ''The World of Animals'' by Dr. Frank Miller is a daily column syndicated in newspapers such as The Washington Post.

Staff writers and editors originate and edit articles for periodicals and pamphlets published by their employers. Staff writers and editors are employed by animal welfare and conservation organizations as well as by commercial publishing firms. Among the more than 150 primary animal welfare, conservation, and environmental quality periodicals prepared by staff writers and editors are *The Humane Society News, Environmental Action, Equus, Dogs, Journal of the American Veterinary Medical Association, Natural History, The Auk,* and *American Birds.*

Environmental writers are concerned with the topics of environmental quality, ecology, and conservation. Environmental writers employed by newspapers and magazines cover a diversity of contemporary events and topics ranging from a report on an oil spill to a technical analysis of the potential implications of a proposed international convention on endangered species. Environmental writers may also be self-employed.

The publicist is concerned with public relations and promotional work. The publicist is an employee or agent of an animal welfare or conservation organization. The publicist authors news releases, letters to the editor, feature articles, and pamphlets. The publicist also coordinates news media coverage of organizational functions and events. The publicist schedules and coordinates public appearances by organizational staff.

The photojournalist combines writing and photography to create a visual story. Most photojournalists specializing in animal welfare and conservation topics work on a freelance basis.

The outdoor writer is concerned with the conservation of natural resources. Outdoor writers are primarily employed as authors of outdoor (hunting/fishing) columns for daily newspapers and magazines. The outdoor writer is usually on the staff of the sports department and may also be assigned to stories about athletic events.

The prospective writer should obtain a college degree in journalism with a double major in animal science or a related discipline. The Dog Writers' Association of America offers partial grants-in-aid to journalism students.

There is keen competition among professional writers for both salaried positions and freelance assignments. There is also little opportunity for upward mobility with regard to promotions for staff employees. Staff writers can anticipate a beginning annual salary of $8,500 to $12,000 while editors may earn in excess of $30,000 in annual income. The fee structure for freelance work has remained basically unchanged for the past fifteen years. The earnings of a freelance writer vary with the quality of the work, its length, and the type of publication in which a manuscript appears. Feature articles of 3,000 words may earn from $50 to $1,500. One-time-use rights to a photograph may pay $7.50 to $100. Flat fees offered for short articles vary from $8 to $100 or may be set at a fixed word rate of approximately $.01 to $.05 per word.

Dr. Michael Fox, Director of The Humane Society's Institute for the Study of Animal Problems, is also a noted author, lecturer, and newspaper columnist.

FORESTER

A district forest ranger inspects the results of a forest improvement project.

The science of forestry relates to the management of timber and other natural resources which occur in association with forest lands. The professional forester is responsible for planning and supervising the acquisition, utilization, and management of forest lands. The best known of the positions for foresters is that of the Federal Forest Ranger. The Ranger is a line officer in charge of a forest district. There may be several forest districts in a National Forest.

Individual stands of woodland may be managed for timber production, recreational use, or wilderness preservation. The forester, in planning and supervising the management of forest areas, is concerned with wildlife habitat. Decisions regarding timber harvest and reforestation affect wildlife food sources and shelter. Through selective planting or thinning of woodlands, the forester may create or enhance wildlife habitat. The careful harvesting of timber may permit the preservation of critical habitat areas.

The duties of a forester are not confined to the production and harvest of timber. Foresters are concerned with the control of diseases and insects which damage trees, watershed protection, flood prevention, firefighting, and wildlife research. Recently, Federal foresters have been researching wildlife food preferences with the intention of determining which species of trees should be planted to provided a palatable and nutritious source of food for wild animals.

The Forest Service of the United States Department of Agriculture, oldest of the Federal conservation agencies, is the major forestry organization in the nation. Among the activities of the Forest Service are the management, protection, and development of the National Forests and National Grasslands; coordination of state and industrial forestry programs; forestry research; and administration of National Wilderness areas.

National Forests are managed with a multiple-use objective intended ''to provide the maximum benefit for the greatest number of people.'' Among the activities which occur in National Forests are mining, livestock grazing, timber harvesting, camping, hunting, and boating.

In excess of 20,000 persons are employed in permanent positions with the Forest Service and an additional 20,000 employees hold seasonal jobs. However, the largest number of foresters are employed by industrial landowners. Approximately 36,000 foresters, plus support personnel, are employed by industrial timber production companies.

National Forest lands comprise one-twelfth of the country's total area and are estimated to contain fifty percent of the wild animals classified as big game species. Wildlife in National Forests are managed by the Forest Service in cooperation with state fish and game departments. The Forest Service does have projects directed toward maintaining and improving wildlife habitat. Historically, the science of forestry has emphasized the consumption utilization of natural resources. Wildlife management programs on forest lands have been concerned with providing optimum hunting opportunities for sportsmen. In recent years the Forest Service has adopted a ''Total Wildlife Program'' approach which actively promotes the non-consumptive enjoyment of wildlife. The Forest Service is currently involved in the protection and management of both endangered and non-game species.

U.S. FOREST SERVICE

Increasingly, attention is being given to wildlife observation and wildlife photography. Yet, the consumptive exploitation of wild animals through game-oriented management programs continues as the principal objective of National Forest wildlife projects.

Traditionally, the professional forester has borne broad responsibility for all management plans and activities affecting forest lands. Today, there is a trend toward specialization. Professional wildlife biologists are being employed to direct those phases of forestry programs which directly relate to wild animals. Currently, the Forest Service employs approximately 350 Wildlife and Fisheries Biologists. Foresters and biologists specializing in wildlife management on forest lands are employed mainly by Federal and state agencies. Only a small number of industrial landowners employ wildlife specialists. Several municipal parks employ foresters in wildlife conservation programs.

A forestry school graduate beginning employment with the Forest Service will start at the GS-5 pay grade. A beginning employee with postgraduate schooling or a ranking in the top ten percent of his or her class, can start at a pay grade of GS-7. A forester with a Ph.D. or job experience will start at a commensurately higher pay grade. The Federal Park Ranger or District Ranger may earn an annual salary of $18,000 to $30,000. The Forest Supervisor for a National Forest can earn $25,000 to $40,000 per year. Regional Foresters and other top administrators are paid $40,000 to $50,000. The upper salary range for foresters employed in the private sector is even higher.

At present, there are limited job opportunities for professional foresters. It is estimated that only fifty percent of new forestry school graduates are finding employment in the forestry profession or related fields. Employment opportunities for foresters are expected to increase only moderately during the next five years.

ATTORNEY AT LAW

The Humane Society's General Counsel discusses the protection of whales with the late Rogers C.B. Morton, then U.S. Secretary of the Interior, and Gilbert Gude, then U.S. Congressman from Maryland.

In the years since publication of *Silent Spring,* concerned citizens have spurred the enactment of environmental quality, conservation, and animal protection legislation. Working at all levels of government, private citizens, individually and through established organizations such as The Humane Society of the United States, have prompted the adoption of legislative controls on a broad spectrum of issues including animal mistreatment, wildlife exploitation, water pollution, community planning and zoning, noise pollution, pesticide use, predator control, and the development of natural areas. Legislative measures

amended or newly enacted by Congress during the current decade include the Marine Mammal Protection Act, Animal Welfare Act, Endangered Species Act, Humane Methods of Slaughter Act, Horse Protection Act, Wild Free Roaming Horses and Burros Act, and Migratory Bird Treaty Act.

The enactment of revolutionary animal protection, conservation, and environmental laws has conveyed to government and industry clearly defined responsibilities and obligations. Increasingly, humane societies, conservation organizations, civic groups, environmental organizations, individual citizens, and neighborhood ad hoc committees are using judicial mechanisms to challange natural resource management plans, animal exploitation schemes, and land development enterprises.

The increase in legislation and litigation relating directly to the welfare of animals and protection of the environment has led to the formation of a legal cadre which specializes in this area of jurisprudence. In this connection attorneys are concerned with both civil and criminal areas of law. General Counsel and Solicitor departments are a common component of staffs among both government agencies and non-profit organizations concerned with the welfare of animals or protection of the environment.

The Federal government is the largest employer of lawyers who specialize in environmental law or related fields of practice. The United States Department of Justice is responsible for all litigation involving the Federal government. The Department of Justice employs two attorneys within its Wildlife Section. An additional forty staff attorneys combine wildlife law with other litigative topics.

Administrative agencies of the Federal government have legal divisions within their staff structures. The agencies principally concerned with animal protection, environmental quality, and conservation are the United States Department of the Interior, United States Department of Agriculture, United States Department of Commerce (National Marine Fisheries Service and National Oceanic and Atmospheric Administration), Environmental Prottection Agency, and the President's Council on Environmental Quality.

The eight attorneys for the Office of the Solicitor within the United States Department of the Interior (USDI) include among their primary functions the tasks of providing liason in litigation with the U.S. Department of Justice, providing legal counsel to staff, interpreting statutes, providing assistance to staff in drafting regulations, preparation of legal opinions, drafting of legislation, review of agreements and contracts, and the instruction of law enforcement personnel. Persons possessing law degrees are employed in many divisions of USDI; however, their duties may be administrative in scope. Attorneys employed by other Federal agencies share similar assignments and duties.

An attorney in the private sector may engage in specialized private practice or may be employed

on the staff of a humane or conservation organization. The attorney in private practice is generally hired on retainer and may serve several organizations and individual clients. The duties of an attorney directly employed by an animal welfare, conservation, or environmental quality organization include a broad range of activities commonly associated with incorporated charitable institutions. The duties of a staff lawyer can include filing articles of incorporation; preparation of briefs, petitions, and suits; estate planning for benefactors; liason with legislators and government agencies; pension planning for staff; preparation of solicitation and registration reports required by state and Federal tax agencies; monitoring government enforcement of standards and regulations; presentation of testimony; lobbying; drafting legislative proposals; providing specialized legal advice to the public; and registration of copyright on publications.

Lawyers associated with animal welfare organizations will also be concerned with criminal investigations into alleged incidents of animal mistreatment. An attorney for a humane society may instruct humane agents in investigative procedure, civil rights, false arrest, libel, slander, defamation, and other aspects of law enforcement. A humane society lawyer may also assist in the prosecution of criminal cases involving state animal mistreatment statutes.

To become an attorney at law a person must obtain a J.D. or LL.M. degree from a school of law. To qualify for admission to a law school, an applicant commonly is required to possess a baccalaureate degree in pre-law or other academic discipline. Law schools commonly require three years of study. Law students intending to specialize in animal welfare, environmental protection, or conservation should pursue courses in taxation, wills and trusts, administrative law, local government law, environmental law, litigation, and legislation. Law school graduates must pass a bar examination and be licensed by the state government before they may practice law.

Compensation for the newly graduated attorney employed by the Federal government is established at the GS-11 pay grade of $19,263. Government lawyers can advance to the GS-15 pay grade level of $49,000. Attorneys employed by charitable organizations receive beginning salaries of $16,000 to $22,000.

SELF-EMPLOYMENT OCCUPATIONS

Horse training is a self-employment occupation popular with persons who are interested in working with animals.

A substantial number of persons who work with animals are self-employed. Common job titles of self-employed persons include: riding instructor, veterinary practitioner, animal handler, groomer, pet shop operator, kennel operator, freelance writer, freelance photographer, stable operator, farrier, dairy farm operator, animal trainer, freelance artist, animal taxi driver, pet supplies manufacturer, pet supplies distributor, exerciser/walker, and consultant.

The basic prerequisites for self-employment are familiarity with the goods or services being offered, working capital, and a need for the goods or services within the community being served. The United States Department of Labor separates self-employed persons into three basic categories: 1) Professional persons who are not businessmen but provide a service requiring special skills. This category includes veterinary practitioners, writers, and artists. 2) Persons in non-specialized, low paying occupations which require few skills and little monetary investment such as the dog walker, pet sitter, or animal taxi driver. 3) Persons who are business proprietors and actually own their establishment such as a pet grooming salon, pet shop, or boarding kennel.

No single job profile can typify the experiences and duties of the self-employed worker. Persons who choose self-employment face work conditions which are substantially different from those of the salaried labor force. Self-employed individuals work longer hours and take less vacation than employees. The self-employed perform a wider variety of functions, both administrative and retail, than salaried workers. The self-employed do earn slightly more income than salaried persons but such earnings may be offset by the absence of fringe benefits such as retirement and medical plans. Persons who are independently employed need to be self-motivated for there is no one to supervise their work.

The freedom and challenge of being their own bosses is a major attraction for the self-employed. There is an opportunity to adjust work hours and schedule to suit personal preferences. There is also the reward of profiting from personal creativity, ability, and devotion to the job. For the self-employed there is also the certainty of gaining entry into the job market.

Although self-employment offers special attractions, this career option is not without pitfalls. The income of a self-employed person may be irregular especially while becoming established. It may be necessary to borrow capital to establish a business. The self-employed person's income hinges upon his or her ability to make sound judgements about the needs and wants to customers. A poor investment or improper business decision can prove costly. According to the United States Department of Commerce, only one in every five businesses started by self-employed persons survives for ten years.

A majority of the self-employment opportunities in working with animals are found in the retail market where goods and services are sold directly to the consumer. The pet trade industry provides the greatest number of opportunities and options for persons with a preference for self-employment. The retail pet shop industry, which includes approximately 6,000 facilities, is dominated by small, independently operated stores. Similarly, most grooming salons and boarding kennels are operated by self-employed persons.

HSUS

A trainer may teach animals to perform tricks as well as working on obedience instruction.

ANIMAL CONTROL OFFICER
HUMANE AGENT

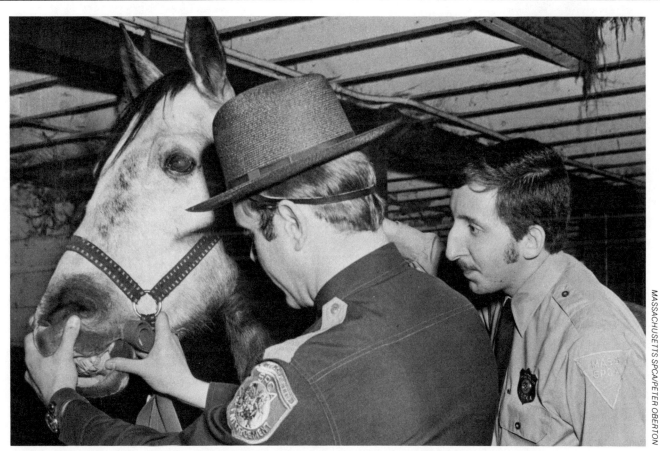

A humane agent and an apprentice cruelty investigator conduct a routine inspection of a horse stable.

The animal control officer and humane agent are the backbone of U. S. animal welfare programs. The animal control officer is responsible for the enforcement of municipal ordinances relating to the keeping and restraint of animals. In the past, the animal control officer was popularly known as a "dog warden." The warden patrolled neighborhood streets in search of stray dogs and impounded all domestic canines found running at large.

The contemporary animal control officer is a professional animal care specialist who has been trained to handle all manner of situations involving pets and pet owners. The animal control officer is concerned with the welfare of the community's animals, both domestic and wild. Animal control officers may conduct routine compliance inspections of pet shops, kennels, stables, and other commercial enterprises to assure that animals are receiving adequate care. Animal control personnel operate animal ambulances. Some officers specialize in the rescue of trapped and injured animals. Officers occasionally conduct community dog obedience and pet care clinics and may address civic groups and school classes. Animal control personnel are

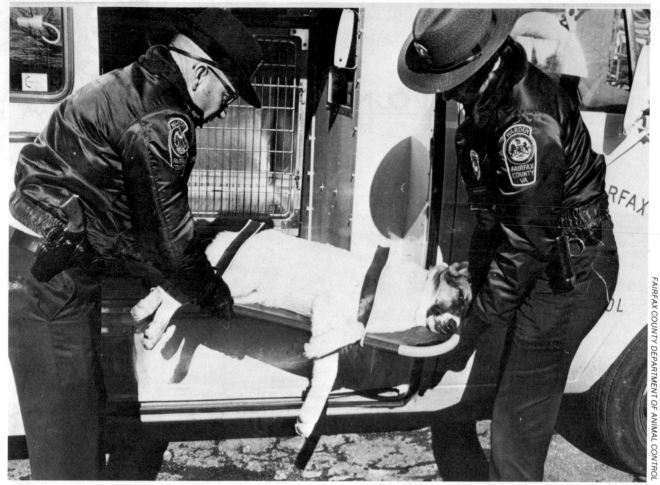

Animal control officers often are responsible for the rescue of injured animals.

responsible for the administration of rabies inoculations and dog license laws. In some communities animal control officers assume the responsibility for investigating alleged incidents of animal mistreatment. In conjunction with the responsibilities of the animal control agency an officer may be assigned to conduct a census of the community dog and cat populations. The animal control officer retains responsibility for the apprehension and impoundment of animals which are running at large in violation of local ordinances and for issuing citations to the owners of offending pets.

The animal control officer is usually an employee of an animal control department. The department is a branch of municipal government. The department of animal control may be an individual agency or a division of the department of health or police department. In Pennsylvania and Connecticut animal control officers are employed by the state Departments of Agriculture.

The work of the animal control officer is complemented by humane agents. The humane agent

is commonly an employee of a local animal welfare agency such as an SPCA or humane society. These individuals are primarily responsible for the enforcement of state and local laws relating to the mistreatment of animals. The humane agent investigates reported incidents of animal abuse, files criminal complaints against offenders, and, with the assistance of legal counsel, prosecutes violations of animal cruelty laws. The humane agent may be expert in the rescue and first aid treatment of injured animals. As with their counterparts in animal control departments, the humane agent may be required to conduct pet care clinics and speak before civic groups.

The duties of the humane agent or animal control officer often overlap with those of other community officials. Municipal park authority personnel and local wildlife conservation officers share in the responsibility for protecting wildlife. Municipal health department workers are concerned with sanitation in pet shops and dog bite incidents.

As female police officers have become accepted,

the number of women humane agents and animal control officers has expanded proportionately. Each year larger numbers of women are entering these professions. While a majority of today's animal control officers and humane agents are male, there are no barriers for a woman who is seeking employment in these professions.

Neither technical schools nor junior colleges offer specialized programs of study for prospective animal control officers or humane agents. Desirable backgrounds for such personnel include undergraduate study in criminology, law enforcement, veterinary technology, or animal science. Most municipalities require applicants for a position as an animal control officer to possess a high school diploma. A similar educational background is required of prospective humane agents.

Humane agents distribute pet food to dog and cat owners during severe winter storm.

On-the-job training is a common condition of employment for novice humane agents and animal control officers. They may be required to complete police indoctrination courses and to serve apprenticeships under experienced colleagues. In

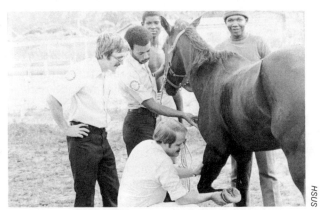

A humane agent checks the condition of a horse which was alleged to have been mistreated.

several states the humane agent is required to obtain local court certification of his or her competence to enforce animal protection laws.

In interviewing job applicants employers generally give preference to persons who have a good general appearance, are capable speakers, remain calm under stress, have an authoritative presence, and possess the ability to make independent judgements.

An animal control officer records a resident's complaint regarding his neighbor's barking dog.

Some rural municipalities employ animal control officers only on a part-time basis. Similarly, animal welfare agencies serving towns or small cities may not require the services of full-time humane agents. Thus full-time positions for animal control officers and humane agents are usually confined to communities with human populations in excess of 100,000 persons. Personnel employed in a part-time capacity earn $3,000 to $5,000 per year. A beginning humane agent or animal control officer is commonly paid $7,500 to $9,000. Experienced personnel can expect to earn approximately $12,000. Animal control departments and humane societies serving major metropolitan centers may pay senior personnel in excess of $16,000 in annual salary and benefits. Salaries do vary in accordance with geographic regions, community size, and agency budgets.

The humane agent and animal control officer do have an opportunity for job advancement. They may be appointed to supervisory positions as chief investigators, assistant shelter managers, shelter managers or executive directors.

VETERINARY TECHNICIAN

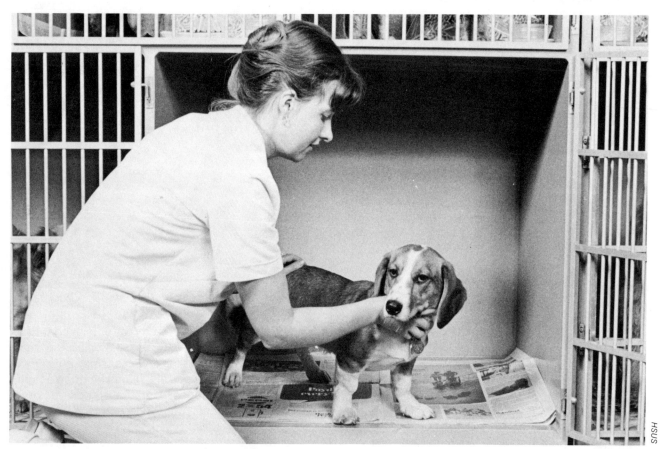

Animal hospitals are the most common employers of veterinary technicians.

HSUS

Animal health care is expanding in thoroughness and complexity; invaluable but time consuming procedures are greatly improving the veterinarian's ability to diagnose and successfully treat animal ailments. At the same time the United States is witnessing an increased demand for veterinary services. Within the past decade the veterinary profession has begun to compensate for the veterinary manpower shortage by employing technicians who have received specialized training in animal health and animal care procedures.

The veterinary technician is primarily employed as an assistant to a veterinarian engaged in private practice. The duties of a veterinary technician may include specimen collection, surgical preparation, laboratory analysis, animal hospital management, emergency first aid treatment, client consultation, surgical nursing, the administration of medication, and the routine care of hospitalized patients. Veterinary technicians have an option of specializing in a particular area of medicine such as surgical nursing, X-ray technology, or laboratory technology. However, there is a limited demand for such specialists. The duties of a technician employed in a veterinary hospital may involve all aspects of animal health care procedures. However, state laws regulating the practice of veterinary medicine prohibit technicians from performing surgery, making diagnoses, or prescribing treatment.

Increasing numbers of trained veterinary technicians are finding employment as paraprofessionals working in veterinary hospitals. The variety of work involved with this profession is restricted only by the scope of the veterinarian's practice and his attitude toward the use of paraprofessionals — some veterinarians restrict the job duties of an assistant to record keeping, animal grooming, housekeeping and other routine tasks, but in progressive veterinary practices technicians are assuming integral roles in the treatment and care of patients.

Employment opportunities for veterinary technicians include a variety of practical and ethical jobs in industry and government. In addition to

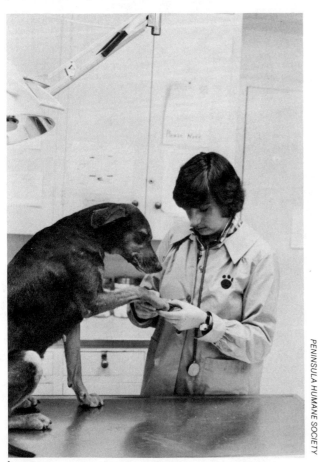

A veterinary technician, employed at an animal shelter, examines a dog which was taken into custody after being mistreated by its owner.

PENINSULA HUMANE SOCIETY

working as assistants in large animal and small animal practices, technicians are now finding employment in animal shelters, zoological parks, horse farms, kennels, veterinary colleges, government diagnostic laboratories, biological research laboratories and other facilities.

Some veterinarians prefer to personally train their personnel; however, an associate degree in animal technology is a valuable and often essential qualification for the person desiring meaningful employment in a veterinary hospital or for the individual interested in exploring job opportunities outside the veterinary clinic. There are currently more than 50 community colleges and universities* offering training for veterinary technicians. A majority of these scholastic programs are two years in duration. A high school diploma is normally a prerequisite for acceptance into an animal technology program of study.

The student veterinary technician receives classroom instruction in animal nutrition, physiology, toxicology, clinical techniques, parasitology, microbiology, animal care, applied anatomy, clinical pathology, pharmacology, radiology, surgical preparation, and animal housing. Most scholastic institutions require that a student receive practical training in a veterinary hospital prior to graduation. Upon successful completion of an animal technology program the graduating student is awarded either a certificate, associate degree or baccalaureate degree depending upon the program of study.

The American Veterinary Medical Association (AVMA) has undertaken the accreditation and standardization of training programs for veterinary technicians. To date, the AVMA has reviewed and accredited thirty-two scholastic programs. The AVMA has also endorsed a proposal for state Veterinary Medical Examining Boards to certify individual technicians. In future years job applicants may be required to pass a licensing examination similar to the testing program that currently exists for registered nurses.

Several state and community veterinary medical associations have established technician training programs for individuals who are unable to enroll in institutional courses. These special classes are normally open only to persons with previous experience as animal hospital attendants. To be eligible for training an applicant must possess a written recommendation from a licensed veterinarian. Programs typically involve eight months of twice-weekly night classes with weekend work in animal hospitals. Persons completing the program of study are awarded animal hospital technician certificates.

The annual starting salaries for certified veterinary technicians vary from $6,500 to $10,000 depending on the training and experience of the employee. Senior veterinary technicians who have risen to managerial positions in shelters, research institutions and animal hospitals are earning $12,000 to $16,000.

The employment of paraprofessionals in the field of veterinary medicine remains a novel program that is viewed with cautious optimism by doctors of veterinary medicine. It is difficult to evaluate future opportunities in this profession. It is known that graduating technicians are encountering minimal difficulty in obtaining employment. It can be presumed that as technicians win greater acceptance within the veterinary profession, the demand for their services and advancement opportunities will increase in proportion to the improved stature of this profession.

----

*Scholastic institutions offering training for veterinary technicians are listed in Appendix I under the titles "Animal Technology" and "Veterinary Technology".

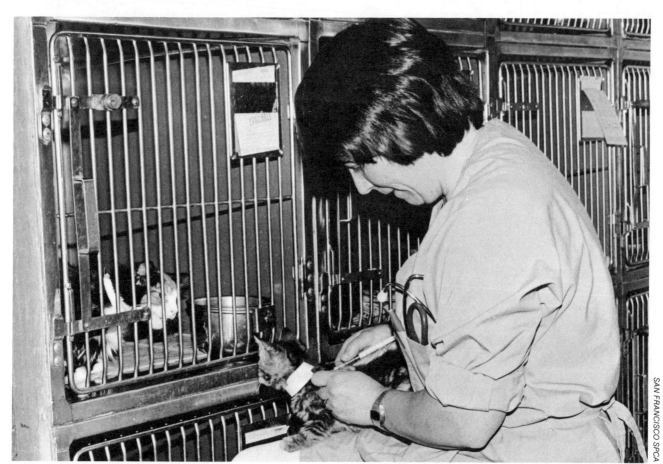

A veterinary technician administers a routine distemper vaccination to a new shelter arrival.

SAN FRANCISCO SPCA

ANIMAL CARE ATTENDANT

An animal care attendant may be assigned the duty of identifying and notifying the owner of a stray pet recovered by the shelter.

The animal care attendant works at the most rudimentary level of the animal care profession. The primary duties of an attendant include the cleaning, grooming, feeding, general observation, and exercising of animals. Auxiliary duties assigned to attendants can include carpentry, gardening, and common labor. Persons working for animal shelters may be assigned duty as an ambulance attendant or nighttime shelter attendant. Attendants working in pet shops may take inventory or serve as cashiers and sales clerks.

Every facility which kennels animals, both domestic and wild, has need of animal care attendants. Among the more common facilities where attendants can find employment are animal shelters, veterinary hospitals, stables, grooming shops, farms, pet shops, kennels, and zoological parks. Regardless of the nature of the establishment, commercial enterprise or charitable institution, the work of the animal attendant is essentially the same.

The working conditions for an animal care attendant might seem unattractive except to those persons with a special affection for animals. The basic

An animal care attendant introduces an adopted shelter dog to its new owner.

SAN FRANCISCO SPCA

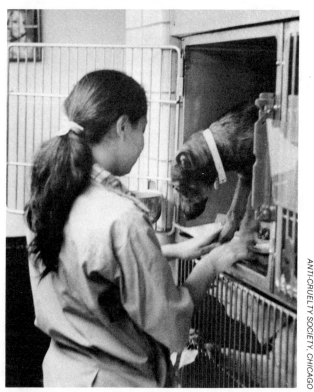

An animal care attendant comforts a frightened animal as it is placed in a shelter cage.

ANTI-CRUELTY SOCIETY, CHICAGO

work of the attendant is dirty, repetitious, demanding, and sometimes even dangerous. Fortunately, those individuals who enjoy working with animals are usually able to overcome the disadvantages commonly associated with the position of animal care attendant. These persons view animals individually and enjoy dealing with the varying temperaments, habits, and responses of each creature in their charge.

There are no scholastic or work experience prerequisites for obtaining employment as an animal care attendant. However, job opportunities and earning potential are significantly enhanced through formal training or the development of special job skills. Community college courses in animal science, business management, zoology, or related subjects will assist the attendant in obtaining employment as well as in job advancement.

The Humane Society of the United States sponsors a two day animal welfare/animal control workshop which provides a basic introduction to animal shelter operations and management. Workshops are conducted several times each year in different regions of the United States (see Chapter 5). Explorer Scout packs and 4-H Clubs also conduct programs which help to prepare young people for jobs as animal care attendants.

There is a high labor turnover among animal care attendants as a result of attrition and advancement. Thus, there is no shortage of job opportunities for persons anxious or willing to enter the job market as animal care attendants. The type of attendant job which a person should choose will depend upon his or her career goals. The prospective attendant should seek employment within that segment of the job market which is most closely related to his or her special interests.

Salaries for animal care attendants are universally poor. Newly hired attendants in non-supervisory positions will earn approximately $450 per month depending upon previous experience and duties. Senior animal shelter and kennel attendants may earn $1,000 or more per month. The attendant who possesses resourcefulness, dedication, and ability can advance rapidly within certain segments of the job market. The animal shelter attendant may become a humane agent, animal control officer, or assistant shelter manager. Frequently, job advancement necessitates that the attendant relocate his or her residence within another community.

ZOO KEEPER

A zoo keeper trains elephants to perform in public shows.

BRONX ZOO

The American Association of Zoological Parks and Aquariums recognizes 197 zoos and 39 aquariums located within the United States. These institutions employ 7,000 full-time plus 4,000 part-time salaried staff. Municipal governments are the primary operators of zoological parks.

Among zoological park staffs, zoo keepers or animal caretakers comprise the major group of personnel directly involved with animal care activities. Keepers are responsible for providing the basic care required to maintain the health of an animal collection. The most important fundamental duties performed by zoo keepers involve the cleanliness and safety of enclosures for animals and the feeding of the animal stock. Keepers assist the zoo veterinarian in administering animal health programs and may also contribute to the design and construction of animal enclosures.

The zoo keeper is more than an animal care attendant. Keepers must possess an understanding of techniques for animal breeding, capture, hygiene, and exhibition. The zoo keeper must have the ability to relate to the needs and temperaments of individual animals—including rare species about

During morning rounds, a zoo keeper greets one of the animals for which he cares.

which there may be minimal recorded knowledge. Changes in an animal's habits, preferences, moods, or behavior serve as indicators of medical problems. Keepers function as trained observers who must detect behavioral changes, determine their cause, and react accordingly.

Keepers are generally assigned to work with a broad group of animals such as mammals, birds, or reptiles. In large zoological parks, keepers may work with a limited collection of animals such as primates, large cats, or dolphins. Keepers with special interests and skills may be assigned as technical specialists, or they may be employed full-time on specific projects such as the captive breeding of a particular species.

A senior keeper manages an animal exhibition building and is responsible for the supervision of other keepers working in that facility. A head keeper works directly with the curator and is responsible for supervising the entire keeper force. In major zoological parks there are head keepers for each curatorial department.

Within the animal attendant profession, zoo keepers have historically had a unique opportunity for advancement. The most common course of job promotion is from keeper to senior keeper, to assistant head keeper, to head keeper, possible to assistant curator, and even, on rare occasions, to zoo director.

Education and experience are important job prerequisites for the person seeking a keeper position with a major zoological park. The Bronx Zoo in New York City only accepts as job applicants individuals with a minimum of one year's college

instruction in zoology or animal husbandry, or, as its equivalent, at least one year's full-time salaried employment in a job involving the care and feeding of animals. The Brookfield Zoo in Chicago receives a sufficient number of applications from college graduates to fill all of their keeper positions.

Preference at major zoological parks for keeper positions is given to college graduates, especially those persons with degrees in zoology or biology. However, since zoo keeping requires extensive on-the-job training and learning by experience, special consideration in hiring is occasionally given to the non-college graduate on the basis of practical experience, exceptional desire, or aptitude for learning. Small zoos are more flexible in their job requirements. However, salaries and advancement opportunities are poorer than in the large, prestigious zoological parks.

The American Association of Zoological Parks and Aquariums is consulting with several community colleges on the development of formal vocation training programs for prospective zoo keepers. Several major zoological parks offer formal keeper training courses as well as on-the-job training programs.

For the individual lacking in formal training, a background of work with farm animals is considered especially desirable. Zoo officials believe that farm experience is indicative of an ability to perform laborious tasks and to handle large animals.

Salaries, job requirements, and job opportunities vary widely among zoological parks and depend upon the size and prestige of individual institutions. Apprentice zoo keepers may earn from $5,000 to $9,000. Headkeepers and other experienced staff receive annual salaries up to $18,000.

WILDLIFE CONSERVATION OFFICER

A conservation officer frees a coyote which had become entangled in a fence.

U.S. FISH AND WILDLIFE SERVICE/RAY RAUCH

Wildlife conservation is broadly defined as the protection and maintenance of wildlife populations. The wildlife conservation officer may also be known as a conservation warden or, most commonly, as a game warden. As the latter title suggests, the wildlife conservation officer is primarily concerned with game species — wild animals which are exploited for commercial and recreational purposes.

State wildlife management agencies, popularly known as fish and game departments, are the foremost employers of wildlife conservation officers.

The principal duties of a conservation officer involve the enforcement of laws and regulations regarding hunting, trapping, and fishing. The wildlife conservation officer may patrol a district in search of game law violators. The officer spot-checks licenses of hunters, trappers, and fishermen. The officer ascertains that license holders do not exceed legal quotas on the taking of wild animals. The wildlife conservation officer investigates reports of game law violations, arrests offenders, and assists in the preparation and prosecution of criminal charges against game law violators.

The work of the wildlife conservation officer is no longer confined to the enforcement of game laws and regulations. Today, conservation officers may perform a variety of tasks relating to the protection and management of wild animals. Conservation officers may be called upon to conduct wildlife census counts; capture and band animals; rescue orphaned and injured wildlife; relocate wild animals; erect and maintain wildlife feeding stations; investigate hunting and boating accidents; control predatory and nuisance wildlife through shooting, trapping and other methods; provide instruction in hunter safety; wildlife habitat restoration and improvement; speak before school classes, civic groups, and hunters' clubs; forest fire detection and control; operate state-owned game breeding farms; issue wildlife holding permits; monitor commercial traffic in wildlife; and inspect private game breeding farms, fish hatcheries, and commercial shooting preserves. An officer may be assigned to a conservation district, state park, game management area, or municipality.

The Special Agent is the federal counterpart to the state wildlife conservation officer. Special Agents are employees of the Division of Law Enforcement for the United States Fish and Wildlife Service. Special Agents are responsible for investigating suspected violations of federal wildlife laws and regulations, arresting offenders, and preparing criminal charges against violators. Special Agents currently enforce ten major federal conservation laws plus other statutes and regulations. Special Agents also investigate applicants for federal wildlife permits. Agent-Pilots may fly enforcement patrols. Unlike state conservation officers, federal agents specialize in law enforcement operations and only occasionally participate in wildlife management activities such as censusing.

In recent years there has been a sharp rise in the minimum job qualification requirements for wildlife conservation officers. Several state fish and game departments now require an applicant for the position of conservation officer to possess a bachelor degree in wildlife biology, forestry, or a related field. Within a class of 24 game conservation officer trainees recently hired by the Pennsylvania Game Department, one trainee possessed a master's degree, thirteen persons held bachelor degrees, two trainees held associate degrees, and six additional trainees had received formal education beyond high school. In lieu of formal education applicants may substitute employment experience in law en-

forcement, farming, game breeding, forestry, or wildlife conservation. Applicants for the position of Special Agent are required to have a bachelor degree in criminal justice, wildlife biology or a related field, or to have an equivalent amount of job experience in wildlife law enforcement.

Jobs for conservation officers and Special Agents are physically demanding and often require strenuous outdoor activity. Several state fish and game departments have established physical requirements which must be met by job applicants.

U.S. FISH AND WILDLIFE SERVICE

Wildlife conservation officers trap geese in nets as part of a wildlife population census count.

Starting salaries for state wildlife conservation officers range from $6,500 to $10,000 depending upon geographic region, experience, training, and duty assignment. The starting pay grade of GS-5 is established for Special Agents; however, a starting employee with extraordinary educational or work experience credentials may start at the GS-7 or GS-9 pay grade. A Special Agent may advance to the GS-14 pay grade level.

The job market for conservation officers is static. There is hope for the expansion of employment opportunities with the introduction of non-game wildlife programs. At present, however, there is intense competition for available positions. Every 2-3 years the Pennsylvania Game Department conducts a class for game conservation officer trainees. There were 1,650 applications for 24 positions in the 1978 graduating class.

FORESTRY TECHNICIAN
FORESTRY AIDE

Forest technicians plant seedlings in an area where trees were cut to produce lumber.

Forestry technicians and forestry aides assist professional foresters in the management of forest resources, including wildlife. The duties of a technician may involve tree measurement, marking trees for harvest or thinning, field research, field supervision of recreational forest land, supervision of road construction and road survey crews, topographic surveys, timber inventories, planting of trees, and the collection and analysis of data. Technicians may be assigned tasks relating to the prevention and detection of forest fires or the protection of wildlife.

Job titles and duties for technicians vary in accordance with specific assignments. The job titles commonly assigned to technicians include: District Fire Control Officer, Survey Fire Control Officer, Survey Party Chief, Recreation Camp Supervisor, and Timber Management Technician.

An applicant for the position of forestry technician with the Forest Service of the United States Department of Agriculture, is required to have three years of general experience in forestry, or to have completed a one- or two-year college program in forest technology at an institution accredited by the Society of American Foresters.

The forestry aide supplements the labor force of technicians. Aides perform a variety of tasks including log scaling, tree measurement, maintenance of scientific data-collecting instruments, road survey crew work, and fire control work. A high school diploma is not required for employment as a forestry aide; however, schooling can be substituted for a portion of the general experience requirement for the position of forestry aide with the Forest Service.

Forest aides and forestry technicians are employed by federal, state, and local government agencies. In the private sector, aides and technicians are principally employed by paper, lumber, and mill companies. These jobs are physically demanding, may require residence in rural locations, and involve extensive outdoor activity.

Forestry aides enter civil service work at the beginning grade of GS-2 or GS-3, depending upon general experience. An aide employed in the private sector will receive a starting salary of $6,000 to $8,000. Technicians with the Forest Service normally begin employment at the GS-5 pay grade. Technicians employed by industry may begin with a salary of $8,000 to $12,000. Experienced technicians can earn $16,000 or more.

Employment opportunities for technicians and aides are expected to expand at a greater rate than those of many other conservation and animal welfare professions. However, regional competition for jobs may develop in some areas as a greater number of students are graduated from forest technology programs.

A forest technician records the result of an experimental project to control insects which bore into trees.

CLERICAL CAREERS

A shelter receptionist and an office manager review the procedure for the redemption of impounded pets.

Clerical careers include a variety of jobs which are essential to the operation of conservation and animal welfare institutions as well as commercial enterprises working with animals. No agency or enterprise can long endure without competent staff to perform basic administrative tasks.

Among the job titles included within the category of clerical careers are secretary, bookkeeper, file clerk, sales clerk, record clerk, office receptionist, switchboard operator, typist, cashier, computer operator, mail clerk, stenographer, voucher examiner, and stock clerk. Clerical personnel working with an animal welfare or conservation organization may be assigned duties which are broader than those tasks commonly associated with a particular job title.

Clerical personnel may be called upon to operate light office equipment such as photocopy machines, duplicators, addressing machines, postage meters, adding machines, telephone consoles, stencil cutting equipment, and mail sorting machines.

A clerical employee working for a community animal welfare organization may be required to provide advice and assistance to the public. This daily interaction with the public makes humane society clerical work less repetitious and less tedious than many other clerical jobs.

Clerical positions are increasingly gaining in status as an avenue of advancement. Clerical jobs are being upgraded in responsibilities and salary. Openings for qualified clerical workers are numerous. Employment opportunities for clerical workers are expected to increase faster than the overall average for conservation and animal welfare occupations. Clerical jobs in conservation and animal welfare are clustered in major metropolitan communities, state capitals, Washington, D.C., and university communities.

ANTI-CRUELTY SOCIETY, CHICAGO

A shelter computer operator consults a printout for information on dog food supplies.

As a rule, a high school diploma is required of applicants for clerical positions. Special training in office procedures and the use and operation of office machines is desirable for clerical personnel. A minimum typing speed of 40 to 60 words per minute is required for secretaries and typists. Jobs involving shorthand normally require that an applicant take dictation at a minimum speed of 80 words per minute for three minutes. Employers in interviewing job applicants give preference to clerical workers who are punctual, reliable, cooperative, outgoing, courteous, tactful, organized, possess mechanical aptitude and good eye-hand coordination, and have a fundamental knowledge of arithmetic, spelling, and punctuation.

The basic job qualification required by the Federal government for a GS-2 clerk typist is a high school diploma or six months of office experience. A beginning pay grade of GS-3 is assigned to the clerk typist with one year of general office experience or who has completed an academic year at a business or secretarial school. A person with exceptional qualifications or experience can be started at the GS-4 pay grade. In general, the salary and advancement opportunities with commercial and charitable institutions are comparable with those of government agencies.

SAN FRANCISCO SPCA

A shelter clerk prepares a medical record for a pet dog treated at the humane society animal hospital.

ADDITIONAL CAREER OPTIONS

Animal nurses specialize in the care of newborn zoo animals.

SAN DIEGO ZOOLOGICAL SOCIETY

The professions profiled in this book provide a broad overview of occupational opportunities in animal welfare, conservation, environmental quality, and industry. Insight is supplied into popular professions which are representative of the job market. However, the person interested in a career working with animals is confronted with a wide choice of occupational options which extend far beyond the job titles profiled in the preceding chapters. Several unusual job options are introduced in this section and still more career alternatives may be discovered by consulting the extensive list of career guidance literature referenced in Appendix II.

Pet Groomers maintain the health, condition and physical appearance of animals' coats, especially dogs. Pet groomers bathe, clip, and style the hair of dogs. Groomers may work in a salon or a mobile van which is specially equipped. Groomers must either serve an apprenticeship or attend a vocational school. A groomer may be an employee of a salon, a self-employed worker, or the owner-operator of a salon.

Kennel Foremen manage the daily operation of commercial kennel facilities where animals are boarded for a fee or bred for sale. The kennel foreman is responsible for the training and supervision of kennel workers, business purchases, and the development of operational procedures. The kennel foreman is a salaried employee retained by the kennel owner.

Boarding Kennel Operators own, rent, or lease kennel facilities at which owned dogs are boarded for a daily or weekly fee. The boarding kennel operator administers the kennel business operation and is usually self-employed.

Cattery Operators own, rent, or lease kennel facilities at which owned cats are boarded for a fee or where cats are bred and raised for sale. The cattery operator administers the kennel business operation and is usually self-employed.

Farriers or blacksmiths fit horses with iron shoes which are designed to protect hooves against injury or excessive wear, to maintain the proper angle of the hoof, and to correct improper gaits. Farriers are usually self-employed.

Stable Managers are responsible for the administration and daily operation of stables where horses are boarded for owners or rented for hire. The stable manager supervises a staff which may offer diverse services including riding instruction, the transport of horses for a fee, and the breeding, breaking, and training of horses. The stable manager may be an employee or may own and operate the facility at which he or she works.

Riding Instructors provide training in the techniques of riding and jumping horses. A riding instructor learns through performance in horse shows and apprenticeship. Riding instructors may offer private lessons, operate a riding school, or work in association with several stables.

Animal Taxi Drivers pick up and transport pets for appointments at grooming salons, veterinary hospitals, and other locations. Animal taxi drivers will also greet and transport pets shipped by commercial airlines. Animal taxi drivers charge a flat rate plus mileage fee. Most animal taxi drivers are self-employed.

Dog Walkers exercise pets for owners who are unable to provide physical activity for their animals. Dog walkers charge an hourly fee and may simultaneously exercise several compatible animals.

Pet Sitters provide care, companionship, and supervision for pets in the absence of their owners. The pet sitter may care for an aged or infirmed animal which cannot be left unattended while the owner shops for groceries or he or she may tend an animal for several days or weeks while the owner is out of town. The pet sitter may keep animals at his or her personal residence or may visit the homes of pet owners for whom they are working. Pet sitters charge hourly, daily, and weekly fees.

Watchmen are employed by zoological parks and animal shelters to guard and patrol the premises as a method of protecting against vandalism and other forms of property damage. Watchmen may also be required to observe animals for symptoms of illness and to alert zoo and shelter staff to nighttime emergencies. Watchmen are paid an annual salary.

Animal Ambulance Drivers operate vehicles equipped for transporting wounded, injured, and infirmed animals to veterinary hospitals and animal shelters. The animal ambulance driver may also be engaged in the rescue of animals which are in precarious predicaments. Animal ambulance drivers are salaried employees of community animal welfare organizations and municipal animal control agencies.

Investigators for national animal welfare organizations such as The HSUS have unique jobs involving unusual duties such as the aerial reconnaissance of a wild horse herd.

Artists are skilled in the technical art of painting and drawing. Artists illustrate manuscripts, create graphic designs for publications, and create interpretive paintings and portraits for public sale. Artists who specialize in paintings or illustrations of animals and nature are usually self-employed.

Photographers are skilled in the technical art of photography. Photographers provide prints for use in illustrating manuscripts, visually document events and incidents relating to animals, and create visual records for use in the taxonomic classification of animals. Photographers may also create interpretive works and portraits of animals for public sale. Photographers are usually self-employed.

Animal Nurses specialize in the care of infant and juvenile animals quartered in the animal nurseries of zoological parks. The animal nurse serves in the role of a foster parent providing for the care and socialization of young zoo animals. Animal nurses receive on-the-job training from zoo veterinarians.

Zoo Tour Guides conduct visitors on narrated tours of zoological parks. Zoo tour guides highlight special exhibits, comment upon the natural history and behavior of zoo animals, and answer questions. In addition to narrating, tours guides may also drive tour buses, trains, monorails, and trams.

Beekeepers or apiarists maintain colonies of bees for the commercial production of honey. Beekeepers also rent colonies of bees to growers for use in pollinating fruit trees, agricultural crops, and berry producing plants. Beekeepers usually are self-employed.

Medical Technologists perform clinical laboratory tests for veterinary hospitals including blood typing, blood analysis and identification of viruses and other organisms which infect animals. Medical technologists are employed by commercial laboratories, veterinary clinics, and veterinary colleges.

Excursion Guides conduct tourists on hikes, raft trips, tours, and safaris into wilderness areas and geographical locations throughout the world. Excursion guides may be employees of a travel agency or wildlife authorities working under contract to a travel agency.

5
EDUCATION, TRAINING, AND EXPERIENCE

This chapter will introduce the reader to seminars, training programs, workshops, and volunteer employment opportunities which provide preparation for a career in animal welfare or conservation work.

Seminars, workshops, and conferences can teach job skills. They also offer valuable insights into the fundamental issues confronting a particular profession. Additionally, these programs provide participants with an opportunity to meet informally with potential employers and to prospect for job openings.

Volunteer or part-time employment programs can provide firsthand exposure to the job duties and daily routine of a professional in a selected career field. Such employment is often considered as fulfilling a portion of the training or experience requirements for a permanent job. Thus, volunteer or part-time service can provide a competitive edge against other job applicants and could be a decisive factor in the hiring of a job applicant to fill a particular position. Volunteers and part-time employees have an opportunity to demonstrate their capabilities to potential employers, and they have a valuable advantage in identifying new job openings.

HUMANE SOCIETY OF THE UNITED STATES
ANIMAL CONTROL WORKSHOP

The Humane Society of the United States sponsors a two-day animal welfare/animal control workshop which is designed as a detailed introduction to contemporary approaches toward the problems of animal mistreatment and animal regulation. The workshop is intended to provide practical advice regarding the structure and administration of community animal welfare and animal control programs. Workshop sessions address the topics of public relations, humane education, pet sterilization, humane society philosophy and goals, cruelty investigation, shelter management, animal handling, and animal welfare laws.

Persons who complete the workshop program are issued a certificate of attendance. A minimum of four workshops are conducted annually in different regions of the United States. Frequently, workshops are held in conjunction with business meetings of state humane society federations. The workshop registration fee is $25*. For additional information write Seminar, HSUS, 2100 L Street, NW, Washington, D.C. 20037.

VIRGINIA POLYTECHNIC INSTITUTE
ANIMAL CONTROL WORKSHOP

The Extension Division of Virginia Polytechnic Institute and State University (V.P.I.) offers a six-session animal control workshop program designed to provide technical information relating to the execution of the daily duties of animal control officers and humane agents. Three workshops are conducted each year. Traditionally, workshop sessions have been held on a particular day of the week for six successive weeks. However, V.P.I. may periodically schedule a workshop to be held on consecutive days during a single week.

The workshop addresses the topics of animal anatomy and physiology, animal behavior, capture techniques, handling techniques, animal care procedures, animal diseases, euthanasia procedures, human relations, injuries and first aid procedures, shelter management methods, and cruelty investigation procedures. Consideration is given to domestic pets, livestock, and wildlife.

The workshop enrollment fee is $35*. For additional information write the Program Leader, Animal Control Workshop, Extension and Continuing Education Division, Virginia Polytechnic Institute and State University, 11440 Isaac Newton Square North, Reston, Virginia 22090.

The Annual Conference of The Humane Society of the United States provides a unique opportunity for receiving training in the various aspects of animal welfare work.

TEXAS A&M UNIVERSITY ANIMAL CONTROL WORKSHOP

The Center for Urban Programs of Texas A&M University each November conducts a five-day short course in Animal Personnel Training. The program includes sessions on human relations, first aid for animals, animal capture techniques, animal control legislation, and kenneling methods. Continuing education credit units are awarded to persons completing the course of study. Priority in course registration is given to persons who are currently employed with humane societies and animal control agencies. To qualify for course enrollment, non-professional personnel must be employed as volunteers with an animal welfare agency, or they must be registered in an animal science or veterinary technology scholastic program, or they must obtain a letter of recommendation from an animal control or animal welfare agency. The course fee is $90*. For additional information write the Project Coordinator, Animal Control Personnel Training Program, Center for Urban Programs, Zachry Engineering Center, Texas A&M University, College Station, Texas 77840.

MASSACHUSETTS SPCA HUMANE AGENT TRAINING PROGRAM

The MSPCA offers an eight-week formal training program for humane agents which includes instruction in ambulance work, animal care, animal handling, euthanasia, humane education, law enforcement, animal capture, and humane society policies and procedures. While the MSPCA program was developed for the training of its own agents, the program is open to all persons interested in careers as humane agents and animal control officers.

To be accepted into the MSPCA program, an applicant must be sponsored by a community animal welfare agency. Alternately, an applicant must have a demonstrated commitment toward the pursuit of a career as a humane agent as evidenced by volunteer work or scholastic study involving an animal science curriculum. The MSPCA program is a personalized course of study modified to accommodate the requirements and interests of individual participants.

The MSPCA also conducts a Humane Executive's

Training Program designed to teach management skills to those persons interested in the pursuit of a career as an executive with an animal welfare organization or animal control agency. The program is free and students receive a stipend from the MSPCA. As of this writing the Humane Executive's Training Program is being restructured. The length of the course and admittance qualifications are to be altered.

For information regarding either The Humane Agent's course or the Humane Executive's Training Program write The President's Administrative Assistant, Massachusetts SPCA, 350 South Huntington Avenue, Boston, Massachusetts 02130.

STUDENT CONSERVATION ASSOCIATION
SEASONAL VOLUNTEER EMPLOYMENT

The Student Conservation Association (SCA) is a non-profit organization that places high school, college, and graduate students in summer volunteer positions with the Forest Service, National Park Service, and other public agencies engaged in conservation work. Assignments are classified to separate placement opportunities for high school students from those for college students. Positions open to college and graduate students include placement as a park assistant or forest assistant working under the direct supervision of National Park Service and Forest Service personnel. The SCA provides a subsistence wage for volunteers. Financial assistance is available to high school students who cannot afford the expense of travel to their locations of summer employment. In the college job placement program transportation is provided to the worksite. Each year the SCA places approximately 300 high school students and 250 college students in volunteer summer employment positions. Applications for placement are accepted from December 1 through March 1 preceding each year's program. Applications received after March 1 will not be considered for that year's program. Additional information and application forms may be obtained by writing the Student Conservation Association, Box 550, Charlestown, New Hampshire 03603.

VOLUNTEERS IN PARKS
VOLUNTEER EMPLOYMENT

Volunteers in Parks is a program of the National Park Service (NPS) that employs citizens in activities relating to the administration and public utilization of national park lands. Volunteers serve in such roles as nature interpreters, environmental educators, and resource management aides. Currently, 9,000 persons are serving as VIP's in national parks, national monuments, national historical sites, and other National Park Service lands. Volunteers may serve on a part-time or intermittent basis, such as an hour a week, one day a week, or on special occasions. There is no salaried compensation for volunteers; however, reimbursement may be provided for certain incidental expenses such as uniforms, transportation, lodging, and subsistence. The VIP program is open to persons of all ages but persons who are under 18 years of age must obtain written permission from their parents or guardians. The establishment of VIP positions depends upon the needs of individual parks, each of which has the authority to independently create VIP jobs. The selection of persons to fill these positions is based upon the skills and qualifications of each applicant. A listing of available VIP positions may be obtained from individual parks or from the appropriate National Park Service Regional Office (see appendix VII). The National Park Service publishes a pamphlet, "Volunteers in Parks," which outlines the VIP program, identifies NPS regions and park areas, and contains a volunteer application form. Copies of the pamphlet may also be obtained from individual parks or from the VIP Coordinator at the appropriate NPS Regional Office.

VOLUNTEERS IN FORESTS
VOLUNTEER EMPLOYMENT

Volunteers in the National Forests is the National Forest Service equivalent of the VIP program. Volunteers are employed in activities relating to the administration and public utilization of national forest land. Volunteers serve without pay on an intermittent or part-time basis. Reimbursement may be provided for certain incidental expenses. The Volunteers in National Forests program currently involves 15,000 persons at approximately 155 locations. Information relating to available VIF positions may be obtained from any national forest or from a regional office of the Forest Service (see appendix).

YOUTH CONSERVATION CORPS
SEASONAL EMPLOYMENT

The Youth Conservation Corps (YCC) is a federally sponsored summer employment program for persons from 15 through 18 years of age. The program is jointly administered by the United States Department of Agriculture's Forest Service and the United States Department of the Interior. YCC summer camps annually involve 40,000 Corps members in more than 1,000 individual projects. Approximately 30 percent of these projects are administered under state grant programs which usually involve the state department of natural resources. Camp programs vary in length from 4-10 weeks but average 8 weeks in duration. YCC participants are paid an average salary of $13 per day. A random selection process is used to choose Corps program participants. However, the program is co-educational with equal numbers of male and female participants. YCC participants may be employed in interpretation, visitor information services, trail maintenance and construction, habitat improvement, erosion control, recreational facilities construction, maintenance and cleanup, or timber stand improvement. Corps members are also involved in environmental awareness field study projects in connection with camp assignments.

For information relating to the current year's YCC camp locations and recruiting areas, write after January 1 to the Youth Conservation Corps., P.O. Box 2975, Washington, D.C. 20013. A pamphlet, "United States Youth Conservation Corps," is available from most national forests and national parks. Inquiries may be addressed to either the Director, Manpower Training and Youth Activities, Office of Management and Budget, United States Department of the Interior, Washington, D.C. 20242; or the Director, Division of Manpower and Youth Conservation Programs, United States Forest Service, United States Department of Agriculture, Washington, D.C. 20250.

JOB CORPS CIVILIAN CONSERVATION CENTER
JOB TRAINING

The emphasis of the Job Corps Civilian Conservation Center is to provide basic education, social skills training, on-the-job vocational skills training, and outdoor conservation work experience for disadvantaged youth. The Job Corps CCC program focuses primarily upon training youth in a trade such as carpentry. Participants may, however, be trained as forestry aides or taught other job skills which qualify them for a career in conservation work. Information relating to the Job Corps Civilian Conservation Center may be obtained from any state employment service office or by writing either the Director, Manpower Training and Youth Activities, Office of Management and Budget, United States Department of the Interior, Washington, D.C. 20242, or the Director, Division of Manpower and Youth Conservation Programs, United States Forest Service, United States Department of Agriculture, Washington, D.C. 20250.

NATIONAL PARK SERVICE
SEASONAL EMPLOYMENT

The National Park Service employs seasonal staff to augment its permanent work force during periods of peak visitor activity at national parks. Seasonal jobs usually involve the summer months. The initial pay grade level for seasonal positions ranges from GS-2 to GS-4. A seasonal employee may serve as a park technician, park aide, park ranger, student assistant, or laborer. Seasonal positions with the National Park Service are difficult to obtain. Applicants for positions far outnumber available jobs. Returning seasonal employees and military veterans are given preference in hiring. Certain seasonal positions require that an applicant take the Summer Employment Examination that is administered by the United States Civil Service Commission.

The area CSC office should be contacted by mid-November to register for the Summer Employment Examination. All seasonal job applicants must file a Standard Form 171/Personal Qualifications Statement with the National Park Service. Forms are available from the Civil Service Commission area office or from the personnel office of any federal agency. Applications for seasonal jobs are accepted from January 1 through February 15 for summer jobs. For parks offering winter employment opportunities for seasonal staff, applications must be submitted between June 1 and July 15. A pamphlet entitled "Seasonal Employment" may be obtained from the Personnel Office, National Park Service, United States Department of the Interior, Washington, D.C. 20240.

FOREST SERVICE
SEASONAL EMPLOYMENT

The Forest Service also employs seasonal staff to augment its permanent work force. Seasonal positions are available at both national forest and research stations. Seasonal jobs usually are confined to the summer months. The initial pay grade level for seasonal positions ranges from GS-2 to GS-5. Seasonal staff primarily serve as forestry aides and forestry technicians. Approximately 20,000 seasonal positions are available annually but the number of persons making application for these jobs greatly exceeds the total number of employment openings. Many positions require that an applicant be 18 years of age.

Personnel are hired according to a merit system which considers previous work experience and years of education. Returning seasonal employees and military veterans are given preference in hiring. Forest Service seasonal job applicants are not required to take the Summer Employment Examination. Summer Seasonal Application Forms are available from most Forest Service offices. Applications must be submitted between January 1 and February 15. For additional information consult Civil Service Commission Form 414/Summer Employment Announcements, which is used each November.

YCC STAFF APPOINTMENTS
SEASONAL EMPLOYMENT

The Youth Conservation Corps program requires an administrative staff of 8,000 counselors and group leaders. To qualify for a position as a YCC summer camp staff member an applicant must be at least 19 years of age. Preferably, applicants should have a natural science background, be knowledgeable with regard to the use of basic carpentry tools, and they should have previous experience working with youths. Each federal and state agency independently hires staff personnel for the YCC programs which it administers. Prospective employers include, among others, the U.S. Fish and Wildlife Service, National Park Service, U.S. Forest Service, and state departments of natural resources. Additional information may be obtained from either the Director, Manpower Training and Youth Activities, Office of Management and Budget, United States Department of the Interior, Washington, D.C. 20242; or the Director, Division of Manpower and Youth Conservation Programs, United States Forest Service, United States Department of Agriculture, Washington, D.C. 20250.

YOUNG ADULT CONSERVATION CORPS
TEMPORARY EMPLOYMENT

In 1977 a new federal conservation employment program was implemented. The Young Adult Conservation Corps is administered by the United States Departments of the Interior, Agriculture, and Labor. The YACC is similar in structure to the Youth Conservation Corps but is directed at persons 16 through 23 years of age. The program will provide employment, usually of 12 months duration, with conservation projects involving national parks, national forests, and other public lands.

Preference in hiring is given to young people who are residents of communities which have high rates of unemployment.

The Young Adult Conservation Corps will soon become the premier federally sponsored temporary employment program. During its first year the YACC offered 22,000 jobs for unemployed men and women.

Information on the National Young Adult Conservation Corps should be available through state employment service offices or contact either the Director, Manpower Training and Youth Activities, Office of Management and Budget, United States Department of the Interior, Washington, D.C. 20242; or the Director, Division of Manpower and Youth Conservation Programs, United States Forest Service, United States Department of Agriculture, Washington, D.C. 20250.

COLORADO STATE UNIVERSITY
CORRESPONDENCE COURSE

Colorado State University offers a 3-credit correspondence course in environmental conservation. NR 120 is an introduction to basic ecological principles. The ten course units include natural resources management, population dynamics, and biotic communities. The course may be started at any time during the year. Tuition costs are $68 plus texts. For information write the Center for Continuing Education, Colorado State University, Fort Collins, Colorado 80523.

UNIVERSITY OF WASHINGTON CORRESPONDENCE COURSE

The University of Washington offers a 5-credit correspondence course entitled "Interpreting The Environment." The program, Forest Management C353, is intended to provide an introduction to the principles and methods of nature interpretation. Course assignments pertain to the operation of visitor information centers, exhibit design for nature centers, construction plans for self-guided nature trails, and techniques for guiding trail walks. Students may enroll in the course at any time during the year. Tuition costs are $100.00 plus texts. For information write Independent Study, 222 Lewis Hall, DW-30, University of Washington, Seattle, Washington 98195.

CORRESPONDENCE SCHOOLS

There are three correspondence schools known to offer training courses for persons with career interests as game wardens, veterinary technicians, or animal control officers. In general, correspondence courses are not comparable in quality to the scholastic programs of study offered by colleges and universities. The most important attribute of personnel engaged in employment involving direct contact with animals is an ability to handle and manage the creatures in their custody. Such ability is difficult to develop without supervised, practical experience.

Most government and private agencies will not accept a certificate from a correspondence school as fulfilling any portion of the basic educational or experience requirements for employment. Such training courses can provide a useful introduction to required job skills. Yet correspondence school programs cannot be recommended as a method of career preparation. Those schools offering applicable career training courses are:

North American School of Animal Science
4500 Campus Drive
Department RJ 084
Newport, California 92663

North American School of Conservation
4500 Campus Drive
Department 21012
Newport, California 92660

Animal Science Institute
519 Little River Station
Miami, Florida 33138

CONFERENCE PROGRAMS

Many professional associations, animal welfare agencies, and conservation organizations conduct annual conferences. These programs often include workshops and general sessions of value to prospective animal protection or conservation workers. Additionally, special seminars, workshops, and conferences are sponsored by government agencies and private institutions. Conference dates are commonly announced in organizational newsletters and special membership mailings. The 3-day annual conference of The Humane Society of the United States is usually held during the month of October.

COMMUNITY CAREER PREPARATION OPPORTUNITIES

This chapter is not written as an all inclusive listing of applicable career preparation programs. The listings in this booklet are necessarily confined to major programs which provide training or job experience opportunities for substantial numbers of future animal welfare and conservation workers. Excluded from this chapter are those community institutions — animal shelters, nature centers, veterinary clinics, zoological parks, and other facilities — which are the most important source of opportunities for volunteer or part-time employment. These institutions are individually operated and will vary substantially with regard to the availability of part-time or volunteer positions, financial remuneration, duties, and the duration of service. Securing a part-time or volunteer position with a community facility requires both persistence and good fortune. It is wise to initiate inquiries and submit applications well in advance of the date when an applicant desires to begin volunteer service or temporary employment.

---

*Registration fees may vary as a result of hotel accommodation charges, meal fees, or materials costs.

THE JOB SEARCH

6

The reader may justifiably be discouraged by the current job outlook within the animal welfare, conservation, and environmental quality professions. During the 1980's there will be limited employment opportunities for persons seeking positions within the occupational specialties involving work with animals. It is anticipated that job seekers will continue to outnumber available positions. Yet, personnel officials and career guidance authorities insist that this job market situation need not pose a significant obstacle to qualified job candidates.

Failure in job hunting is often the result of a disorganized or minimal effort or a person's insistance in pursuing job openings for which they are unqualified. Many job hunters are inclined to randomly mail applications to every potential employer whom they are able to identify and then idly await invitations to interview for job openings. This saturation mailing technique rarely produces favorable results. Employers receive large volumes of unsolicited job applications. Typically, such inquiries are acknowledged by a form letter and discarded or filed. When a job opening does occur, it is unlikely that a personnel official will review hundreds of unsolicited resumes for the purpose of providing past applicants with an opportunity to interview for the position.

There are five elements which are basic to a successful job search by qualified applicants: the proper strategy, effective research, obtaining interviews, successful interviewing, and negotiating a satisfactory job offer.

CREDENTIALS AND QUALIFICATIONS

A career working with animals occasionally can be achieved by the individual, although lacking in formal training or job skills, who is able to demonstrate a special aptitude and commitment for a particular position. However, education and experience remain primary factors in successful job placement. It is important for the student who aspires to a career in animal welfare, conservation, environmental quality, or animal industry to obtain the proper scholastic training for his or her desired career.

It is beneficial to apply for student or associate membership in appropriate professional associations. Enrollment can provide access to membership job placement services such as the job opportunities lists referenced in Appendix IV. Membership publications will keep the job seeker informed of events and institutional program developments which may be of critical importance to the job seeker. Membership in a professional association can be cited in a resume as a personal achievement.

Participation in workshops and seminars can enhance the personal qualifications of a job seeker especially if successful completion of the program results in an award of college credits or a certificate of completion.

Honors, awards, published articles, and other activities may also provide an advantage against job competition. The more impressive a person's credentials the better will be his or her opportunity for placement within a profession.

PERSONAL ASSESSMENT

It is important that the job applicant precisely define his or her job interests. Preliminary to initiating a job search, the prospective worker must determine specific job preferences, salary requirements, acceptable localities of residence, and work environment requirements.

STUDY OF THE JOB MARKET

The person planning a career working with animals should review and compare as many job options as possible. An individual should not rush into a job search but rather should conduct a preliminary investigation of the job market. In this initial phase of the job search, obtain information on potential employers with regard to their policies, organizational values, management style, and internal structures. The job seeker should develop a basic knowledge of the operations and programs of employers with whom they intend to apply for a position. Individuals should schedule appointments with staff members in the service of potential employers to informally discuss job titles and associated duties, responsibilities, qualifications, and employment opportunities, Also, question staff members as to the techniques which they used to obtain employment. It is possible a staff member who is impressed by a job seeker will assist that person in obtaining a position with his or her employer.

Executive search firms, school placement offices, union personnel offices and other traditional job placement services are unlikely to provide productive assistance in identifying job openings involving work with animals. However, there is a hidden, unadvertised job market which may be discovered by consulting annual budgets and institutional literature. Budget increases which provide funds for additional staff are a useful indicator of forthcoming job openings. Publications detailing program plans may also serve as a guide to potential job openings. Announcements of retirements, resignations, and promotions are another indicator of possible job opportunities.

When initiating a formal job search the prospective worker should narrow his or her list of potential employers to those institutions which may provide job opportunities consistent with that person's goals and objectives. Most job seekers have limited financial resources and, therefore, should focus their energies upon those employers and employment opportunities of genuine interest. Do not waste time, postage, or personal finances in an unpromising effort to canvass the entire job market with copies of a personal resume.

ATTITUDE

Among qualified job applicants personal attitude may be the single most important attribute in determining who will obtain employment within their chosen profession. The prospective worker should conduct a job search with self-reliance, enthusiasm, self-confidence, tactful assertiveness, and courage. The job seeker will need a solid sense of self-respect for his or her talents and qualifications. Individuals should pursue job applications with the attitude that they are capable of making a valuable contribution to the employer who hires them. To obtain a job prospective workers must sell themselves. Self-promotion requires that persons have confidence in their abilities and be able to transmit that attitude in posture, behavior, and writing.

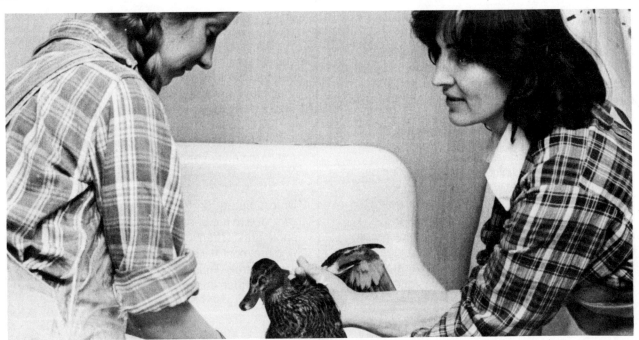

FRED STEVENSON

Volunteer workers, such as this oiled bird rescue trainee receiving instructions from a humane society official, have a distinct advantage in identifying new job openings.

WRITTEN COMMUNICATION

A job seeker's initial contact with a prospective employer commonly occurs in the form of written communication. The principal forms of written communication are a personal letter of introduction and the application for employment. The personal letter of introduction is intended as an inquiry into the availability of employment opportunities with a particular institution or business enterprise. The letter of introduction should express a person's interests in terms of possibilities, opportunities and challenges rather than emphasizing job titles, duties, or tasks. The application for employment is used to formally apply for a particular job opening.

When applying for a job the applicant will frequently be requested to submit a resume. The effective resume translates skills, training, and job history into quantifiable, specific accomplishments. A resume should never understate a person's job qualifications. The resume should be neatly typed, properly punctuated, and grammatically correct.

INTERVIEWING

The interview provides for a personal exchange of information between the employer and job applicant. The interview should provide an opportunity for both the employer to consider a job application and for the applicant to evaluate the job opening.

The importance of polished interview skills should not be overlooked. The interviewee should communicate self-confidence, enthusiasm, aptitude, knowledge, and interest. The interviewee should be conversant with the employer's programs and policies. The job applicant must be able to articulate his or her own career goals. The interviewee should focus responses to questions on how he or she can best meet the requirements of the job.

The basic techniques of job interviewing can be learned through books which are available in libraries and guidance counselling departments. Career counsellors suggest that job seekers rehearse their interviews. Counsellors also recommend that interviewees take notes during the interview and ask the employer questions regarding the specific duties and responsibilities of the job.

PERSISTENCE

It is erroneous to presume that the ideal position will be awaiting a person at that precise moment when they initiate a job search. There is a slow rate of turnover among many of the professions discussed in this book. Small staffs and low rates of attrition contribute to a job market situation which does not offer promise of immediate success in obtaining employment.

Individuals should not anticipate a rush of invitations to interview for jobs within days of having placed an advertisement or having mailed job applications. The job seeker should recognize that there may be an absence of job openings at a given moment during the year. In fact, there are seasonal fluctuations in job openings. It may be necessary for an applicant to address follow-up letters, or telephone potential employers to advise them of his or her continuing interest in job openings. Applicants should request an opportunity to interview with an institution even in the absence of an immediate job opening. The interview will provide an opportunity to gain insight into forthcoming positions as well as becoming acquainted with the individual on staff responsible for hiring. In maintaining the active status of a job application the job seeker should be cautious not to be obtrusive by placing unreasonable demands upon the time of the person responsible for hiring.

OBJECTIVITY

The job seeker must be realistic in his or her expectations for employment. The prospective worker should not pursue positions for which that individual is significantly underqualified. The job seeker should not persist in obtaining placement with an employer who has clearly expressed disinterest in that person or who has unequivocally indicated an absence of job opportunities.

Unfortunately, preferred jobs are not necessarily awarded to the best qualified or most dedicated job applicants. Often jobs are won by those applicants who are most skilled in the techniques of conducting a job search. Thus, the astute job seeker will carefully plan and coordinate his or her job search.

APPENDICES

APPENDIX I
Scholastic Programs

There are diverse educational options for the student contemplating a career in animal welfare or conservation. Scholastic programs are offered by community colleges, universities, and vocational schools. Programs of study vary in length from six months to nine years.

This appendix is presented as an introduction to unique curricula which provide specialized preparation for a career in animal welfare, environmental quality, or conservation. Programs of study, course offerings, and degree awards are continuously revised by educational institutions. The scholastic programs listed in this appendix reflect only a portion of the educational options available to high school graduates. Excluded from listing are common curricula in the biological sciences and other programs of study routinely offered by educational institutions.

Several universities permit students to pursue independent study programs which are specially designed to fulfill the educational requirements for particular career fields. For detailed information on the programs of study, coursework, or entrance requirements of an educational institution consult the current school catalog or contact the Office of the Registrar.

In preparing this appendix every effort has been made to avoid errors and omissions. However, The Humane Society of the United States cannot guarantee the accuracy of the information provided to our office nor can The HSUS attest to the relative merits of courses offered by individual educational institutions. Certain scholastic programs are accredited by professional associations such as the American Veterinary Medical Association and the Society of American Foresters. The reputability of an educational institution may also be determined by contacting one of the six regional educational associations: Western Association of Schools and Colleges, New England Association of Schools and Colleges, Middle States Association of Colleges and Secondary Schools, North Central Association of Colleges and Schools, Northwestern Association of Secondary and High Schools, or the Southern Association of Colleges and Schools.

In general, scholastic programs for which a certificate is offered upon completion are one year in length. Associate degree programs are two years in length. Bachelor degree programs are four years in length. A master's degree requires two years of postgraduate study after obtaining a baccalaureate degree and a Ph.D. requires an additional one or two years of study.

Several scholastic programs do not directly result in a degree award. An educational institution may require that a student transfer to a cooperating university after the second or third year of study. The appropriate degree is awarded by the educational institution at which the student completes his or her final year of study. The student entering a preprofessional program may apply for admittance to a professional school after his or her junior year. The undergraduate institution will award such a student a baccalaureate degree upon successful completion of the first year of study at the professional school. Some non-vocational programs of study are designed for the student who intends to enter the job market after one or two years of study. No degree is awarded to the student enrolled in such a program.

DIRECTORIES OF SCHOLASTIC PROGRAMS

AIBS Directory of Bioscience Departments and Faculties in the United States and Canada, edited by Peter Gray. New York: Halsted Press, 1976, $25.00.

University Curricula in the Marine Sciences and Related Fields; Academic Years 1979-1980, 1980-1981, by the Interagency Committee on Marine Science and Engineering of the Federal Council for Science and Technology. Rockville, Maryland: National Sea Grant Program of the National Oceanic and Atmospheric Administration, 1979, complimentary.

Baron's Profile of American Colleges, revised edition, by the College Division of Baron's Educational Series, Incorporated. Woodbury, New York: Baron's Educational Series, Inc., 1976, $15.25 ($5.95 paperback).

Comparative Guide To American Colleges, by James Cass and Max Birnbaum. New York: Harper & Row, 1977, $17.50 ($8.95 paperback).

Lovejoy's Career and Vocational School Guide, 5th Edition, by Clarence E. Lovejoy. New York: Simon and Schuster, 1978, $9.95 ($4.95 paperback).

Lovejoy's College Guide, 12th Edition, by Clarence E. Lovejoy. New York: Simon and Schuster, 1976, $4.95 paperback.

Directory of Professional Preparation Programs in Recreation, Parks, and Related Areas. The National Recreation and Park Association. Arlington, Virginia, 1973, $3.00.

List of Accredited Programs in Landscape Architecture. The American Society of Landscape Architects, Washington, D.C., Annual, complimentary.

Colleges and Universities Offering Planning and Related Degree Programs. The American Society of Planning Officials, Chicago, Illinois; or The American Institute of Planners, Washington, D.C., 1979, complimentary.

Forestry Schools in the United States. The Forest Service, U.S. Department of Agriculture, Washington, D.C., 1975, $.35.

EDUCATIONAL INSTITUTIONS

Alabama

Alabama Agricultural and Mechanical College
  Normal, Alabama 35762
  Biology: *B.S.*
  Pre-Veterinary Medicine: *B.S.*
  Zoology: *B.S.*

Alabama State University
  Montgomery, Alabama 36101
  Biology: *B.A., B.S.*
  Biology (Marine Biology): *B.A.*
  Recreation: *B.S.*
  Recreation Leadership: *A.S.*

Athens College
  Athens, Alabama 35611
  Biology: *B.S.*
  Zoology: *B.S.*

Auburn University
  Auburn, Alabama 36830
  Agricultural Business & Economics: *B.S., M.S.*
  Agricultural Engineering: *B.S., M.S., Ph.D.*
  Agricultural Journalism: *B.S.*
  Animal & Dairy Science: *B.S., M.S., Ph.D.*
  Animal & Dairy Science (Pre-Veterinary Medicine): *B.S.*
  Biological Sciences (Botany): *B.S., M.S., Ph.D.*
  Biological Sciences (Microbiology): *B.S., M.S., Ph.D.*
  Earth Sciences: *B.S.*
  Fisheries & Allied Aquacultures: *M.S., Ph.D.*
  Forestry (Forest Management): *B.S., M.S., Ph.D.*
  Geology: *B.S.*
  Horticulture: *B.S., M.S.*
  Large Animal Surgery & Medicine: *M.S.*
  Pathology & Parasitology: *M.S.*
  Recreation: *B.S., M.S.*
  Small Animal Surgery & Medicine: *M.S.*
  Toxicology: *M.S.*
  Veterinary Medicine: *D.V.M.*
  Zoological Sciences (Entomology): *B.S., M.S., Ph.D.*
  Zoological Sciences (Fisheries): *B.S., M.S., Ph.D.*
  Zoological Sciences (Marine Biology): *B.S., M.S., Ph.D.*
  Zoological Sciences (Wildlife Management): *B.S., M.S., Ph.D.*
  Zoological Sciences (Zoology): *B.S., M.S., Ph.D.*

Birmingham Southern College
  Birmingham, Alabama 35204
  Biology: *B.S.*

Daniel Payne College
  Birmingham, Alabama 35212
  Biology: *A.A., A.S.*
  Veterinary Medicine: *Non-Degree*

John C. Calhoun State Community College
  Decatur, Alabama 35602
  Agricultural Science: *A.S.*
  Biological Sciences: *A.S.*

Northeast Alabama State Junior College
  Rainsville, Alabama 35986
  Agricultural Business & Economics: *A.S.*
  Agricultural Engineering: *A.S.*
  Agricultural Science (Agricultural Journalism): *A.S.*
  Agricultural Science (Animal Science): *A.S.*
  Agricultural Science (Dairy Science): *A.S.*
  Biological Science (Botany): *A.S.*
  Biological Science (Entomology): *A.S.*
  Biological Science (Fisheries Management): *A.S.*
  Biological Science (Wildlife Management): *A.S.*
  Biological Science (Zoology): *A.S.*
  Forestry: *A.S.*
  Pre-Veterinary Medicine: *A.S.*

Northwest Alabama State Junior College
  Phil Campbell, Alabama 33581
  Agricultural Science: *A.A., A.S.*
  Agricultural Vocational Education: *A.S.*
  Biology: *A.A., A.S.*

Oakwood College
  Huntsville, Alabama 35800
  Biology: *B.A.*
  Pre-Veterinary Medicine: *B.G.S.*

Snead State Junior College
  Boaz, Alabama 35957
  Agricultural Science: *A.S.*
  Pre-Forestry: *A.S.*
  Veterinary Hospital Technology Program: *A.A.S.*

Troy State University
  Troy, Alabama 36081
  Biology: *B.S.*
  Marine Biology: *B.S.*
  Microbiology: *B.S.*
  Zoology: *B.S.*

Tuskegee Institute
  Tuskegee Institute, Alabama 36088
  Animal Genetics: *B.S., M.S.*
  Animal Husbandry: *B.S., M.S.*
  Animal Pathology: *M.S.*
  Animal Physiology: *M.S.*
  Animal Science: *B.S., M.S.*
  Biology: *B.S.*
  Dairy Science: *B.S., M.S.*
  Veterinary Anatomy: *M.S.*
  Veterinary Bacteriology: *M.S.*
  Veterinary Medicine: *D.V.M.*
  Veterinary Microbiology: *M.S.*

University of Alabama in Tuscaloosa
  University, Alabama 35486
  Biology: *B.S., M.S., Ph.D.*
  Marine Science: *M.S.*

University of Alabama in Birmingham
Birmingham, Alabama 35233
Biochemistry: *M.S., Ph.D.*
Biology: *B.S., M.S., Ph.D.*
Natural Science: *B.*

University of Montevallo
Montevallo, Alabama 35115
Biology: *B.S.*

University of North Alabama
Florence, Alabama 35630
Agriculture (Pre-Professional): *Non-Degree*
Biology (General): *B.A., B.S., M.S.*
Biology (Marine): *B.A., B.S.*
Biology (Professional): *B.A., B.S.*
Forestry (Pre-Professional): *Non-Degree*
General Science: *B.A., B.S.*
Veterinary Medicine (Pre-Professional): *Non-Degree*

Alaska

University of Alaska - Fairbanks
Fairbanks, Alaska 99701
Biological Sciences: *B.A., B.S., M.A.T., M.S., Ph.D.*
Biological Sciences (Botany): *M.S.*
Biological Sciences (Zoology): *M.S.*
Earth Science: *B.A.*
Fisheries Biology: *B.S., M.S., Ph.D.*
General Science (Biological Science): *B.S.*
Natural Resources Management: *B.S.*
Wildlife (Wildlife Management Biologist): *B.S., M.S., Ph.D.*
Wildlife (Wildlife Research Biologist): *B.S., M.S., Ph.D.*

Sheldon Jackson College
Sitka, Alaska 99835
Aquaculture Technician: *A.S., Certificate*
Forestry Technician: *A.S.*

Arkansas

Arkansas College
Batesville, Arkansas 72501
Biology: *B.A.*
Cytotechnology (Pre-Professional): *Non-Degree, B.A.*
Environmental Health: *B.A.*
Environmental Science: *B.A.*
Veterinary Medicine (Pre-Professional): *Non-Degree, B.A.*

Arkansas State University - Beebe Campus
Beebe, Arkansas 70212
Agriculture: *A.A.*
Agriculture (Agricultural Business & Economics): *Non-Degree*
Agriculture (Agricultural Education): *Non-Degree*
Agriculture (Agronomy): *Non-Degree*
Agriculture (Animal Science): *Non-Degree*
Agriculture (General Agriculture): *Non-Degree*
Agriculture (Horticulture): *Non-Degree*
Biological Science: *A.A.*

Arkansas State University
Jonesboro, Arkansas 72467
Agricultural Science (Animal Science): *B.S.*
Agricultural Science (General): *B.S.*
Agricultural Science (Plant Science): *B.S.*

Agricultural Science (Pre-Veterinary Medicine): *Non-Degree*
Applied Agricultural Science (Agri-Business): *B.S.*
Applied Agricultural Science (Agri-Education): *B.S.*
Biology: *B.S., M.S.*
Botany: *B.S.*
General Science (Biology): *B.S.Ed.*
Wildlife Management: *B.S.*
Zoology: *B.S.*

Arkansas Tech University
Russellville, Arkansas 72801
Agricultural Business: *B.S.*
Biological Science: *B.S.*
Biology: *B.S.*
Fisheries - Wildlife Management: *B.S.*
Geology: *B.S.*
Park Administration: *B.S.*
Pre-Veterinary Medicine: *B.S., Non-Degree*
Recreation Administration: *B.S.*

College of The Ozarks
Clarkesville, Arkansas 72830
Biology: *B.S.*
Medical Technology: *B.S.*
Natural Science: *B.S.*
Pre-Forestry: *B.S.*
Pre-Veterinary Medicine: *B.S.*

University of Arkansas
Fayetteville, Arkansas 72701
Agriculture (Agricultural Business): *B.S.A.*
Agriculture (Agricultural Economics): *B.S.A.*
Agriculture (Agronomy): *B.S.A.*
Agriculture (Animal Nutrition): *B.S.A.*
Agriculture (Animal Science): *B.S.A.*
Agriculture (Dairy Science): *B.S.A.*
Agriculture (Domestic Animal Biology): *B.S.A.*
Agriculture (Environmental Science): *B.S.A.*
Agriculture (General Agriculture): *B.S.A.*
Agriculture (Horticulture): *B.S.A.*
Agriculture (Landscape Design & Urban Horticulture): *B.S.A.*
Agriculture (Vocational Agriculture Education): *B.S.A.*

University of Arkansas at Monticello
Monticello, Arkansas 71655
Agriculture (Pre-Agriculture): *Non-Degree*
Agriculture: *B.S.*
Biology: *B.S.*
Forestry (Forest Administration): *B.S.*
Forestry (Forest Management): *B.S.*
Forestry (Forest Science): *B.S.*
Forestry (Forest Wildlife Management): *B.S.*
Wildlife & Fisheries Science: *B.S.*

University of Arkansas at Pine Bluff
Pine Bluff, Arkansas 71604
Agricultural Education: *Certificate, B.S.*
Agriculture: *B.S.*
Agriculture (Animal Sciences): *B.S.*
Agriculture (Plant & Soil Science): *B.S.*
Biology: *B.A., B.S., B.S.T.*

University of Arkansas at Little Rock
  Little Rock, Arkansas 72204
  Biology: *B.S., B.S.Ed.*
  Environmental Health: *B.S.*
  Health, Physical Education & Recreation (Recreational Education): *B.S.*
  Veterinary Medicine: *Non-Degree*

University of Central Arkansas
  Conway, Arkansas 72032
  Biology: *B.A., B.S., B.S.Ed., M.S., M.S.E.*
  Pre-Veterinary Medicine: *Non-Degree*

Arizona

Arizona State University
  Tempe, Arizona 85281
  Agriculture (Agricultural Industry): *B.S., M.S.*
  Agriculture (Biological-Agricultural Science): *B.S., M.S.*
  Agriculture (Environmental Resources in Agriculture): *B.S., M.S.*
  Agriculture (Pre-Veterinary Medicine): *B.S.*
  Botany and Microbiology: *B.S., M.S., Ph.D.*
  Botany (Biology): *B.S., M.S., Ph.D.*
  Botany and Microbiology (Botany): *B.S., M.S., Ph.D.*
  Botany and Microbiology (Microbiology): *B.S., M.S., Ph.D.*
  Geology: *B.S., B.A.Ed., M.S., Ph.D.*
  Zoology: *B.S., M.S., Ph.D.*
  Zoology (Entomology): *B.S., M.S., Ph.D.*
  Zoology (Wildlife Biology): *B.S., M.S., Ph.D.*

Arizona Western College
  Yuma, Arizona 85364
  Agriculture (Professional): *A.A.*
  Agricultural Business Management: *A.A.S.*
  Animal Science: *A.A.S.*
  Earth Science: *A.A.*
  Earth Science (Engineering Geology): *A.A.*
  Earth Science (Geology): *A.A.*
  Earth Science (Geophysics): *A.A.*

Eastern Arizona College
  Thatcher, Arizona 85552
  Agriculture (Occupational): *A.A.S.*
  Agriculture (Agri-Business): *A.A.S.*
  Agriculture (Production Agriculture): *A.A.S.*
  Agriculture (Professional): *A.A.*
  Biology: *A.A.*
  Biology (Biological Science): *A.A.*
  Biology (Wildlife Biology): *A.A.*
  Forestry: *A.A.*

Mesa Community College
  Mesa, Arizona 85201
  Agri-Business, Sales & Service: *A.A.*
  Agricultural Production & Management: *A.A.*

Navajo Community College
  Chinle, Arizona 86503
  Natural Sciences (Pre-Forestry): *A.A., A.A.S., Certificate*
  Natural Sciences (Pre-Veterinary Medicine): *A.A., A.A.S., Certificate*
  Natural Science (Pre-Wildlife Management): *A.A., A.A.S.*

Northern Arizona University
  Flagstaff, Arizona 86011
  Biology: *B.S., M.S.*
  Biology, Secondary Education: *B.S.Ed., M.A.Ed.*
  Botany: *B.S., Ph.D.*
  Earth Science: *B.S.Ed., M.A.Ed., M.S.*
  Forestry: *B.S., M.S.F.*
  Geochemistry: *B.S.*
  Geology (General): *B.S.*
  Geology (Applied): *B.S.*
  Microbiology (Applied): *M.S.*
  Pre-Veterinary Medicine: *Non-Degree*
  Recreation Resource Management: *B.S.*
  Zoology: *B.S., Ph.D.*

Northland Pioneer College
  Holbrook, Arizona 86025
  Agriculture: *A.S., A.A.S.*
  Forestry: *A.S., A.A.S., Certificate*

Scottsdale Community College
  Scottsdale, Arizona 85251
  Biology: *A.A.*
  Equine Training & Range Management: *A.A., Certificate*
  Geology: *A.A.*
  Pre-Forestry: *A.A., Non-Degree*
  Recreational Leadership: *Non-Degree*

University of Arizona
  Tucson, Arizona 85721
  Agriculture (General - Natural Resources): *B.S., M.S.*
  Agriculture (Agricultural Economics): *B.S., M.S.*
  Agriculture (Agricultural Education): *B.S., M.Ag.Ed., M.S.*
  Agriculture (Animal Health Service): *B.S., M.S.*
  Agriculture (Entomology): *B.S., M.S., Ph.D.*
  Agriculture (Fisheries): *B.S., M.S., Ph.D.*
  Agriculture (Horticulture): *B.S., M.S., Ph.D.*
  Agriculture (Natural Resource Recreation): *B.S.*
  Agriculture (Plant Pathology): *B.S., M.S., Ph.D.*
  Agriculture (Plant Sciences): *B.S., M.S.*
  Agriculture (Range Management): *B.S., M.S., Ph.D.*
  Agriculture (Soil & Water Science): *B.S., M.S., Ph.D.*
  Agriculture (Watershed Management): *B.S., M.S., Ph.D.*
  Agriculture (Wildlife Ecology): *B.S., M.S., Ph.D.*
  Animal Physiology: *M.S., Ph.D.*
  Biology (General): *B.S., M.S., Ph.D.*
  Botany: *M.S., Ph.D.*
  Cellular & Developmental Biology: *B.S., M.S., Ph.D.*
  Earth Sciences (Water Resources Administration): *B.S., M.S., Ph.D.*
  Ecology & Developmental Biology: *B.S., M.S., Ph.D.*
  Microbiology: *M.S., Ph.D.*
  Plant Protection: *M.S.*
  Poultry Science: *M.S.*

California

Allan Hancock College
  Santa Maria, California 93454
  Agricultural Inspection Services: *A.S.*
  Animal Science: *A.S.*
  General Agri-Business: *A.S.*

Antelope Valley College
Lancaster, California 93534
Animal Science: *Certificate*
Landscape & Park Management: *Certificate*
Natural Resources: *Certificate*
Recreation: *Certificate*

Bakersfield College
Bakersfield, California 93305
Animal Husbandry: *A.A.*
Forestry & Wildlife Management: *A.A.*
Horticulture: *A.A.*

Barstow College
Barstow, California 92311
Biology: *A.A., A.S.*
Botany: *A.A., A.S.*
Physiology: *A.A., A.S.*
Zoology: *A.A., A.S.*

Butte Junior College
Oroville, California 95938
Agriculture: *A.A.*
Agriculture (Agricultural Biology): *A.A.*
Agriculture (Agricultural Business): *A.A.*
Agriculture (Agricultural Engineering): *A.A.*
Agriculture (Agronomy): *A.A.*
Agriculture (Animal Husbandry): *A.A.*
Agriculture (General Agriculture): *A.A.*
Agriculture (Horticulture): *A.A.*
Agriculture (Natural Resources): *A.A.*
Agriculture (Park Administration): *A.A.*
Agriculture (Poultry Science): *A.A.*
Agriculture (Pre-Forestry): *A.A.*
Agriculture (Pre-Veterinary Medicine): *A.A.*
Agriculture (Soil Science): *A.A.*
Agricultural Business: *Certificate, A.A.*
Agricultural Inspection: *Certificate, A.A.*
Animal Science: *Certificate, A.A.*
Landscape Maintenance and Horticulture: *Certificate, A.A.*
Natural Resources: *Certificate, A.A.*
Parks & Recreation: *Certificate, A.A.*

Cabrillo College
Aptos, California 95003
Wildlife Law Enforcement: *Certificate*

California Baptist College
Riverside, California 92504
Biology: *B.A., B.S.*

California Institute of Technology
Pasadena, California 91125
Cell Biology: *Ph.D.*
Developmental Biology: *Ph.D.*
Environmental Engineering: *M.S., Ph.D.*
Immunology: *Ph.D.*
Molecular Biology: *Ph.D.*
Neurobiology: *Ph.D.*
Psychobiology: *Ph.D.*

California Lutheran College
Thousand Oaks, California 91360
Biological Sciences: *B.A., B.S.*

California Polytechnic State University, San Luis Obispo
San Luis Obispo, California 93407
Agriculture Management: *B.S.*
Agriculture Science: *B.S.*
Agriculture Engineering: *B.S.*
Animal Science: *B.S.*
Dairy Science: *B.S.*
Natural Resource Management: *B.S.*

California State College, Stanislaus
Turlock, California 95380
Botany: *B.A., B.S.*
Entomology: *B.A., B.S.*
Marine Biology: *B.A., B.S.*
Zoology: *B.A., B.S.*

California State Polytechnic University, Pomona
Pomona, California 91768
Agricultural Business Management: *B.S.*
Agricultural Engineering: *B.S.*
Agronomy: *B.S.*
Animal Science: *B.S.*
Biology: *B.S., M.S.*
Botany: *B.S.*
Earth Science: *B.S.*
Microbiology: *B.S.*
Park Administration: *B.S.*
Soil Science: *B.S.*
Zoology: *B.S.*

California State University, Chico
Chico, California 95927
Agriculture: *B.S.*
Agriculture (Animal Science): *B.S.*
Agriculture (Dairy Science): *B.S.*
Agriculture (Range Management): *B.S.*
Geology: *B.A.*
Physical Sciences (Earth Science): *M.A.*
Pre-Veterinary (Biological Sciences): *B.A.*
Pre-Veterinary (Animal Sciences): *B.S.*
Recreation Administration: *B.A., M.A.*

California State University, Dominquez Hills
Carson, California 90747
Pre-Veterinary (Biological Science): *B.A., M.A.*

California State University, Fresno
Fresno, California 93740
Agriculture Science: *B.S.*
Animal Science: *B.S.*
Animal Veterinary Technician: *B.S.*
Biology: *B.A., M.A.*
Biology (Biological Science): *B.A., M.A.*
Biology (Botany): *B.A., M.A.*
Biology (Environmental Biology): *B.A., M.A.*
Biology (Functional Biology): *B.A., M.A.*
Biology (Microbiology): *B.A., M.A.*
Biology (Zoology): *B.A., M.A.*
Geology: *B.A., M.A.*
Plant Science: *B.S.*
Pre-Veterinary Science: *B.S.*
Recreation Administraion: *B.S.*

California State University at Fullerton
  Fullerton, California 92634
    Biological Science: *B.A., M.A.*
    Biological Science (Botany): *B.A., M.A.*
    Biological Science (Cellular & Molecular Biology): *B.A., M.A.*
    Biological Science (Ecology): *B.A., M.A.*
    Biological Science (Genetics): *B.A., M.A.*
    Biological Science (Marine Biology): *B.A., M.A.*
    Biological Science (Microbiology): *B.A., M.A.*
    Biological Science (Zoology): *B.A., M.A.*
    Earth Science: *B.A.*
    Environmental Studies: *M.S.*

California State University, Hayward
  Hayward, California 94542
    Biological Science: *B.S., M.A.*
    Earth Science: *B.S., M.S.*
    Recreation: *B.S.*

California State University, Long Beach
  Long Beach, California 90804
    Biology: *B.A.*
    Botany: *B.S.*
    Earth Science: *B.S.*
    Entomology: *B.A.*
    Marine Science: *B.S.*
    Microbiology: *B.S.*
    Recreation: *B.A.*
    Zoology: *B.S.*

California State University, Los Angeles
  Los Angeles, California 90032
    Biology: *B.A., B.S., M.S.*
    Biology: *M.S.*
    Biology (Animal Behavior): *M.S.*
    Biology (Botany): *M.S.*
    Biology (Entomology): *M.S.*
    Biology (Invertebrate Zoology): *M.S.*
    Biology (Marine Zoology): *M.S.*
    Biology (Parasitology): *M.S.*
    Biology (Vertebrate Zoology): *M.S.*
    Biology (Wildlife Management): *M.S.*
    Environmental Biology: *B.S.*
    Microbiology: *B.A., M.S.*
    Recreation: *B.S., M.S.*

California State University, Northridge
  Northridge, California 91330
    Biology: *B.A., M.A.*
    Earth Science: *B.A.*

California State University, Sacramento
  Sacramento, California 95819
    Animal Biology: *B.A., B.S.*
    Biological Conservation: *B.A., M.S.*
    Environmental Biology: *B.A., B.S.*
    Environmental Health: *B.S.*
    Environmental Studies: *B.A.*
    Recreation/Park Administration: *B.S., M.S.*

Canada College
  Redwood City, California 94061
    Biological Technology: *A.S.*
    Pre-Veterinary Medicine: *Non-Degree*
    Wildlife Management: *Non-Degree*

Cerritos College
  Norwalk, California 90650
    Biology: *A.A.*
    Botany: *A.A.*
    Forestry: *A.A.*
    Microbiology: *A.A.*
    Wildlife Management: *A.A.*
    Zoology: *A.A.*

College of the Canyons
  Valencia, California 91355
    Biology: *A.S.*
    Biology (Cellular & Molecular Biology): *A.S.*
    Biology (Environmental Biology): *A.S.*
    Biology (General Biology): *A.S.*
    Environmental Control: *Certificate*
    Natural Resources: *A.S.*
    Natural Resources (Pre-Forestry): *A.S.*
    Natural Resources (Range Management): *A.S.*
    Natural Resources (Wildlife Management): *A.S.*
    Pre-Veterinary Medicine: *Non-Degree*
    Recreation: *A.S.*

College of the Desert
  Palm Desert, California 92260
    Agricultural Business: *A.A., Certificate*
    Landscape Architecture: *A.A., Certificate*
    Natural Resources: *A.A., Certificate*
    Parks/Recreation Management: *A.A., Certificate*
    Plant Science: *A.A., Certificate*
    Veterinary Science: *A.A., Certificate*

College of the Redwoods
  Eureka, California 95501
    Agri-Business: *Certificate*
    Animal Science: *Certificate*
    Farm Management: *Certificate*
    Forest Technology: *Certificate*
    Horticulture: *Certificate*
    Range Management: *Certificate*

College of the Sequoias
  Visalia, California 93277
    Agriculture: *A.A., A.S.*
    Agriculture Engineering Technology: *A.A., A.S., Non-Degree*
    Agriculture (Agri-Business): *A.A., A.S., Non-Degree*
    Agriculture (Animal Science Technology): *A.A., A.S., Non-Degree*
    Agriculture (Plant Science Technology): *A.A., A.S., Non-Degree*
    Agriculture (Pre-Agriculture): *A.A., A.S., Non-Degree*
    Agriculture (Pre-Recreation): *A.A., A.S., Non-Degree*
    Biological Science: *A.A., A.S.*

Columbia College
  Columbia, California 95301
    Biology: *A.A.*
    Forestry Technology: *Certificate*
    Natural Resources: *A.A.*
    Natural Resources Technology: *Certificate*

Cosumnes River College
  Sacramento, California 95823
  Agriculture: *A.S.*
  Agriculture (Agricultural Business): *A.S.*
  Agriculture (Animal Science): *A.S.*
  Agriculture (Plant Science): *A.S.*
  Agri-Business Technology: *Certificate*
  Animal Health Technology: *Certificate*
  Animal Science Technology: *Certificate*
  Plant Science Production Technology: *Certificate*

El Camino College
  El Camino College, via Torrance, California 90506
  Biological Sciences: *A.A.*
  Biological Sciences (Botany): *A.A.*
  Biological Sciences (Microbiology): *A.A.*
  Biological Sciences (Zoology): *A.A.*
  Geology: *A.A.*

Feather River College
  Quincy, California 95971
  Biological Science: *A.A.*
  Forest Resource Technology: *A.S.*
  Forest Resource Technology (Park Technician): *A.S.*
  Forest Resource Technology (Timber Technician): *A.S.*
  Forest Resource Technology (Wildlife Technician): *A.S.*
  Zoology: *A.*

Foothill College
  Los Altos Hills, California 94022
  Animal Health Technician: *A.A.*

Fullerton College
  Fullerton, California 92634
  Biological Technician: *A.A.*
  Oceanographic Technology: *A.A.*

Gavilan College
  Gilroy, California 95020
  Life Sciences (Biology): *A.*
  Life Sciences (Botany): *A.*
  Life Sciences (Conservation): *A.*
  Life Sciences (Ecology): *A.*
  Life Sciences (Entomology): *A.*
  Life Sciences (Fish & Wildlife Management): *A.*
  Life Sciences (Forestry): *A.*
  Life Sciences (Game Management): *A.*
  Life Sciences (Pre-Veterinary Medicine): *A.*
  Life Sciences (Range Management): *A.*

Hartnell College
  Salinas, California 93901
  Animal Sciences: *Certificate*

Humbolt State University
  Arcata, California 95521
  Biology: *B.A., M.A.*
  Botany: *B.A.*
  Environmental Resource Engineering: *B.S.*
  Fisheries: *B.S., M.S.*
  Forestry: *B.S., M.S.*
  Natural Resources: *M.S.*
  Natural Resource Planning & Interpretation: *B.S.*
  Oceanography: *B.S.*
  Range Management: *B.S.*
  Watershed Management: *M.S.*
  Wildlife Management: *B.S.*
  Zoology: *B.A.*

Immaculate Heart College
  Los Angeles, California 90027
  Biology: *B.A., M.A.*
  Physical Sciences: *B.A.*

Imperial Valley College
  Imperial, California 92251
  Animal Science: *A.S.*
  Life Science: *A.A., A.S.*
  Physical Science: *A.A., A.S.*
  Plant Science: *A.S.*
  Recreation: *A.S.*
  Soil & Water Technology: *A.S.*

International College
  Westwood, California 90024
  Animal Ethology - Humane Ethics: *M., D.*

Lassen College
  Susanville, California 96130
  Agri-Business: *A.A.*
  Forestry: *A.A.*
  Forestry (Forestry Aide): *A.A.*
  Forestry (Forest Recreation): *A.A., Certificate*
  Forestry (Forestry Technician): *A.A.*
  Forestry (Pre-Forestry): *Non-Degree*
  Forestry (Pre-Forestry Management): *Non-Degree*
  Pre-Agriculture: *Non-Degree*
  Pre-Environmental Resources: *Non-Degree*
  Pre-Wildlife Management: *Non-Degree*

LaVerne College
  LaVerne, California 91750
  Biology: *B.A., B.S.*
  Biology (Biology & Environmental Studies): *B.A., B.S.*
  Biology (Environmental Management): *B.A., B.S.*

Lone Mountain College
  San Francisco, California 94115
  Biology: *B.A.*
  Biology (Animal Behavior): *B.A.*
  Biology (Ecology): *B.A.*
  Biology (Vertebrate Zoology): *B.A.*

Long Beach City College
  Long Beach, California 90808
  Biological Science: *A.S.*

Los Angeles City College
  Los Angeles, California 90029
  Earth Science: *A.A.*
  Recreation: *A.A.*

Los Angeles Pierce College
  Woodland Hills, California 91364
  Agricultural Business: *A.S.*
  Animal Health Technology: *A.S.*
  Animal Science: *A.S., Certificate*
  Crop Production: *A.S.*
  Dairy Science: *A.S.*
  General Agriculture: *A.S.*
  Horticulture: *A.S.*
  Natural Resources Management: *A.S.*
  Natural Resources Science: *A.S.*

Los Angeles Valley College
  Van Nuys, California 91401
  Recreation (Municipal Recreation & Parks): *A.A.*

Loyola Marymount University
    Los Angeles, California 90045
    Biology: *M.A.T.*

Merced College
    Merced, California 95341
    Animal Science: *A.A., Certificate*
    Plant Science: *A.A., Certificate*
    Pre-Veterinary Medicine: *Non-Degree*

Merritt College
    Oakland, California 94619
    Biological Sciences: *A.A., A.S.*
    Biological Sciences (Biology): *A.A., A.S.*
    Biological Sciences (Botany): *A.A., A.S.*
    Biological Sciences (Ecology): *A.A., A.S.*
    Biological Sciences (Entomology): *A.A., A.S.*
    Biological Sciences (Forestry): *A.A., A.S.*
    Biological Sciences (Marine Technology): *A.A., A.S.*
    Biological Sciences (Zoology): *A.A., A.S.*
    Earth Sciences (Oceanography): *A.A., A.S.*
    Environmental Studies: *A.A., A.S.*
    Recreation & Leisure Services: *A.A., A.S.*

Modesto Junior College
    Modesto, California 95350
    Agriculture: *A.A., A.S.*
    Agriculture (Animal Science): *A.A., A.S.*
    Agriculture (Dairy Science): *A.A., A.S.*
    Agricultural Technology: *Certificate*
    Agricultural Technology (Agricultural Lab Tech):
        Certificate
    Agricultural Technology (Forestry Tech): *Certificate*
    Agricultural Technology (Recreational Land Manage-
    ment Tech): *Certificate*

Monterey Peninsula College
    Monterey, California 93940
    Recreation: *Certificate*

Moorpark College
    Moorpark, California 93021
    Exotic Animal Training & Management: *A.S.*
    Exotic Animal Care & Handling: *Certificate*

Mount San Antonio College
    Walnut, California 91789
    Agricultural Technology: *A.S.*
    Animal Health Technology: *A.S.*
    Animal Science: *A.S.*
    Biology: *B.S.*
    Botany: *B.S.*
    Dairy Science: *A.S.*
    Environmental Studies: *B.S.*
    Forestry Technology: *A.S.*
    Livestock Management: *Certificate*
    Livestock Production: *A.S.*
    Pet Science: *A.S.*
    Plant Science Technology: *A.S.*
    Poultry Science: *A.S.*
    Pre-Veterinary Medicine: *B.S.*
    Wildlife Conservation: *A.S.*
    Wildlife Management: *B.S.*

Naval Postgraduate School
    Monterey, California 93940
    Oceanography: *B.S., M.S., Ph.D.*

Ohlone College
    Freemont, California 94537
    Environmental Technology: *A.A.*

Orange Coast College
    Costa Mesa, California 92626
    Animal Health Technology: *A.A.*
    Animal Science: *A.A.*
    Marine Technology: *A.A.*

Pacific College
    Fresno, California 93702
    Animal Science: *B.S., M.S.*
    Animal Science (Agri-Business): *B.S., M.S.*
    Animal Science (Animal Science Communication -
        Journalism): *B.S., M.S.*
    Animal Science (Dairy Husbandry): *B.S., M.S.*
    Animal Science (Poultry Science): *B.S., M.S.*
    Biology: *B.S.*
    Biology (Physiology): *B.S.*
    Biology (Zoology): *B.S.*

Palomar College
    San Marcos, California 92069
    Zoology: *A.*

Pasadena City College
    Pasedena, California 91106
    Forestry - Technical: *A.A.*

Pepperdine University
    Malibu, California 90265
    Biology: *B.A., B.S.*
    Natural Science: *B.A., B.S.*
    Recreation Education: *B.S.*

Pitzer College
    Claremont, California 91711
    Biology: *B.A.*
    Environmental Studies: *B.A.*
    Natural Sciences: *B.A.*

Pomona College
    Claremont, California 91711
    Biology: *B.A.*
    Biology (Botany): *B.A.*
    Biology (Zoology): *B.A.*

Reedley College
    Reedley, California 93654
    Agri-Business: *A.S.*
    Animal Science: *A.S.*
    Forest and Park Technology: *A.S.*
    Forest and Park Technology (Forest Recreation): *A.S.*
    Forest and Park Technology (Interpretation): *A.S.*
    Forest and Park Technology (Municipal Recreation/
        Parks): *A.S.*
    Forest and Park Technology (Outdoor Education): *A.S.*
    Forest and Park Technology (Outdoor Recreation): *A.S.*
    Forest and Park Technology (Park Management): *A.S.*
    Plant Science - Agronomy: *A.S.*

San Bernardino Valley College
    San Bernardino, California 92403
    Biology: *A.A.*
    Botany: *A.A.*
    Zoology: *A.A.*
    Pre-Veterinary: *Non-Degree*

San Diego City College
San Diego, California 92101
Animal Technician: *A.A.S.*
Biology: *A.A.*
Biology (Pre-Agriculture): *A.A.*
Biology (Pre-Forestry): *A.A.*
Biology (Pre-Veterinary Medicine): *A.A.*
Recreational Leadership: *A.A.*

San Diego Evening College
San Diego, California 92101
Life Science: *A.A.*
Recreational Leadership: *Certificate*

San Diego State University
San Diego, California 92182
Biology: *M.S.* *
Ecology: *Ph.D.*
Psychology: *M.A.* *
Zoology: *M.S.* *, *B.S.*

San Francisco State University
San Francisco, California 94132
Biology: *B.A., M.A.*
Biology (Ecology & Systematic): *B.A., M.A.*
Biology (Physiology & Behavioral): *B.A., M.A.*
Biology (Microbiology): *B.A., M.A.*
Biology (Marine): *B.A., M.A.*
Recreation: *B.A., M.S.*

San Joaquin Delta College
Stockton, California 95204
Agri-Business: *A.A., Certificate*
Agriculture & Natural Resources: *A.A.*
Agriculture & Natural Resources (Agricultural Engineering & Mechanics): *A.A.*
Agriculture & Natural Resources (Agricultural Production-Plant & Animal): *A.A.*
Agriculture & Natural Resources (Forestry): *A.A.*
Agriculture & Natural Resources (Natural Resources Management): *A.A.*
Agriculture & Natural Resources (Wildlife & Fish Management): *A.A.*
Animal Husbandry: *Certificate*
Animal Science: *A.A.*
Animal Science Production & Technology: *A.A.*
Natural Resources Management: *Certificate*

San Jose State University
San Jose, California 95192
Behavioral Science: *B.A.*
Biological Science: *B.A., M.S., M.A.*
Environmental Studies: *B.A., B.S., M.S.*
Entomology: *B.S.*
Geology: *M.A., M.S.*
Material Science: *M.A., M.S.*
Microbiology: *B.S.*
Natural Science: *B.A.*
Recreation: *M.A., M.S.*
Zoology: *B.A.*

Santa Rosa Junior College
Santa Rosa, California 95401
Agri-Business: *A.S., Certificate*
Agriculture: *A.S.*
Animal Science: *A.S., Certificate*
Earth Sciences: *A.S.*
Forest Recreation: *Certificate*

Forestry: *A.S.*
Forest Technology: *Certificate*
Ornamental Horticulture: *A.S., Certificate*
Plant Science: *A.S., Certificate*

Shasta College
Redding, California 96001
Agri-Business: *A.A.*
Agriculture: *Non-Degree*
Biological Science: *Non-Degree*
Engineering Technology: *A.A.*
Environmental Conservation: *Non-Degree*
Fisheries Technology: *A.A.*
Forestry: *Non-Degree*
Game Management: *Non-Degree*
Geology: *Non-Degree*
Horse Husbandry: *Certificate*
Natural Resources: *A.A., Non-Degree*
Oceanography: *Non-Degree*
Ornamental Horticulture: *A.A.*
Production Agriculture: *A.A.*
Recreation: *A.A.*
Recreation (Park & Environmental Recreation): *A.A.*
Recreational Administration: *Non-Degree*
Veterinary Medicine: *Non-Degree*

Sierra College
Rocklin, California 95677
Agri-Business: *Certificate*
Agriculture, General: *A.A., A.S., Certificate*
Agriculture, General (Animal Husbandry): *A.A., A.S., Certificate*
Forest Technology: *A.A., A.S., Certificate*
Horse Husbandry: *Certificate*
Horticulture: *A.A., A.S.*
Landscaping & Horticulture: *Certificate*

College of the Siskiyous
Weed, California 96094
Agricultural Crop Production: *A.A., A.S., Certificate*
Animal Science: *A.A., A.S., Certificate*
Business Agriculture: *A.A., A.S., Certificate*
Dairy Husbandry: *A.A., A.S., Certificate*
Forestry Assistant: *A.A., A.S., Certificate*
Forestry Technician: *A.A., A.S., Certificate*
General Agriculture: *A.A., A.S., Certificate*
Natural Resources (Water Resources Management): *A.A., A.S., Certificate*
Natural Resources (Wildlife Management): *A.A., A.S., Certificate*
Pre-Forestry: *A.A., A.S., Certificate*

Sonoma State University
Rohnert Park, California 94928
Biology: *B.A., M.A.* *
Biology (Parks & Recreation): *B.A.*
Biology (Animal Behavior): *B.A.*
Biology (Marine Biology): *B.A.*
Biology (Pre-Veterinary): *B.A.*
Environmental Studies - Planning Emphasis: *B.A.*
Geology: *B.A., B.S.*

Southwestern College
Chula Vista, California 92010
Forestry: *Non-Degree*
Zoology: *Non-Degree*

Stanford University
  Stanford, California 94305
  Biological Sciences: *B.S., M.S., Ph.D.*
  Environmental Earth Sciences: *B.S., M.S.*
  Land Resource Planning: *B.S.*

U.S. International University - San Diego
  San Diego, California 92131
  Biology (Marine Sciences): *B.A.*
  Natural Sciences: *B.A.*
  Natural Sciences (Pre-Veterinary Medicine): *B.A.*
  Service Industries Management (Outdoor Recreation): *B.S.*

University of California - Berkeley
  Berkeley, California 94720
  Botany: *B.S., M.S.*
  Conservation of Natural Resources: *B.S.*
  Forestry: *B.S., M.F.*
  Range Management: *M.S.*
  Wildland Resource Science: *M.S., Ph.D.*
  Zoology: *B.S., M.S., Ph.D.*

University of California - Davis
  Davis, California 95616
  Agricultural Chemistry: *M.S., Ph.D.*
  Agricultural Science & Management: *B.S.*
  Agronomy: *M.S.*
  Animal Genetics: *M.S., Ph.D.*
  Animal Nutrition: *M.S., Ph.D.*
  Avian Sciences: *B.S., M.S.*
  Biological Sciences: *A.B., B.S.*
  Botany: *M.S., Ph.D.*
  Ecology: *M.S., Ph.D.*
  Entomology: *M.S., Ph.D.*
  Environmental Studies: *B.S.*
  Horticulture: *M.S.*
  Microbiology: *M.A., Ph.D.*
  Plant Protection/Pest Management: *M.S.*
  Range Management: *M.S.*
  Range and Wildlands Science: *B.S.*
  Soil Science: *M.S., Ph.D.*
  Veterinary Medicine: *D.V.M.*
  Water Science: *M.S.*
  Wildlife & Fisheries Biology: *B.S., M.S. *, Ph.D.*
  Zoology: *M.A., Ph.D.*

University of California - Irvine
  Irvine, California 92717
  Biological Sciences: *B.S., M.A.T., M.S., Ph.D.*
  Biological Sciences (Developmental Cell Biology): *B.S., M.A.T., M.S., Ph.D.*
  Biological Sciences (Ecology & Evolutionary Biology): *B.S., M.A.T., M.S., Ph.D.*
  Biological Sciences (Molecular Biology & Biochemistry): *B.S., M.A.T., M.S., Ph.D.*
  Biological Sciences (Psychobiology): *B.S., M.A.T., M.S., Ph.D.*
  Ecology: *B., M.*
  Social Ecology: *B.A., M.A., Ph.D.*

University of California - Los Angeles
  Los Angeles, California 90024
  Bacteriology: *B.A.*
  Biology: *B.A., M.S., C. Phil., Ph.D.*
  Environmental Science & Engineering: *D. Env.*
  Geography-Ecosystems: *B.A.*
  Geology: *B.S., M.S., C. Phil., Ph.D.*
  Geology Engineering: *B.S*
  Geochemistry: *M.S., Ph.D.*
  Geological Paleobiology: *M.S., Ph.D.*
  Geological Studies (Non-Renewable Natural Resources): *B.S.*
  Microbiology: *Ph.D.*
  Microbiology & Immunology: *M.S.*

University of California - Riverside
  Riverside, California 92502
  Biology: *A.B., B.S., M.A., Ph.D.*
  Botany: *Ph.D.*
  Entomology: *A.B., B.S., M.S., Ph.D.*
  Environmental Studies: *A.B., B.S.*
  Genetics: *Ph.D.*
  Geological Sciences: *M.S., Ph.D.*
  Geology: *A.B., B.S.*
  Paleobiology: *A.B., B.S.*
  Pest Management: *M.S.*
  Plant Science: *A.B., B.S., M.S.*
  Psychobiology: *A.B., B.S.*
  Soil Science: *B.S., M.S., Ph.D.*
  Systems Ecology: *B.S.*

University of California - San Diego
  La Jolla, California 92037
  Biology: *M.S., Ph.D.*
  Earth Science: *M.S., Ph.D.*
  Oceanography: *M.S., Ph.D.*

University of California - Santa Barbara
  Santa Barbara, California 93010
  Biological Sciences: *B.A., M.A., Ph.D.*
  Biological Sciences (Aquatic Biology): *B.A., M.A., Ph.D.*
  Biological Sciences (Environmental Biology): *B.A., M.A., Ph.D.*
  Biological Sciences (Evolutionary Biology): *B.A., M.A., Ph.D.*
  Biological Sciences (Physiology & Cellular Biology): *B.A., M.A., Ph.D.*
  Biology: *B.A.*
  Environmental Studies (Inter-departmental): *B.A.*

University of California - Santa Cruz
  Santa Cruz, California 95060
  Earth Sciences: *B.A.*
  Environmental Planning: *B.A.*
  Environmental Studies: *B.A.*
  Marine Studies: *B.A.*
  Natural History: *B.A.*
  Natural Sciences: *B.A.*
  Pre-Forestry: *Non-Degree*
  Pre-Landscape Architecture: *Non-Degree*
  Pre-Urban Planning: *Non-Degree*
  Pre-Veterinary Medicine: *Non-Degree*
  Psychobiology: *B.A.*

University of the Pacific
  Stockton, California 95204
  Biological Sciences: *B.A., B.S., M.S.*
  Biology: *B.S.*
  Chemistry: *B.S.*
  Geology: *B.A., B.S.*
  Geophysics: *B.S.*
  Marine Science: *M.S.*
  Recreation Education: *B.A., M.A.*

University of Redlands
  Redlands, California 92374
  Biology: *B.*
  Geology: *B.*

University of Southern California
  Los Angeles 90007
  Biological Sciences: *B.S., M.S., Ph.D.*
  Environmental Engineering: *M.S.*
  Environmental Social Sciences: *Certificate*
  Geological Science: *B.S., M.S., Ph.D.*
  Microbiology: *Ph.D.*
  Psychobiology: *B.S.*

Victor Valley College
  Victorville, California 92392
  Agriculture: *A.A., A.S.*
  Biology: *A.A., A.S.*
  Environmental Science: *A.A.S.*
  Geology: *A.A., A.S.*

West Coast University
  Los Angeles, California 90020
  Environmental Science: *M.S.*

West Hills Community College
  Coalinga, California 93210
  Agriculture: *Non-Degree*
  Agriculture-Business: *A.A., Non-Degree*
  Animal Husbandry: *A.A., Non-Degree*
  Biology: *Non-Degree*
  Dairy Husbandry: *A.A., Non-Degree*
  Geology: *Non-Degree*

Westmont College
  Santa Barbara, California 93103
  Biology: *B.A.*
  Natural Sciences: *B.A.*

West Valley College
  Saratoga, California 95070
  Park Management Technology: *A.S., Certificate*
  Pre-Forestry: *Non-Degree*

Yuba College
  Marysville, California 95091
  Agricultural Technology: *A.S., Certificate*
  Agricultural Technology (Agri-Business): *A.S.,
    Certificate*
  Agricultural Technology (Animal Science): *A.S.,
    Certificate*
  Animal Health Technician: *A.S.*
  Life Science: *A.A., A.S.*
  Recreation Technician: *A.S.*

Colorado

Adams State College
  Alamosa, Colorado 81102
  Biology: *B.A., B.S.*
  Earth Science: *B.A., B.S.*
  Earth Science Education: *M.A.*
  Environmental Science: *B.A., B.S.*
  Geology: *B.A., B.S.*
  Natural Science: *B.A., B.S.*
  Pre-Veterinary Medicine: *Non-Degree*
  Recreation: *B.A.*

Bel-Rea Institute of Animal Technology
  Denver, Colorado 80231
  Animal Technician: *A.S.*

Colorado Mountain College - West Campus
  Glenwood Springs, Colorado 81601
  Animal Health Technology: *A.A., A.A.S.*
  Biological Science: *A.A.*
  Farm & Ranch Management: *A.A.S., Certificate*
  Natural Resources Management: *Certificate*
  Recreation Leadership: *Certificate*
  Recreation Supervision: *A.A.S.*

Colorado State University
  Fort Collins, Colorado 80521
  Agriculture: *B.S., M.Ag., M.S., Ph.D.*
  Agriculture (Agricultural Business): *B.S., M.Ag.,
    M.S., Ph.D.*
  Agriculture (Agricultural Economics): *B.S., M.Ag.,
    M.S., Ph.D.*
  Agriculture (Agricultural Industries Management): *B.S.,
    M.Ag., M.S., Ph.D.*
  Agriculture (Agricultural Systems Management): *B.S.,
    M.Ag., M.S., Ph.D.*
  Agriculture (Agricultural Journalism): *B.S., M.Ag.,
    M.S., Ph.D.*
  Agriculture (Biological-Agricultural Science): *B.S.,
    M.Ag., M.S., Ph.D.*
  Agriculture (Farm and Range Management): *B.S.,
    M.Ag., M.S., Ph.D.*
  Agriculture (General Agriculture): *B.S., M.Ag.,
    M.S., Ph.D.*
  Agriculture (Horticulture): *B.S., M.Ag., M.S., Ph.D.*
  Agriculture (Production Agriculture): *B.S., M.Ag.,
    M.S., Ph.D.*
  Agriculture (Vocational Agriculture): *B.S., M.Ag.,
    M.S., Ph.D.*
  Agriculture (World Agriculture): *B.S., M.Ag., M.S., Ph.D.*
  Agricultural Economics: *B.S., M.Ag.*
  Agricultural Engineering: *B.S.*
  Agricultural Engineering (Agricultural Industries
    Management): *B.S.*
  Agricultural Economics (Agricultural Journalism): *B.S.*
  Agronomy: *B.S., M.Ag., M.S., Ph.D.*
  Agronomy (Soil Resources & Conservation): *B.S.,
    M. Ag., M.S., Ph.D.*
  Agronomy (Soil Science): *B.S., M.Ag., M.S., Ph.D.*
  Animal Science: *B.S., M.Ag., M.S., Ph.D.*
  Animal Science (Industries Management): *B.S., M.Ag.,
    M.S., Ph.D.*
  Animal Science (Production): *B.S., M.Ag., M.S., Ph.D.*
  Animal Science (Science): *B.S., M.Ag., M.S., Ph.D.*
  Avian Science: *B.S., M.Ag., M.S., Ph.D.*

Bio-Agricultural Science: *B.S.*
Botany & Plant Pathology: *B.S., M.S., Ph.D.*
Fishery Biology: *B.S., M.S., Ph.D.*
Forest Biology: *B.S., M.F., M.S., Ph.D.*
Forest Management Science: *B.S., M.F., M.S., Ph.D.*
Forestry - Business: *B.S., M.F., M.S., Ph.D.*
Geology: *B.S., M.S., Ph.D.*
Geology (Environmental Geology): *B.S., M.S., Ph.D.*
Horticulture: *B.S., M.Ag., M.S., Ph.D.*
Landscape Horticulture: *B.S., M.Ag., M.S., Ph.D.*
Medical Technology & Microbiology: *Non-Degree*
Microbiology: *B.S., M.S., Ph.D.*
Natural Resources Management: *B.S., M.F., M.S., Ph.D.*
Range Science: *B.S., M.S., Ph.D.*
Range Science (Land Rehabilitation): *B.S., M.S., Ph.D.*
Range Science (Range Animal Nutrition): *B.S., M.S., Ph.D.*
Range Science (Range Ecology): *B.S., M.S., Ph.D.*
Range Science (Range Ecosystem Management): *B.S., M.S., Ph.D.*
Range Science (Range Forest Management): *B.S., M.S., Ph.D.*
Range Science (Range Land Planning): *B.S., M.S., Ph.D.*
Recreation Resources: *B.S., M.S., Ph.D.*
Recreation Resources (Conservation Education): *B.S., M.S., Ph.D.*
Recreation Resources (Environmental Interpretation): *B.S., M.S., Ph.D.*
Recreation Resources (Outdoor Recreation): *B.S., M.S., Ph.D.*
Recreation Resources (Park & Recreation Administration): *B.S., M.S., Ph.D.*
Veterinary Medicine: *D.V.M., Non-Degree*
Veterinary Science: *Non-Degree*
Watershed Sciences: *B.S., M.S., Ph.D.*
Watershed Sciences (Forest Watershed Management): *B.S., M.S., Ph.D.*
Watershed Sciences (Hydrology): *B.S., M.S., Ph.D.*
Wildlife Biology: *B.S., M.S., Ph.D.*
Wildlife Biology (Administrative): *B.S., Ph.D.*
Wildlfie Biology (Research): *B.S., M.S., Ph.D.*
Zoology & Entomology: *B.S., M.S., Ph.D.*

Community College of Denver
Lakewood, Colorado 80215
Environmental Control Technology: *Certificate*
Horticulture: *A.A.*
Recreational Leadership: *Certificate*

Fort Lewis College
Durango, Colorado 81301
Agricultural Science: *A.A.*
Biology (General Biology): *B.S.*
Biology (Natural History): *B.S.*
Forestry (Fish Management): *Non-Degree*
Forestry (Forest Management): *Non-Degree*
Forestry (Range Management): *Non-Degree*
Geology: *B.S.*
Pre-Agriculture: *Non-Degree*

Lamar Community College
Lamar, Colorado 81052
Agriculture: *A.A.*
Agricultural Business: *A.A.*
Horse Training Management: *A.A.*

Mesa College
Grand Junction, Colorado 81501
Agriculture (General): *A.S.*
Agriculture (Professional): *A.S., B.S.*
Animal - Plant Management: *B.S.*
Animal Science: *A.S.*
Biology (Applied): *A.S., B.S.*
Biology (General): *A.S.*
Botany, General (Biology): *A.S.*
Environmental Geoscience: *B.S.*
Geology: *A.S., B.S.*
Leisure & Recreational Studies: *B.A.*
Natural Resources: *A.S., B.S.*
Pre-Veterinary Medicine: *A.S.*
Range Management: *A.S.*
Recreation: *A.A., B.A.*
Zoology: *A.S.*

Metropolitan State College
Denver, Colorado 80204
Biology (Botany): *B.A., B.S.*
Biology (Environmental Biology): *B.A., B.S.*
Biology (Microbiology): *B.A., B.S.*
Biology (Zoology): *B.A., B.S.*
Earth Science (Land Use): *B.A., B.S.*
Recreation (Outdoor Recreation): *B.A.*
Recreation (Recreation & Park Administration): *B.A.*

Regis College
Denver, Colorado 80221
Biology: *B.S.*
Ecology: *B.S.*
Environmental Studies - Human Ecology: *B.S.*
Psychology: *B.A., B.S.*

University of Colorado
Boulder, Colorado 80302
Biological Sciences (Cellular Biology): *B.A., M.A., M.S., Ph.D.*
Biological Sciences (Environmental Biology): *B.A., M.A., M.S., Ph.D.*
Biological Sciences (Developmental Biology): *B.A., M.A., M.S., Ph.D.*
Biological Sciences (Molecular Biology): *B.A., M.A., M.S., Ph.D.*
Biological Sciences (Organismic Biology): *B.A., M.A., M.S., Ph.D.*
Biological Sciences (Population Biology): *B.A., M.A., M.S., Ph.D.*
Environmental Conservation: *B.A.*
Geological Sciences: *B.A., M.A., M.S., Ph.D.*
Microbiology: *B.A., M.A., M.S., Ph.D.*
Recreation: *B.S.*

University of Southern Colorado
Pueblo, Colorado 81001
Agriculture: *A.A.*
Biology: *B.S.*

University of Northern Colorado
Greeley, Colorado 80631
Biological Sciences: *B.A., M.A., Ed.S., D.A.*
Botany: *B.A., M.A.*
Earth Sciences (Oceanography): *M.A.*
Outdoor Education: *M.A.*
Pre-Veterinary Medicine: *Non-Degree*

Recreation (Recreation & Park Administration): *B.S.,*
  M.A.
Zoology: *B.A., M.A.*

Western State College
  Gunnison, Colorado 81230
  Biology: *B.A., M.A.*
  Geology: *B.A., M.A.*
  Recreation: *B.A.*

Connecticut

Fairfield University
  Fairfield, Connecticut 06430
  Biology: *B.S.*

Mitchell College
  New London, Connecticut 06320
  Recreation: *A.A., A.S.*

Northwestern Connecticut Community College
  Winsted, Connecticut 06098
  Behavioral Sciences: *A.A.*
  Biology: *A.A.*
  Environmental Technology: *A.S.*
  Park Management & Design: *A.S.*
  Recreational Leadership: *A.S.*

Post College
  Waterbury, Connecticut 06708
  Recreational Leadership: *A.A., A.S.*

Quinnipiac College
  Hamden, Connecticut 06518
  Biology: *B.A.*
  Environmental Health Technology: *B.S.*
  Laboratory Animal Technology: *B.S.*

Southern Connecticut State College
  New Haven, Connecticut 06515
  Biology (Pure Science): *M.S.*
  Biology (Aquatic Biology): *B.A., B.S.*
  Biology (Biological Technology): *B.A., B.S.*
  Biology (Botany): *B.A., B.S.*
  Biology (Environmental Biology): *B.A., B.S.*
  Biology (General Biology): *B.A., B.S.*
  Biology (Microbiology): *B.A., B.S.*
  Biology (Physiology): *B.A., B.S.*
  Biology (Zoology): *B.A., B.S.*
  Earth Science (Environmental Earth Science):
    B.A., B.S.
  Earth Science (Geology): *B.A., B.S.*
  Earth Science (Oceanography): *B.A., B.S.*
  Recreation: *B.S., M.S.*
  Science & Environmental Education: *M.S.*

University of Connecticut
  Storrs, Connecticut 06268
  Agricultural Education: *B.S.*
  Agricultural Economics: *B.S., M.S., Ph.D.*
  Agronomy (Plant Science): *B.S., M.S., Ph.D.*
  Agronomy (Soil Science): *B.S., M.S.*
  Animal Industries: *M.S.*
  Animal Science: *B.S.*
  Biological Science: *B.A., B.S., M.S., Ph.D.*
  Cell Biology: *M.S., Ph.D.*
  Dairy Bacteriology: *Ph.D.*
  Dairy Technology: *M.S.*
  Developmental Biology: *M.S., Ph.D.*

Ecology: *Ph.D.*
Ecology & Biological Control: *Ph.D.*
Entomology: *M.S., Ph.D.*
Environmental Engineering: *Ph.D.*
Environmental Horticulture: *B.S.*
Geology: *M.S., Ph.D.*
Microbiology: *M.S., Ph.D.*
Morphology & Physiology: *Ph.D.*
Natural Resource Conservation: *B.S., M.S.*
Ocean Engineering: *M.S., Ph.D.*
Oceanography: *M.S., Ph.D.*
Parasitology: *Ph.D.*
Physiology & Reproduction: *Ph.D.*
Renewable Natural Resource Conservation: *M.S.*
Zoology: *M.S., Ph.D.*

Wesleyan University
  Middletown, Connecticut 06457
  Biology: *B.A., M.A., Ph.D.* *
  Earth Science: *B.A., M.A.*
  Environmental Science: *B.A., M.A.*

Yale University
  New Haven, Conneticut 06511
  Forestry: *M.F.*
  Forest Science: *M.F.S., Ph.D.*
  Forestry & Environmental Studies: *M.S., M.Phil., Ph.D.*
  Natural Science (Biology): *B.A., B.S.*
  Natural Science (Geology): *B.A., B.S.*

Delaware

Delaware State College
  Dover, Delaware 19901
  Biology: *B.S.*
  Biology (Park Management and Recreation): *B.S.*
  Biology (Soil & Water Management): *B.S.*
  Biology (Vegetation Management): *B.S.*
  Biology (Wildlife Management): *B.S.*
  Natural Resources (General Resource Management):
    B.S.
  Natural Resources Technology: *B. Tech.*
  Pre-veterinary Management: *B.S.*

University of Delaware
  Newark, Delaware 19711
  Agricultural Science (Agricultural Economics):
    A.S., B.S.
  Agricultural Science (Agricultural Education): *A.S., B.S.*
  Agricultural Science (Animal & Poultry Science):
    A.S., B.S.
  Agricultural Science (Ecology): *A.S., B.S.*
  Agricultural Science (Entomology): *A.S., B.S.*
  Agricultural Science (Entomology & Plant Pathology):
    A.S., B.S.
  Agricultural Science (General Agriculture): *A.S., B.S.*
  Agricultural Science (Parks & Recreation Adminis-
    tration): *A.S., B.S.*
  Agricultural Science (Plant Science): *A.S., B.S.*
  Biological Science: *A.A., B.A.*
  Geology: *B.A., B.S.*
  Marine Studies (Chemical Oceanography): *M.S., Ph.D.*
  Marine Studies (Marine Affairs): *M.S., Ph.D.*
  Marine Studies (Marine Biology & Geology):
    M.S., Ph.D.
  Marine Studies (Ocean Engineering): *M.S., Ph.D.*
  Marine Studies (Physical Oceanography): *M.S., Ph.D.*

District of Columbia

The Catholic University of America
   Washington, D.C. 20064
   Biology: *B.S., M.S., Ph.D.*
   Environmental Sciences: *B.S.*
   Ocean Engineering: *B.S., M.S., Ph.D.*
   Oceanography: *B.S.*

The George Washington University
   Washington, D.C. 20052
   Biological Sciences: *B.A., B.S., M.S., Ph.D.*
   Biological Sciences (Zoology): *B.A., B.S., M.S., Ph.D.*
   Environmental Law: *J.D., LL.M., S.J.D.*
   Environmental Studies: *B.A., B.S.*
   Microbiology: *M.S., Ph.D.*
   Ocean Engineering: *B., M.*
   Oceanography: *B.S.*

Georgetown University
   Washington, D.C. 20007
   Biology: *B.S., M.S., Ph.D.*
   Microbiology: *Ph.D.*

Howard University
   Washington, D.C. 20059
   Botany: *M.S.*
   Cell Biology: *Ph.D.*
   Genetics: *Ph.D.*
   Mammalogy: *Ph.D.*
   Microbiology: *Ph.D.*
   Zoology: *M.S., Ph.D.*

University of the District of Columbia
   Washington, D.C. 20009
   Earth Science/Geoscience: *B.S.*
   Environmental Ecology: *B.S.*
   Geoscience: *B.S.*
   Horticulture: *B.S.*
   Oceanography: *B.S.*
   Oceanography (Geological Oceanography): *B.S.*
   Oceanography (Physical Oceanography): *B.S.*

Florida

Brevard Community College
   Cocoa, Florida 32924
   Pre-Forestry: *A.A., A.S.*
   Pre-Veterinary Medicine: *A.A., A.S.*

Broward Community College
   Fort Lauderdale, Florida 33314
   Pre-Recreation: *A.A.*
   Veterinary Medical Assisting: *A.S., V.M.A.*
   Veterinary Medicine: *A.A.*

Chipola Junior College
   Marianna, Florida 32446
   Pre-Agriculture: *Non-Degree*
   Pre-Forestry: *Non-Degree*

Florida Agricultural & Mechanical University
   Tallahassee, Florida 32307
   Agricultural-Business: *Non-Degree*
   Animal Breeding: *Non-Degree*
   Animal Science: *B.S.*
   Aquatic Environment: *B.S.*
   Biology: *B.S., B.A.*

Botany: *Non-Degree*
Earth Science: *Non-Degree*
General Agriculture: *B.S.*
General Entomology: *B.S.*
Pre-Forestry: *Non-Degree*
Veterinary Technician: *A.S.V.T.*

Florida Institute of Technology
   Melbourne, Florida 32901
   Aquaculture: *B.S.*
   Bio-Environmental Oceanography: *M.S.*
   Biological Oceanography: *B.S., M.S.*
   Biological Science: *M.S., Ph.D.*
   Chemical Oceanography: *B.S., M.S.*
   Ecology: *B.S.*
   Environmental Science: *M.S.*
   Environmental Science Technology: *B.S.*
   Environmental Technology: *A.S., B.S.*
   General Biology: *B.S.*
   Marine Biology: *B.S.*
   Oceanography: *B.S., M.S., Ph.D.*
   Ocean Engineering: *B.S., M.S.*
   Oceanographic Technology: *A.S., B.S.*
   Offshore Marine Technology: *A.S.*
   Physical Oceanography: *B.S., M.S.*

Florida Southern College
   Lakeland, Florida 33802
   Biology: *B.A., B.S.*
   Pre-Forestry: *B.S.*

Florida State University
   Tallahasee, Florida 32306
   Biological Science: *B.S., B.A., M.S., Ph.D.*
   Meteorology: *B.S., B.A., M.S., Ph.D.*
   Oceanography: *M.S., Ph.D.*

Lake City Community College
   Lake City, Florida 32055
   Forest Engineering Technology: *A.S.*
   Forest Technology: *A.S.*
   Park Technology: *A.S.*

Nova University
   Fort Lauderdale, Florida 33314
   Oceanography: *D.*

Palm Beach Junior College
   Lake Worth, Florida 33460
   Marine Biology: *A.A.*
   Pre-Veterinary: *A.A.*
   Zoology: *A.A.*

Santa Fe Community College
   Gainesville, Florida 32602
   Biological Parks Technology: *A.A., A.S.*
   Environmental Science: *A.S.*
   Recreational Leadership: *A.A., A.S.*

Seminole Community College
   Sanford, Florida 32771
   Agriculture: *A.A.*
   Animal Science: *A.A.*
   Biology: *A.A.*
   Botany: *A.A.*
   Forestry: *A.A.*
   Geology: *A.A.*
   Microbiology: *A.A.*
   Plant Science: *A.A.*
   Zoology: *A.A.*

St. Petersburg Junior College
St. Petersburg, Florida 33733
Veterinary Technology: *A.S.*

University of Florida
Gainesville, Florida 32611
Agriculture: *B.A., M.Ag., M.S., M.S.T., M.A.M.R.D., Ph.D.*
Agriculture (Agricultural Engineering): *B.S.*
Agriculture (Agronomy): *B.S.*
Agriculture (Animal Science): *B.S.*
Agriculture (Dairy Science): *B.S.*
Agriculture (Entomology & Nematology): *B.S.*
Agriculture (Laboratory Animal Science): *B.S.*
Agriculture (Plant Pathology): *B.S.*
Agriculture (Soil Science): *B.S.*
Agriculture (Veterinary Science): *B.S.*
Forestry: *B.S.F.R.C., M.S., M.F.R.C.*
Range Ecosystems Management: *B.S.F.R.C., M.S., M.F.R.C.*
Resource Conservation: *B.S.F.R.C., M.S., M.F.R.C.*
Veterinary Medicine: *D.V.M.*

University of Miami
Coral Gables, Florida 33124
Atmospheric Science: *M.S., Ph.D.*
Biology: *A.B., B.S., M.S., Ph.D.*
Chemical Oceanography: *M.S., Ph.D.*
Fisheries: *Ph.D.*
Fisheries & Applied Estuarine Ecology: *M.S., Ph.D.*
Geology: *A.B.*
Marine Biology: *M.S., Ph.D.*
Marine Geology and Geophysics: *M.S., Ph.D.*
Microbiology: *B.S., M.S., Ph.D.*
Ocean Engineering: *M.S.*
Physical Oceanography: *M.S., Ph.D.*

University of South Florida
Tampa, Florida 33620
Natural Science (Biology): *B.A., B.S., Ph.D.*
Natural Science (Botany): *B.A., B.S., M.A.*
Natural Science (Marine Science): *M.S.*
Natural Science (Microbiology): *B.A., B.S., M.A.*
Natural Science (Zoology): *B.A., B.S., M.A.*

University of West Florida
Pensacola, Florida 32504
Biology: *B.S., M.S., M.S.T.*
Biology (Biology Education): *B.S.*
Biology (General Biology): *B.S.*
Biology (Marine Biology): *B.S.*
Biology (Pre-Veterinary): *B.S.*
Botany: *Non-Degree*
Microbiology: *Non-Degree*
Oceanography: *Non-Degree*
Zoology: *Non-Degree*

Georgia

Abraham Baldwin Agricultural College
Tifton, Georgia 31794
Agri-Business Technology: *A.Ag.*
Agriculture: *A.S.*
Agricultural Engineering: *A.S.*
Agri-Science Technology: *A.Ag.*
Agri-Science Technology (Livestock Option): *A.Ag.*
Biology: *A.S.*

Environmental Health: *A.S.*
Forest Technology: *A.F.T.*
Forestry: *A.S.*
Wildlife Management: *A.S.*
Wildlife Technology: *A.S.*
Veterinary Medicine: *A.S.*

Brewton-Parker College
Mount Vernon, Georgia 30445
Forestry: *A.A., Non-Degree*
Recreation: *A.A., Non-Degree*
Veterinary Medicine: *Non-Degree*

Emory University
Atlanta, Georgia 30322
Biology (Aquatic): *B.A., B.S., M.S., Ph.D.*
Biology (Estuarine Ecology): *B.A., B.S., M.S., Ph.D.*
Biology (Systems Ecology): *B.A., B.S., M.S., Ph.D.*
Biology (Terrestrial): *B.A., B.S., M.S., Ph.D.*
Geology: *B.A., B.S.*

Fort Valley State College
Fort Valley, Georgia 31030
Animal Husbandry: *B.*

Gainesville Junior College
Gainesville, Georgia 30501
Agriculture: *A.S.*
Biological Science: *A.S.*

Georgia College
Milledgeville, Georgia 31061
Biology: *A.B., B.S., M.Ed., M.S.*
Biology (Aquatic Ecology Option): *A.B., B.S., M.Ed., M.S.*
Environmental Science: *B.S.*
Pre-Veterinary Medicine: *A.B., B.S., Non-Degree*
Recreation (Outdoor): *B.S.*

Georgia Southern College
Statesboro, Georgia 30458
Biology: *B.A., B.S., M.S.*
Biology (Biological Oceanography): *B.A., B.S., M.S.*
Biology (Environmental Biology): *B.A., B.S., M.S.*
Geology: *B.A., B.S.*
Pre-Veterinary Medicine: *B.A., B.S., Non-Degree*
Recreation (Camping & Outdoor): *B.S.*

Georgia State University
Atlanta, Georgia 30303
Biology: *M.S., M.A.T.*
Biological Sciences: *B.S.*
Geology: *B.S.*
Psychology: *B.A., B.S., M.A., Ph.D.*
Recreation: *B.S.*

Kennesaw College
Marietta, Georgia 30061
Agriculture: *A.S.*
Agricultural Engineering: *A.S.*
Biology: *A.S.*
Forestry: *A.S.*
Pre-Veterinary Medicine: *A.S.*
Recreation: *A.S.*

Mercer University
Macon, Georgia 31207
Biology: *B.A., B.S.*
General Science (Environmental Science):
Non-Degree
Pre-Forestry: *Non-Degree*
Recreation: *B.A., B.S.*

Shorter College
Rome, Georgia 30161
Biology: *B.A., B.S.*
Earth Science: *B.A., B.S.*
Natural Science (Environmental): *B.S.*
Pre-Veterinary Medicine: *Non-Degree*
Recreation Management: *B.S.*

South Georgia College
Douglas, Georgia 31533
Agriculture: *Non-Degree*
Agricultural Business: *A.S.*
Agricultural Engineering: *Non-Degree*
Agricultural Science: *A.S.*
Biology: *A.S.*
Botany: *A.S.*
Community Recreation: *A.S.*
Forestry: *A.S.*
Geology: *A.S.*
Outdoor Recreation: *A.S.*
Pre-Veterinary Science: *A.S.*
Recreational Leadership: *A.S.*
Zoology: *A.S.*

University of Georgia
Athens, Georgia 30602
Agriculture: *B.S.A.*
Agricultural Education: *B.S.A., M.Ed.*
Agronomy: *B.S.A., M.S., Ph.D.*
Anatomy (Veterinary): *M.S.*
Animal Nutrition: *Ph.D.*
Animal Science: *B.S.A., M.S., Ph.D.*
Avian Medicine: *M.S.*
Biological Sciences: *B.A., B.S.*
Botany: *B.A., B.S., B.S.A., M.S., Ph.D.*
Dairy Science: *B.S.A., M.S.*
Ecology: *Ph.D.*
Entomology: *B.A., B.S., B.S.A., M.S., Ph.D.*
Forest Resources: *M.S., Ph.D.*
Geology: *B.A., B.S., M.S., Ph.D.*
Horticulture: *B.S.A., M.S.*
Microbiology: *B.A., B.S., B.S.A., M.S., Ph.D.*
Park & Recreation Administration: *M.Ed., Ed.D.*
Pharmacology (Veterinary): *M.S., Ph.D.*
Physiology (Veterinary): *M.S., Ph.D.*
Plant Pathology & Plant Genetics: *B.S.A., M.S., Ph.D.*
Plant Protection & Pest Management: *M.S.*
Plant Sciences: *Ph.D.*
Poultry Science: *B.S.A., M.S., Ph.D.*
Pre-Veterinary Medicine: *B.S.A.*
Psychology: *B.A., B.S.*
Veterinary Parasitology: *M.S., Ph.D.*
Veterinary Pathology: *M.S., Ph.D.*
Zoology: *B.A., B.S., M.S., Ph.D.*

Hawaii

University of Hawaii - Honolulu
Honolulu, Hawaii 96822
Animal Science: *B.M.*
Cooperative Fishery Unit: *M.S., Ph.D.*
Entomology: *B., M., Ph.D.*
Ichthyology:
Ocean Engineering: *M.*
Oceanography: *M., Ph.D.*
Zoology: *B.S., M.S.*, Ph.D.**

Idaho

Idaho State University
Pocatello, Idaho 83201
Biology (Biology or Zoology): *B.S., M.S., D.A., Ph.D.*
Botany: *B.A.*
Conservation: *B.S.*
Geolory: *B.A., B.S., M.S.*
Microbiology: *B.S., M.S.*
Park & Recreation Management: *B.A., B.S.*
Pre-Veterinary Medicine: *Non-Degree*
Sociology (Recreation): *B.A.*

Ricks College
Rexburg, Idaho 83440
Animal Science: *A.*

University of Idaho
Moscow, Idaho 83843
Agribusiness: *B.S.Ag.Econ., B.S. An. Sc., B.S. Soil Sc.*
Agricultural Engineering: *B.S.Ag.E., M.S. Engineering, Ph.D.*
Agricultural, General: *B.S.Gen.Ag.*
Animal Sciences: *B.S.An.Sc., M.S.*
Biological Sciences: *M.Nat.Sc.*
Biology: *B.A., B.S., M.A.T.*
Botany: *B.A., B.S., M.S., Ph.D.*
Earth Science: *M.Nat.Sc., M.A.T.*
Entomology: *B.S.Ent., M.S., Ph.D.*
Fishery Resources: *B.S.Fish. Res., M.S.*
Forest Resources: *B.S.For.Res., M.S.*
Forestry, Wildlife & Range Sciences: *Ph.D.*
Geology: *B.S.Geol., M.S., Ph.D.*
Landscape Horticulture: *B.S.Pl.Sc.*
Natural Resources Development: *B.S.Ag.Econ.*
Plant Science: *B.S.Pl.Sc., M.S., Ph.D.*
Range-Livestock Management: *B.S.An.Sc.*
Range Resources: *B.S.Range Res., M.S.*
Recreation: *B.S.Rec.*
Rural & Community Development: *B.S.Ag.Econ.*
Soil Science: *B.S.Soil Sci., M.S., Ph.D.*
Veterinary Science: *B.S.Vet Sci., M.S.*
Wildlife Recreation Management: *B.S. Wildlife Rec. Mgt., M.S.*
Wildlife Resources: *B.S.Wildl.Res., M.S.*
Zoology: *B.A., B.S., M.S., Ph.D.*

Illinois

Agustana College
Rock Island, Illinois 61201
Biology: *B.A.*
Veterinary Studies (Pre-Professional): *Non-Degree*

Bradley University
  Peoria, Illinois 61606
  Biology: *B.A., B.S.*
  Environmental Science: *B.S.*

Danville Junior College
  Danville, Illinois 61832
  Agriculture: *A.A., A.S., A.A.S.*
  Forestry: *A.A., A.S., A.A.S.*
  Pre-Veterinary Medicine: *A.A.S.*

Eastern Illinois University
  Charleston, Illinois 61920
  Botany: *B.S., M.S.*
  Botany Education: *M.S.*
  Earth Science: *B.S.*
  Environmental Biology: *B.S.*
  Pre-Veterinary Medicine: *Non-Degree*
  Zoology: *B.S., M.S.*
  Zoology Education: *M.S.*

Elmhurst College
  Elmhurst, Illinois 60126
  Biology: *B.A., B.S.*
  Veterinary Medicine (Pre-Professional): *B.A., B.S.*

Eureka College
  Eureka, Illinois 61530
  Biological Science (Biology): *B.S.*

George Williams College
  Downers Grove, Illinois 60515
  Applied Behavioral Sciences: *B.S.*
  Biology: *B.S.*
  Leisure & Environmental Resources Administration:
    M.S.
  Natural Sciences (Pre-Veterinary): *B.A.*
  Recreational Services: *B.S.*

Illinois State University
  Normal, Illinois 61761
  Agri-Business: *B.S.*
  Agriculture: *B.S.*
  Biological Sciences: *B.A., B.S., M.S., Ph.D.*
  Environmental Health: *B.S.*
  Recreation & Park Administration: *B.S.*

Illinois Valley Community College
  Oglesby, Illinois 61348
  Agriculture: *Non-Degree, A.A., A.S.*
  Biological Sciences: *Non-Degree, A.A., A.S.*
  Pre-Veterinary Sciences: *Non-Degree, A.A., A.S.*

Joliet Junior College
  Joliet, Illinois 60436
  Agriculture: *A.S.*
  Horticulture: *A.A.S.*
  Veterinary Medicine (Pre-Professional): *Non-Degree*

Lake Land College
  Mattoon, Illinois 61939
  Agriculture: *A.A., A.S.*
  Biological Science: *A.A., A.S.*
  Biological Science (Pre-Fishery & Wildlife): *Non-Degree, A.A., A.S.*
  Biological Science (Pre-Forestry): *Non-Degree, A.A., A.S.*
  Pre-Veterinary: *Non-Degree, A.A., A.S.*
  Recreation: *Non-Degree, A.A., A.S.*

Lincoln College
  Lincoln, Illinois 62656
  Biology: *A.A.*
  Geography & Earth Science: *A.A.*

Mayfair College (City College of Chicago)
  Chicago, Illinois 60630
  Recreation Leadership: *Certificate*

Millikin University
  Decatur, Illinois 62522
  Biology: *B.A., B.S.*
  Environmental Studies: *B.A., B.S.*

Monmouth College
  Monmouth, Illinois 61462
  Biology: *A.A., B.A.*

Moraine Valley Community College
  Palos Hills, Illinois 60465
  Biology: *A.A., A.S., A.A.S.*
  Natural Sciences: *A.A., A.S., A.A.S.*
  Recreational Leadership Program: *A.A., A.S., A.A.S.*

Northern Illinois University
  De Kalb, Illinois 60115
  Biological Sciences: *B.S.*

Olivet Nazarene College
  Kankakee, Illinois 60901
  Biology: *A.B., B.S.*
  Botany: *A.B., B.S.*
  Physical Science: *A.B., B.S.*
  Physical Sciences (Ecology): *A.B., B.S.*
  Zoology: *A.B., B.S.*

Parkland College
  Champaign, Illinois 61820
  Agriculture: *A.S.*
  Recreation Areas & Facilities Specialist: *A.A.S.*
  Veterinary Technology: *A.*

Principia College
  Elsah, Illinois 62028
  Biology: *B.A., B.S.*
  Earth Sciences: *B.A., B.S.*
  Environmental Sciences: *B.A., B.S.*
  Environmental Studies: *B.A.*

Rock Valley College
  Rockford, Illinois 61101
  Agriculture: *A.S.*
  Earth Sciences: *A.S.*
  Recreational Leadership: *A.A.S.*
  Veterinary Medicine (Pre-Professional): *A.S.*

Southeastern Illinois College
  Harrisburg, Illinois 62946
  Agricultural Production Management: *A.A.S.*
  Forestry Technology: *A.A.S.*

Southern Illinois University - Carbondale
  Carbondale, Illinois 62901
  Agricultural Education: *B.S.*
  Agricultural Education (Agricultural Production & Products): *B.S.*
  Agricultural Education (Agricultural Resources): *B.S.*
  Agricultural Education (Forestry): *B.S.*
  Agriculture (General): *B.S.*
  Agriculture (Environmental Studies): *B.S.*

Animal Industries: *B.S., M.S., Ph.D.*
Biological Sciences: *B.A., B.S., M.S.*
Botany: *B.A., B.S.*
Forestry: *B.S., M.S., Ph.D.*
Forestry (Forest Resources Management): *B.S., M.S., Ph.D.*
Forestry (Forest Science): *B.S., M.S., Ph.D.*
Forestry (Forestry Environmental Assessment): *B.S., M.S., Ph.D.*
Forestry (Outdoor Recreation Resources Management): *B.S., M.S., Ph.D.*
Forestry (Urban Forest Management): *B.S., M.S., Ph.D.*
Microbiology: *B.A.*
Physiology: *B.A.*
Plant & Soil Science: *B.S., M.S.*
Zoology: *B.A., B.S., M.S. *, Ph.D. **
Zoology (Pre-Veterinary Medicine): *B.A., B.S.*

Trinity Christian College
Palos Heights, Illinois 60463
Biological Science: *B.A.*

Triton College
River Grove, Illinois 60171
Biological Sciences: *A.S.*
Pre-Veterinary: *A.S.*
Recreational Leadership: *Certificate*

University of Chicago
Chicago, Illinois 60637
Anatomy: *M.S., Ph.D.*
Anatomy (Cell, Tissue & Molecular Biology): *M.S., Ph.D.*
Anatomy (Ecology): *M.S., Ph.D.*
Anatomy (Experimental Embryology & Reproductive Biology): *M.S., Ph.D.*
Anatomy (Evolutionary Genetics): *M.S., Ph.D.*
Anatomy (Evolutionary Morphology): *M.S., Ph.D.*
Anatomy (Functional Morphology): *M.S., Ph.D.*
Anatomy (Human Biology): *M.S., Ph.D.*
Anatomy (Neurobiology): *M.S., Ph.D.*
Anatomy (Paleontology & Systematics): *M.S., Ph.D.*
Anatomy (Primatology): *M.S., Ph.D.*
Behavioral Sciences: *M.S., Ph.D.*
Biological Sciences: *A.B.*
Biological Sciences (Developmental Biology): *A.B.*
Biological Sciences (Evolutionary Biology): *A.B.*
Biological Sciences (Evolutionary Ecology): *A.B.*
Biological Sciences (Molecular Genetics): *A.B.*
Biological Sciences (Neurobiology): *A.B.*
Biological Sciences (Social Behavior of Animals): *A.B.*
Biology: *M.S., Ph.D.*
Biology (Animal Behavior): *M.S., Ph.D.*
Biology (Ecology): *M.S., Ph.D.*
Biology (Genetics): *M.S., Ph.D.*
Biology (Molecular, Cellular & Developmental Biology): *M.S., Ph.D.*
Biology (Population & Evolutionary Biology): *M.S., Ph.D.*
Evolutionary Biology: *M.S., Ph.D.*
Evolutionary Biology (Anatomy): *B.S., Ph.D.*
Evolutionary Biology (Botany): *M.S., Ph.D.*
Evolutionary Biology (Ecology): *M.S., Ph.D.*
Evolutionary Biology (Paleontology): *M.S., Ph.D.*
Evolutionary Biology (Theoretical Biology): *M.S., Ph.D.*

Evolutionary Biology (Zoology): *M.S., Ph.D.*
Geophysical Sciences: *A.B.*
Immunology: *Ph.D.*
Microbiology: *M.S., Ph.D.*
Microbiology (Physiology): *M.S., Ph.D.*

University of Chicago at Chicago Circle
Chicago, Illinois 60630
Biological Sciences: *B.A., B.S., M.S. *, Ph.D. **
Pre-Veterinary Medicine (Pre-Professional): *B.A., B.S.*

University of Illinois at Urbana-Champaign
Urbana, Illinois 61801
Agriculture: *B.S.*
Agronomy: *B.S., M.S., Ph.D.*
Animal Science: *B.S., M.S., Ph.D.*
Biology: *M.S., Ph.D.*
Biology (Environmental Biology): *M.S., Ph.D.*
Biology (Microbiology): *B.S., M.S., Ph.D.*
Biology (Plant Pathology): *M.S., Ph.D.*
Botany: *M.S., Ph.D.*
Dairy Science: *B.S., M.S., Ph.D.*
Entomology: *B.S., M.S., Ph.D.*
Forest Science: *B.S.*
Leisure Studies: *B.S.*
Recreation & Parks Administration (Recreation): *M.S.*
Physical Education (Recreation): *Ph.D.*
Veterinary Medicine: *M.S., Ph.D., D.V.M.*
Zoology: *B.S., M.S., Ph.D.*

Wabash Valley College (Illinois Eastern Junior Colleges)
Mount Carmel, Illinois 62863
Agri-Business: *A.A.S.*
Conservation & Outdoor Recreation: *A.A.S.*
Management of Agricultural Production: *A.A.S.*

Western Illinois University
Macomb, Illinois 61455
Agricultural Science: *B.S., B.S.T.*
Agricultural Science (Forestry): *Non-Degree*
Agricultural Science (Veterinary Medicine): *Non-Degree*
Biological Sciences (Biology): *B.S., B.S.T.*
Recreation & Park Administration: *B.S.*

Wilbur Wright College (City College of Chicago)
Chicago, Illinois 60634
Agriculture: *A.A.*
Horticulture: *Certificate*
Recreation Leadership: *Certificate*

Indiana

Ball State University
Muncie, Indiana 47306
Biology: *B.A., B.S., M.A., M.S., M.A.Ed.*
Botany: *B.A., B.S.*
Earth Science: *M.A., M.S.*
Geology: *B.A., B.S.*
Institute For Environmental Studies: *Non-Degree*
Natural Resources: *B.S., M.A., M.S.*
Natural Resources (General Resources Management): *B.S., M.A., M.S.*
Natural Resources (Fishery Resources): *B.S., M.A., M.S.*
Natural Resources (Water Quality): *B.S., M.A., M.S.*
Natural Resources (Natural Resources Interpretation): *B.S., M.A., M.S.*

Natural Resources (Environmental Conservation):
  B.S., M.A., M.S.
Science: *B.A., B.S.*
Zoology: *B.A., B.S.*

Butler University
  Indianapolis, Indiana 46208
  Biology: *M.S.*
  Botany: *B.A., B.S., M.S.*
  Pre-Forestry: *B.S., Non-Degree*
  Zoology: *B.A., B.S., M.S.*

DePauw University
  Greencastle, Indiana 46135
  Bacteriology & Botany: *B.A.*
  Earth Sciences: *B.A.*
  Zoology: *B.A., M.A.*

Goshen College
  Goshen, Indiana 46526
  Biology: *B.A.*
  Natural Science: *B.A.*
  Recreational Leadership: *Certificate*

Indiana State University
  Terre Haute, Indiana 47809
  Conservation: *B.S., M.S., Ph.D.*
  Earth Science: *B.A., B.S.*
  Geology: *B.A., B.S.*
  Life Sciences: *B.A., B.S.*
  Pre-Veterinary Medicine: *B., Non-Degree*

Indiana University — Bloomington
  Bloomington, Indiana 47401
  Biological Sciences: *B.A., B.S.*
  Biological Sciences (Cell Biology): *B.A., B.S.*
  Biological Sciences (Genetics): *B.A., B.S.*
  Biological Sciences (Developmental Biology): *B.A., B.S.*
  Biological Sciences (Organismal Biology): *B.A., B.S.*
  Biological Sciences (Physiology): *B.A., B.S.*
  Biological Sciences (Environmental Biology): *B.A., B.S.*
  Biology: *M.A.T.*
  Earth Science: *M.A.T.*
  Geology: *B.A., B.S.*
  Microbiology: *B.A., B.S., M.A., Ph.D.*
  Plant Sciences: *M.A., Ph.D.*
  School of Public and Environmental Affairs: *B.S., M.P.A.*
  Zoology: *B.A., M.A., Ph.D.*

Indiana University — Purdue University at Fort Wayne
  Fort Wayne, Indiana 46805
  Agricultural Science: *Non-Degree*
  Agronomy: *Non-Degree*
  Animal Sciences: *Non-Degree*
  Biological Sciences: *B.S., M.S.*
  Biological Sciences (Botany): *B.S., M.S.*
  Biological Sciences (Ecology): *B.S., M.S.*
  Biological Sciences (Microbiology): *B.S., M.S.*
  Biological Sciences (Zoology): *B.S., M.S.*
  Conservation: *Non-Degree*
  Cytotechnology: *Non-Degree*
  Earth Science: *A.B., B.S.*
  Entomology: *Non-Degree*
  Environmental Science: *M.S.*
  Forestry: *B.S.*
  Forestry (Forest Management): *B.S.*
  Forestry (Forest Recreation): *B.S.*

Forestry (Urban Forestry): *B.S.*
Forestry (Wildlife Management): *B.S.*

Manchester College
  North Manchester, Indiana 46962
  Biology: *B.A., B.S.*
  Environmental Studies: *B.A., B.S.*

Purdue University
  West Lafayette, Indiana 47907
  Agricultural Economics: *B.S., M.S., Ph.D.*
  Agronomy: *B.S., M.S., Ph.D.*
  Animal Science: *B.S., M.S., Ph.D.*
  Botany & Plant Pathology: *B.S., M.S.*
  Entomology: *B.S., M.S., Ph.D.*
  Forestry & Natural Resources: *B.S., M.S., M.F., Ph.D.*
  Forestry & Natural Resources (Forest Engineering):
    B.S., M.S., M.F., Ph.D.
  Forestry & Natural Resources (Forest Management):
    B.S., M.S., M.F., Ph.D.
  Forestry & Natural Resources (Forest Recreation):
    B.S., M.S., M.F., Ph.D.
  Forestry & Natural Resources (Urban Forestry): *B.S.,*
    M.S., M.F., Ph.D.
  Horticulture: *B.S., M.S., Ph.D.*
  Pre-Veterinary Medicine: *Non-Degree*
  Recreation Resources: *B.S., M.S.*
  Soil & Crop Science: *B.S.*
  Veterinary Medicine: *D.V.M.*
  Veterinary Medicine (Large Animal Clinics): *M.S.*
  Veterinary Medicine (Pathology & Public Health): *M.S.,*
    Ph.D.
  Veterinary Medicine (Small Animal Clinics): *M.S.*
  Veterinary Medicine (Veterinary Anatomy): *M.S., Ph.D.*
  Veterinary Medicine (Veterinary Microbiology):
    M.S., Ph.D.
  Veterinary Medicine (Veterinary Physiology & Pharma-
    cology): *M.S., Ph.D.*
  Veterinary Medicine/Agriculture: *B.S., D.V.M.*
  Veterinary Technology: *A.A.S.*
  Wildlife Management: *B.S.*
  Wildlife Science: *B.S.*

Purdue University — Calumet Campus
  Hammond, Indiana 46323
  Agriculture: *Non-Degree*
  Biology: *B.S.*
  Forestry: *Non-Degree*
  Pre-Veterinary Science: *Non-Degree*

Purdue University — North Central Campus
  Westville, Indiana 46391
  Agriculture: *B.A., B.S.*
  Forestry: *B.A., B.S.*
  Recreation: *B.A., B.S.*

Taylor University
  Upland, Indiana 46989
  Biology: *B.A., B.S.*
  Biology (Biology): *B.A., B.S.*
  Biology (Botany): *B.A., B.S.*
  Biology (Zoology): *B.A., B.S.*
  Natural Resources (Fisheries & Wildlife): *Non-Degree*
  Natural Resources (Forestry): *Non-Degree*
  Natural Resources (Park Management): *Non-Degree*
  Natural Resources (Resource Development):
    Non-Degree

University of Evansville
  Evansville, Indiana 47702
  Biology: *A., B.A., B.S.*
  Pre-Veterinary (Pre-Professional): *Non-Degree*

Iowa

Drake University
  Des Moines, Iowa 50311
  Biology: *B.A., M.A.*
  Earth Science: *B.A.*
  Marine Science: *B.A.*
  Veterinary Medicine: *Non-Degree*

Hawkeye Institute of Technology
  Waterloo, Iowa 50704
  Animal Science: *A.*

Iowa State University
  Ames, Iowa 50010
  Agriculture Business: *B.S.*
  Agricultural Economics: *M.S., Ph.D.*
  Agricultural Education: *B.S., M.S., Ph.D.*
  Agricultural Engineering: *B.S., M.Eng., M.S., Ph.D.*
  Agricultural Journalism: *B.S.*
  Agronomy: *B.S., M.S., Ph.D.*
  Animal Science: *B.S., M.S., Ph.D.*
  Biology: *B.S.*
  Botany: *B.S., M.S., Ph.D.*
  Dairy Science: *B.S.*
  Earth Science: *B.A., B.S., M.S., Ph.D.*
  Entomology: *B.S., M.S., Ph.D.*
  Fisheries & Wildlife Biology: *B.S., M.S., Ph.D.*
  Geology: *B.A., B.S., M.S., Ph.D.*
  Horticulture: *B.S., M.S., Ph.D.*
  Immunobiology: *M.S., Ph.D.*
  International Agriculture: *B.S.*
  Molecular, Cellular & Developmental Biology:
    M.S., Ph.D.
  Pest Management: *B.S.*
  Plant Pathology: *B.S., M.S., Ph.D.*
  Veterinary Anatomy: *M.S., Ph.D.*
  Veterinary Clinical Sciences: *M.S.*
  Veterinary Medicine: *D.V.M.*
  Veterinary Microbiology: *M.S., Ph.D.*
  Veterinary Pathology: *M.S., Ph.D.*
  Veterinary Physiology: *M.S., Ph.D.*
  Veterinary Preventative Medicine: *M.S.*
  Water Resources: *M.S., Ph.D.*
  Zoology: *B.S., M.S., Ph.D.*

University of Iowa
  Iowa City, Iowa 52242
  Anatomy: *M.S., Ph.D.*
  Botany: *B.A., M.S., Ph.D.*
  Environmental Engineering: *M.S., Ph.D.*
  Geology: *B.A., B.S.*
  Microbiology: *B.S., M.S., Ph.D.*
  Recreational Education: *B.S., M.A.*
  Zoology: *B.A., M.S., Ph.D.*

University of Northern Iowa
  Cedar Falls, Iowa 50613
  Biology: *B.A., M.A.*
  Earth Science: *M.A.*
  Geology: *B.A.*
  Recreation: *B.A.*
  Science (Environmental Planning): *B.A.*

Western Iowa Technical Community College
  Sioux City, Iowa 51102
  Animal Science: *Certificate*

Kansas

Colby Community College
  Colby, Kansas 67701
  Animal Science: *A.S.*
  Animal Technology: *A.A.S.*
  Companion Animal Care Curriculum: *Certificate*
  Conservation/Wildlife Management: *A.S.*
  Farm and Ranch Management: *A.S.*
  Horse Production: *A.S.*
  Pre-Veterinary Medicine: *A.A.*
  Zoology: *A.S.*

Emporia State University
  Emporia, Kansas 66801
  Biology: *B.A., B.S.. M.S.. M.S.Ed.* '
  Biology (Botany): *B.A., B.S., M.S., M.S.Ed.*
  Biology (Environmental Biology): *B.A., B.S., M.S.,*
    M.S.Ed.
  Biology (General Biology): *B.A., B.S., M.S., M.S.Ed.* '
  Biology (Microbiology & Cellular Biology): *B.A., B.S.,*
    M.S., M.S.Ed. '
  Biology (Zoology): *B.A., B.S., M.S., M.S.Ed.* '
  Earth Science: *B.A.. B.S., M.S.*
  Pre-Agriculture: *Non-Degree*
  Pre-Veterinary Medicine: *Non-Degree*
  Recreation: *M.S.Ed.*

Fort Hays State University
  Hays, Kansas 67601
  Agriculture: *B.A., B.S.*
  Agriculture (Animal Sciences): *B.A., B.S.*
  Biology: *B.A., B.S.*
  Biology (Resource Management): *B.A., B.S.*
  Biology (Wildlife): *B.A., B.S.*
  Pre-Forestry: *Non-Degree*
  Zoology: *B.A., B.S.*

Highland Community Junior College
  Highland, Kansas 66035
  Agriculture: *A.A., A.S., A.A.S., Non-Degree*
  Biology: *A.A., A.S., A.A.S., Non-Degree*
  Cytotechnology: *A.A., A.S., A.A.S.*
  Forestry & Conservation: *A.A., A.S., A.A.S.,*
    Non-Degree
  Veterinary Medicine: *Non-Degree*

Hutchinson Community Junior College
  Hutchinson, Kansas 67501
  Agriculture: *A.A., Non-Degree*
  Biological Sciences: *A.A., Non-Degree*
  Cytotechnology: *A.A., Non-Degree*
  Forestry: *A.A., Non-Degree*
  Veterinary Medicine: *A.A., Non-Degree*

Kansas State University
  Manhattan, Kansas 66506
  Agriculture: *B.S.*
  Agronomy: *B.S., M.S., Ph.D.*
  Animal Science: *B.S., M.S., Ph.D.*
  Biology: *B.S., M.S., Ph.D.*
  Crop Protection: *B.S., M.S.*
  Dairy Production: *B.S.*
  Entomology: *B.S., M.S., Ph.D.*

Feed Science and Management: *B.S.*
Fisheries & Wildlife Biology: *A.B., B.S.*
Horticulture: *B.S.*
Natural Resources Management: *B.S.*
Plant Pathology: *B.S., M.S., Ph.D.*
Poultry Science: *B.S., M.S.*
Pre-Forestry: *Non-Degree*
Pre-Veterinary Medicine: *Non-Degree*
Recreation: *A.B., B.S.*
Veterinary Medicine: *B.S., D.V.M.*

Kansas Wesleyan University
Salina, Kansas 67401
Biology: *A.B.*

Pratt Community Junior College
Pratt, Kansas 67124
Agriculture: *A.A., A.S., A.A.S., Non-Degree*
Agriculture (Agriculture Economics): *A.A., A.S., A.A.S., Non-Degree*
Agriculture (Agricultural Education): *A.A., A.S., A.A.S., Non-Degree*
Agriculture (Agronomy): *A.A., A.S., A.A.S., Non-Degree*
Agriculture (Animal Husbandry): *A.A., A.S., A.A.S., Non-Degree*
Agriculture (Entomology): *A.A., A.S., A.A.S., Non-Degree*
Agriculture (Farm Management): *A.A., A.S., A.A.S., Non-Degree*
Agriculture (Forestry): *Non-Degree*
Agriculture (Horticulture): *A.A., A.S., A.A.S., Non-Degree*
Agriculture (Wildlife Management): *A.A., A.S., A.A.S., Non-Degree*
Pre-Veterinary Medicine: *A.A., A.S., A.A.S., Non-Degree*

St. John's College
Winfield, Kansas 67156
Natural Science: *A.A.*

Sterling College
Sterling, Kansas 67579
Biology: *B.A.*

Tabor College
Hillsboro, Kansas 67063
Biology: *B.A.*

University of Kansas
Lawrence, Kansas 66045
Animal Natural History: *B.A., B.S.*
Biology: *B.A., B.S., M.S., Ph.D.*
Botany: *B.A., B.S.*
Cellular Biology: *B.S.*
Ecology: *B.A.*
Entomology: *B.S., M.A.*, M.S.*, Ph.D.**
Environmental Health: *B.A.*
Environmental Studies: *B.S.*
Herpetology: *B.S.*
Human Biology: *B.A.*
Mammalogy: *B.S.*
Microbiology: *B.S., M.S., Ph.D.*
Organismal Biology: *B.S.*
Ornithology: *B.S.*
Paleontology: *B.A.*
Physiology: *B.S.*
Recreation (Outdoor): *B.S.Ed.*

Systematics & Ecology: *B.S.. M.S.*, Ph.D.**
Tropical Biology: *B.S.*
Water Resources Engineering: *M.S.*
Water Resource Science: *M.S.*
Zoology: *B.S., M.S., Ph.D.*

Wichita State University
Wichita, Kansas 67208
Psychology: *M.A.**

Kentucky

Berea College
Berea, Kentucky 40404
Agriculture: *A.B., B.S.*
Biology: *A.B.*

Eastern Kentucky University
Richmond, Kentucky 40475
Agriculture: *B.S.*
Agriculture (Dairy Herd Management): *A.A., B.S.*
Biology: *B.S., M.A., M.S.*
Earth Science: *B.S., M.A.*
Environmental Resources: *B.S.*
Microbiology: *B.S.*
Pre-Forestry: *Non-Degree*
Pre-Veterinary Medicine: *Non-Degree*
Recreation & Park Administration: *B.S., M.S.*
Recreation Supervision: *A.A.*
Wildlife Management: *B.S.*

Morehead State University
Morehead, Kentucky 40351
Agriculture: *A.S., B.S.*
Agriculture (Animal Science): *B.S.*
Biology: *B.S., M.S.*
Environmental Studies: *B.S.*
Pre-Forestry: *Non-Degree*
Pre-Veterinary: *Non-Degree*
Recreation: *A., B.S.*
Veterinary Technology: *A.A.S.*

Murray State University
Murray, Kentucky 42071
Aquatic Biology: *B.S., M.S.*
Agriculture: *B.S., M.S.*
Animal Sciences: *B.S., M.S.*
Biological Sciences: *B.S., M.S., M.A.*
Pre-Forestry: *B.S.*
Pre-Veterinary: *B.S.*
Recreation & Park Administration: *B.S., M.A.*
Wildlife Biology: *B.S., M.S.*

Pikeville College
Pikeville, Kentucky 41501
Biology: *B.S.*
Medical Technology: *B.S.*

Southeastern Christian College
Winchester, Kentucky 40391
Natural Science: *A.*

Spalding College
Louisville, Kentucky 40203
Biology: *A.B.*
Medical Technology: *B.S.*

Thomas More College
Ft. Mitchell, Kentucky 41017
Biology: *B.S.*
Medical Technology: *B.S.*
Pre-Professional (Veterinary): *B.S.*

University of Kentucky
Lexington, Kentucky 40506
Animal Science: *B.S., M.S., M.S. Ag., Ph.D.*
Biological Sciences: *Ph.D.*
Entomology: *B.S., M.S., M.S. Ag., Ph.D.*
Forestry: *B.S.*
Microbiology: *B.S., M.S., Ph.D.*
Pre-Veterinary Medicine: *B.S.*
Recreation: *B.S.*
Veterinary Science: *Ph.D.*
Zoology: *B.S., M.S., Ph.D.*

University of Louisville
Louisville, Kentucky 40208
Aquatic Biology: *Ph.D.*
Biology: *B.A., M.S., Ph.D.*
Water Resources: *M.S., Ph.D.*
Zoology: *B.S.*

Western Kentucky University
Bowling Green, Kentucky 42101
Aquatic Biology: *Ph.D.*
Agriculture (Animal Science): *B.S.*
Agriculture (Conservation — Rural Recreation): *B.S.*
Agriculture (Dairy Science): *B.S.*
Agriculture: *A.A., B.S., M.A., M.S.*
Biology: *B.S., M.A.*
Pre-Veterinary Medicine: *B.S.*
Wildlife Ecology and Conservation: *B.S.*

Louisiana

Louisiana State University and Agricultural & Mechanical
College
Baton Rouge, Louisiana 70803
Animal Science: *B.S., M.S., Ph.D.*
Cooperative Fishery Unit: *M.S.*
Cooperative Wildlife Research Unit: *M.S.*
Dairy Science: *B.S., M.S., Ph.D.*
Entomology: *B.S.*
Entomology (Animal & Plant Protection): *B.S.*
Fisheries: *M.S.*
Forestry: *B.S., M.S., M.F., Ph.D.*
Forestry (Wildlife Management): *B.S., M.S.*
Marine Studies: *M.S., Ph.D.*
Natural Science: *M.N.S.*
Physiology: *M.S.*, Ph.D.**
Poultry Science: *B.S., M.S., Ph.D.*
Veterinary Medicine: *M.S., Ph.D., D.V.M.*
Zoology: *B.S., M.S.*, Ph.D.**
Zoology (Mammalogy): *B.S., M.S.*, Ph.D.**

Louisiana State University Medical Center
New Orleans, Louisiana 70112
Parasitology: *M., Ph.D.*

Louisiana Tech University
Ruston, Louisiana 71270
Animal Husbandry: *B.*
Animal Science: *B.S.*
Dairy Science: *B.*
Forestry: *B.S., M.F., Ph.D.*
Pre-Veterinary Medicine: *Non-Degree*
Conservation/Wildlife Management: *B.*
Zoology: *B.S., M.S.*

McNeese State University
Lake Charles, Louisiana 70609
Agronomy: *B.S.*
Animal Science: *B.*
Environmental Science: *B.S., M.S.*
Forestry: *B.S.*
General Resources Management: *B.S.*
Marine Biology: *B.S.*
Wildlife Management: *B.S.*
Zoology: *B.S.*

Nicholls State University
Thibodaux, Louisiana 70301
Animal Science: *B.S., M.*

Northeast Louisiana University
Monroe, Louisiana 71209
Animal Science: *B.S.*
Pre-Veterinary Medicine: *Non-Degree*

Northwestern State University of Louisiana
Natchitoches, Louisiana 71457
Animal Science: *B.*
Animal Technician: *A.S.*
Biological Science: *M.S.*
Outdoor Education: *M.S.*
Recreation: *B.S., M.S.*
Wildlife Management: *B.S.*
Zoology: *B.S., M.S.*

Southeastern Louisiana University
Hammond, Louisiana 70401
Animal Science: *B.S.*
Pre-Veterinary Medicine: *B.S.*
Zoology: *B.S.*

Southern University & Agricultural & Mechanical College
Baton Rouge, Louisiana 70813
Animal Science: *B.*
Dairy Science: *B.*

University of Southwestern Louisiana
Lafayette, Louisiana 70501
Animal Science: *B.*

Tulane University of Louisiana
New Orleans, Louisiana 70118
Engineering Management (Resource Management):
B.S.
Environmental Biology (Ecology and Systematics):
B.S., M.S., Ph.D.
Zoology: *B.S., M.S., Ph.D.*

Maine

Colby College
  Waterville, Maine 04901
  Biology: *B.A.*
  Environmental Studies: *B.A.*
  Geology: *B.A.*
  Geology-Biology: *B.A.*

Southern Maine Vocational-Technical Institute
  South Portland, Maine 04106
  Marine Science: *Certificate, A.*

Unity College
  Unity, Maine 04988
  Conservation-Law Enforcement: *A.A.S.*
  Environmental Science: *B.S.E.S.*
  Environmental Science: *B.S.E.S.*
  Environmental Science (Aquatic Biology): *B.S.E.S.*
  Environmental Science (Conservation Law): *B.S.E.S.*
  Environmental Science (Forest Resources): *B.S.E.S.*
  Wildlife & Fisheries Technology: *A.A.S., B.S.*
  Wildlife & Fisheries Technology (Fisheries):
    A.A.S., B.S.
  Wildlife & Fisheries Technology (Wildlife): *A.A.S., B.S.*

University of Maine at Orono
  Orono, Maine 04473
  Animal Agricultural Technology: *A.S.*
  Animal and Veterinary Sciences: *B.S.*
  Animal Medical Technology: *A.S.*
  Animal Nutrition: *Ph.D.*
  Animal Sciences: *B.S., M.S.*
  Biology: *B.S.*
  Botany & Plant Pathology: *B.S.*
  Cooperative Fishery Unit: *M.S.*
  Cooperative Wildlife Research Unit: *B.S., M.S., Ph.D.*
  Entomology: *B.S.*
  Forest Engineering: *B.S.*
  Forestry: *B.S., M.S., Ph.D.*
  Microbiology: *B.S.*
  Natural Resource Management: *B.S.*
  Oceanography: *M.S., Ph.D.*
  Plant Science: *B.S., M.S., Ph.D.*
  Recreation & Parks: *B.S.*
  Wildlife Management: *B.S., M.S., Ph.D.*
  Zoology: *B.S., M.S., Ph.D.*

University of Maine at Presque Isle
  Presque Isle, Maine 04769
  Environmental Studies (Geo-Ecology): *B.S.*
  Geology: *Non-Degree*
  Life Science: *B.A.*
  Life Science & Agriculture: *Non-Degree*
  Life Science (Agricultural Engineering): *Non-Degree*
  Life Science (Animal & Veterinary Science):
    Non-Degree
  Life Science & Agriculture (Biology): *Non-Degree*
  Life Science (Forest Engineering): *Non-Degree*
  Life Science & Agriculture (Forest Management &
    Science): *Non-Degree*
  Life Science & Agriculture (Natural Resource Manage-
    ment): *Non-Degree*
  Life Science & Agriculture (Plant & Soil Science):
    Non-Degree
  Life Science & Agriculture (Wildlife Management &
    Science): *Non-Degree*
  Recreation: *A.A., B.S., Certificate*

Maryland

Anne Arundel Community College
  Arnold, Maryland 21012
  Ocean Engineering: *A.*

Charles County Community College
  La Plata, Maryland 20646
  Estuarine Technology: *A.A.*
  Horticulture: *Certificate*

Chesapeake College
  Wye Mills, Maryland 21679
  Agriculture: *Certificate*
  Recreation: *A.A.*
  Recreation (Outdoor): *A.A.*

Community College of Baltimore — Liberty Campus
  Baltimore, Maryland 21215
  Recreation Leadership: *A.A.*
  Therapeutic Recreation: *A.A.*

Essex Community College
  Baltimore, Maryland 21237
  Animal Science Technology: *A.A.*

Frostburg State College
  Frostburg, Maryland 21532
  Biology: *B.A., B.S., M.S., M.Ed.*
  General Science (Earth Science): *B.A., B.S.*
  Recreation: *B.A., B.S.*
  Wildlife Fisheries Management: *B.A., B.S., M.S.*

Garrett Community College
  McHenry, Maryland 21701
  Conservation: *Non-Degree*
  Wildlife-Fisheries Management: *Non-Degree*
  Wildlife Management Technology: *A.*

Loyola College
  Baltimore, Maryland 21210
  Pre-Veterinary Medicine: *B.*

Prince George's Community College
  Largo, Maryland 20870
  Recreation Leadership & Parks: *A.A.*

The Johns Hopkins University
  Baltimore, Maryland 21218
  Environmental Engineering: *M.S.E., Ph.D.*
  Environmental Health Sciences: *M.S., Ph.D., Dr.PH,
    Sc.D.*
  Natural Resources, Environmental Economics: *M.S.
    Ph.D.*
  Pathology: *M.S.*, Ph.D.**
  Vertebrate Ecology: *M.S., Ph.D., Sc. D.*
  Waterfowl Biology: *M.S., Ph.D., Sc. D.*

United States Naval Academy
  Annapolis, Maryland 21402
  Marine Engineering: *B.S.*
  Ocean Engineering: *B.S.*
  Oceanography: *B.S.*
  Resources Management: *B.S.*

University of Maryland at College Park
   College Park, Maryland 20742
   Agricultural Engineering: *B.S., M.S., Ph.D.*
   Agriculture and Resource Economics: *B.S., M.S.,*
      Ph.D.
   Agriculture, General: *B.S.*
   Agronomy: *B.S.*
   Animal Sciences: *B.S., M.S., Ph.D.*
   Biological Sciences: *B.S.*
   Botany: *B.S.*
   Conservation & Resource Development: *B.S.*
   Entomology: *B.S., M.S., Ph.D.*
   Geology: *B.S.*
   Horticulture: *B.S.*
   Microbiology: *B.S.*
   Pre-Forestry: *Non-Degree*
   Pre-Veterinary Medicine: *Non-Degree*
   Recreation: *B.S., M.A., Ph.D.*
   Zoology: *B.S., M.S., Ph.D.*

University of Maryland — Baltimore County
   Baltimore, Maryland 21228
   Biological Sciences: *B.S.*
   Psychology: *M.A. ***

University of Maryland Eastern Shore
   Princess Anne, Maryland 21853
   Natural Sciences: *B.S.*

Massachusetts

Becker Junior College
   Worcester, Massachusetts 01609
   Veterinary Assistant: *A.S.*

Clark University
   Worchester, Massachusetts 01610
   Biology: *M.A. *, Ph.D. ***

Harvard University
   Cambridge, Massachusetts 01238
   Forestry: *M.F.*
   Landscape Architecture: *M.L.A.*

Holliston Junior College
   Holliston, Massachusetts 01746
   Animal Technology: *A.A.S.*

Holliston Junior College, Lenox Campus
   Lenox, Massachusetts 01240
   Kennel Management: *Certificate*

Holyoke Community College
   Holyoke, Massachusetts 01040
   Veterinary and Animal Science Career: *A.S.*

Massachusetts Institute of Technology
   Cambridge, Massachusetts 02139
   Cell Biology & Physiology: *M., Ph.D.*
   Ocean Engineering: *B., M., Ph.D.*
   Oceanography: *M., Ph.D.*

Northeastern University
   Boston, Massachusetts 02115
   Outdoor Recreation Education & Conservation: *B.S.,*
      M.S.

Springfield College
   Springfield, Massachusetts 01109
   Environmental Studies: *B.S.*
   Natural Resources: *B.S.*

University of Massachusetts at Amherst
   Amherst, Massachusetts 01003
   Animal Husbandry: *M.S., Ph.D.*
   Animal Science: *A.S., B.S., M.S., Ph.D.*
   Entomology: *B.S.*
   Environmental Sciences: *B.S.*
   Fisheries Biology: *B.S.*
   Forestry: *B.S., M.S., Ph.D.*
   Laboratory Animal Management: *A.S.*
   Marine Science: *M.*
   Natural Resource Studies: *B.S.*
   Ocean Engineering: *M., Ph.D.*
   Park Management: *A.S.*
   Plant Pathology: *B.S.*
   Plant & Soil Sciences: *B.S.*
   Veterinary Medicine: *M.*
   Wildlife Biology: *B.S., M.S., Ph.D.*
   Zoology: *M., Ph.D.*

University of Massachusetts at Boston
   Boston, Massachusetts 02125
   Biology: *M.S. ***

Woods Hole Oceanographic Institute
   Woods Hole, Massachusetts 02543
   Oceanography: *Ph.D.*

Michigan

Albion College
   Albion, Michigan 49224
   Biology: *B.S.*

Andrews University
   Berrien Springs, Michigan 49104
   Biology: *B.S.*
   Veterinary Medicine (Pre-Professional): *Non-Degree*
   Zoology: *B.S.*

Central Michigan University
   Mt. Pleasant, Michigan 48859
   Biology: *B.S., M.S.*
   Earth Science: *B.S.*
   Environmental Systems: *B.S.*
   Recreation & Park Administration: *B.S.*

Eastern Michigan University
   Ypsilanti, Michigan 48197
   Biology: *B.S.*
   Biology (Aquatic Biology): *B.S.*
   Biology (Microbiology): *B.S.*
   Biology (Physiology): *B.S.*
   Pre-Forestry: *B.S.*
   Recreation: *B.S.*

Ferris State College
   Big Rapids, Michigan 49307
   Environmental Health: *A.A.S., B.S.*
   Pesticide Technology: *A.A.S.*

Gogebic Community College
   Ironwood, Michigan 49938
   Natural Resources: *Non-Degree*
   Parks & Recreation Management: *A.*
   Pre-Veterinary Medicine: *Non-Degree*

Grand Rapids Jr. College
   Grand Rapids, Michigan 49502
   Natural Resources (Pre-Professional): *Non-Degree*
   Veterinary (Pre-Professional): *Non-Degree*

Lake Superior State College
  Sault Sainte Marie, Michigan 49783
  Agriculture (Pre-Professional): *Non-Degree*
  Biology: *B.A.*
  Earth Science: *B.A., B.S.*
  Environmental Science: *B.S.*
  Natural Resources Technology: *A.S.*
  Veterinary Medicine (Pre-Professional): *Non-Degree*

Michigan Technological University
  Houghton, Michigan 49931
  Biological Sciences: *B.S., M.S., Ph.D.*
  Forestry: *B.S., M.S.*
  Forestry (Conservation): *B.S., M.S.*
  Forestry (Forest Science): *B.S., M.S.*
  Forestry (Recreation Resource Management):
    B.S., M.S.
  Forestry (Urban Forestry): *B.S., M.S.*
  Forestry (Wildlife Ecology): *B.S., M.S.*

Michigan State University
  East Lansing, Michigan 48824
  Agricultural Biochemistry: *B.S.*
  Agricultural Economics: *M.S., Ph.D.*
  Agriculture and Natural Resource Education: *B.S.*
  Agriculture and Natural Resource Communication:
    B.S.
  Anatomy: *M.S., Ph.D.*
  Animal Husbandry: *B.S., M.S., Ph.D.*
  Biochemistry: *B.S., M.S.*
  Crop & Soil Science: *B.S., M.S., Ph.D.*
  Dairy Science: *B.S., M.S., Ph.D.*
  Earth Science: *B.S.*
  Entomology: *M.S., Ph.D.*
  Entomology (Aquatic Insects): *M.S., Ph.D.*
  Entomology (Bees & Pollination): *M.S., Ph.D.*
  Entomology (Ecology): *M.S., Ph.D.*
  Entomology (Forest Entomology): *M.S., Ph.D.*
  Entomology (Insect Biochemistry): *M.S., Ph.D.*
  Entomology (Morphology): *M.S., Ph.D.*
  Entomology (Nematology): *M.S., Ph.D.*
  Entomology (Physiology): *M.S., Ph.D.*
  Entomology (System Science): *M.S., Ph.D.*
  Entomology (Toxicology): *M.S., Ph.D.*
  Fisheries & Wildlife: *B.S., M.S., Ph.D.*
  Forestry: *B.S., M.S., Ph.D.*
  Geology: *M.S., M.A.T., Ph.D.*
  Horticulture: *B.S., M.S., Ph.D.*
  Microbiology: *M.S.*
  Natural Resource & Environmental Education: *B.S.*
  Park & Recreation Resources: *B.S., M.S.*
  Pathology: *M.S., Ph.D.*
  Physiology: *M.S., Ph.D.*
  Poultry Science: *B.S., M.S., Ph.D.*
  Resource Development: *B.S., M.S., Ph.D.*
  Veterinary Medicine: *D.V.M.*
  Veterinary Medicine (Anatomy): *M.S., Ph.D.*
  Veterinary Medicine (Large Animal Surgery & Medi-
    cine): *M.S.*
  Veterinary Medicine (Pathology): *M.S., Ph.D.*
  Veterinary Medicine (Pharmacology): *M.S., Ph.D.*
  Veterinary Medicine (Physiology): *M.S., Ph.D.*
  Veterinary Medicine (Small Animal Surgery & Medi-
    cine): *M.S.*
  Zoology: *M.S., Ph.D.*

Montcalm Community College
  Sidney, Michigan 48885
  Biology: *Non-Degree*
  Pre-Veterinary: *Non-Degree*
  Zoology: *Non-Degree*

Northern Michigan University
  Marquette, Michigan 49855
  Biology (Pre-Professional): *B.A., B.S., M.A.*
  Biology (Water Science): *B.A., B.S., M.A.*
  Science: *A.S.*

University of Michigan
  Ann Arbor, Michigan 48109
  Conservation and Outdoor Education: *B., M.*
  Environmental Education: *B.S., M.S., Ph.D.*
  Environmental Psychology: *B.S.*
  Environmental Science: *B.S.*
  Environmental Studies: *B.S.*
  Fisheries: *B.S., M.S., Ph.D.*
  Forestry: *B.S., M.S., Ph.D., M.F.*
  Forestry Recreation: *B.S., M.S., Ph.D.*
  Landscape Architecture: *B.L.A., M.L.A., Ph.D.*
  Natural Resources: *B.S., M.S., Ph.D.*
  Outdoor Recreation: *B.S., M.A., Ph.D.*
  Resource Ecology: *B.S., M.S., Ph.D.*
  Resource Policy: *B.S., M.S., Ph.D.*
  Resource Management: *B.S., M.S., Ph.D.*
  Wildlife: *B.S., M.S., Ph.D.*
  Wildlife Management: *Ph.D.*

University of Michigan — Flint
  Flint, Michigan 48503
  Biology (Botany & Zoology): *Certificate, A.B.*
  Environmental Studies: *A.B.*

Wayne County Community College
  Detroit, Michigan 48201
  Animal Health Technology: *A.S.*

Wayne State University
  Detroit, Michigan 48202
  Biology: *B.A., B.S., M.S.*, Ph.D.*, M.A.**
  Environmental Studies: *B.A.*
  Geology: *B.A., B.S., M.S.*
  Recreation & Park Services: *B.S.*

Western Michigan University
  Kalamazoo, Michigan 49008
  Biology: *M.A.*
  Biology (Botany): *M.A.*
  Biology (Genetics): *M.A.*
  Biology (Microbiology): *M.A.*
  Biology (Physiology): *M.A.*

Minnesota

Bethany Lutheran College
  Mankato, Minnesota 56001
  Biology: *A.A., Diploma*
  National Resources & Conservation: *A.A., Diploma*

Mankato State University
  Mankato, Minnesota 56001
  Biology: *B.A., B.S., B.S.T., M.A., M.S.*
  Earth Science: *B.A., B.S., B.S.T.*
  Environmental Studies Institute: *B.S., B.S.T., M.A.*
  Pre-Agriculture: *Non-Degree*
  Pre-Forestry: *Non-Degree*

Pre-Veterinary Medicine: *Non-Degree*
Recreation, Park & Community Education: *B.S.*
Water Quality & Pollution Control Technology: *A.S.*

Medical Institute of Minnesota
Minneapolis, Minnesota 55404
Animal Health Technology: *A.S.*

University of Minnesota - Twin Cities
Minneapolis, Minnesota 55455, St. Paul 55108
Agricultural Economics: *M.S., Ph.D.*
Agricultural Education: *M.S.*
Agricultural Engineering: *M.S.Ag.E., M.Ag.E., Ph.D.*
Agronomy: *M.S., Ph.D.*
Animal Physiology: *M.S., Ph.D.*
Animal Science: *M.S., Ph.D.*
Botany: *B.S., M.A., M.S., Ph.D.*
Ecology & Behavorial Biology: *B.S.*
Ecology & Behavorial Biology: *B.S.*
Ecology: *M.S., Ph.D.*
Entomology: *M.S., Ph.D.*
Environmental Health: *M.S., Ph.D.*
Fisheries: *M.S., Ph.D.*
Forestry: *M.S., M.F., Ph.D.*
Geo-Engineering: *M.S.Geo.E., M.Geo.E.*
Geology: *M.S., Ph.D.*
Geology & Geophysics: *B.A.*
Horticulture: *M.S., Ph.D.*
Microbiology: *B.S., M.S., Ph.D.*
Plant Breeding: *M.S., Ph.D.*
Plant Pathology: *M.S., Ph.D.*
Plant Physiology: *M.S., Ph.D.*
Psychology: *B.A.*
Recreation and Park Administration: *M.A.*
Soil Science: *M.S., Ph.D.*
Veterinary Anatomy: *M.S., Ph.D.*
Veterinary Medicine: *M.S., Ph.D.*
Veterinary Microbiology: *M.S., Ph.D.*
Veterinary Parasitology: *M.S., Ph.D.*
Veterinary Physiology & Pharmacology: *M.S., Ph.D.*
Veterinary Surgery, Radiology & Anesthesiology:
    M.S., Ph.D.
Wildlife: *M.S., Ph.D.*
Zoology: *M.S., Ph.D.*

University of Minnesota - Duluth
Duluth, Minnesota 55812
Biology: *B.A., B.S.*
Earth Science: *B.A.*
Geology: *B.S.*
Pre-Agricultural Education: *Non-Degree*
Pre-Agriculture: *Non-Degree*
Pre-Fishery & Wildlife Management: *Non-Degree*
Pre-Forestry: *Non-Degree*
Pre-Veterinary Medicine: *Non-Degree*
Recreation (Community & Outdoor): *B.A.A., B.A.S.*

University of Minnesota - Technical College
(Crookston Campus)
Crookston, Minnesota 56716
Agricultural Business: *A.A.S.*
Agricultural Production: *A.A.S.*
Agricultural Production (Dairy): *A.A.S.*
Agricultural Production (Diversified Agricultural
    Production): *A.A.S.*
Agricultural Services Technology: *A.A.S.*
Agronomy: *A.A.S.*

Animal Technology: *A.A.S.*
Animal Technology (Dairy Science): *A.A.S.*
Animal Technology (Light Horse Management): *A.A.S.*
Mechanized Agricultural Management: *A.A.S.*
Natural Resources Technology: *A.A.S.*
Natural Resources Technology (Natural Resources
    Conservation): *A.A.S.*
Natural Resources Technology (Biology Laboratory
    Technology): *A.A.S.*
Natural Resources Technology (Park & Recreational
    Area Management): *A.A.S.*
Plant & Soil Technology: *A.A.S.*

University of Minnesota - Technical College - Waseca
Waseca, Minnesota 56093
Animal Health Technology: *A.S.*
Animal-Industry Related Technology: *A.S.*
Animal Science: *A.S.*
Light Horse Management: *A.S.*

Vermilion Community College
Ely, Minnesota 55731
Conservation Technology: *Certificate, A.*
Conservation Technology (Park Management
    Option): *A.*

Winona State University
Winona, Minnesota 55987
Biology: *B.A., B.S.*
Earth Science: *B.S.*
Geology: *B.S.*
Pre-Veterinary Medicine: *Non-Degree*
Recreation: *B.S.*

Mississippi

Hinds Junior College
Raymond, Mississippi 39154
Animal Technician: *A.A.S.*

Mississippi State University
Mississippi State, Mississippi 39762
Agricommunications: *B.S., M.S., M.Ag.*
Agriculture, General: *B.S., M.S., M.Ag.*
Agronomy (Crop Science): *B.S., M.S., M.Ag., Ph.D.*
Agronomy (Soil Science): *B.S., M.S., M.Ag., Ph.D.*
Animal Science: *B.S., M.S., M.Ag., Ph.D.*
Botany: *PhD.*
Dairy Science (Dairy Production): *B.S., M.Ag.,
    M.S., Ph.D.*
Dairy Science (Dairy Manufacturing): *B.S., M.Ag.,
    M.S., Ph.D.*
Entomology: *B.S., M.Ag., M.S., Ph.D.*
Forest Resources (Fishery Management): *B.S.,
    M.S., Ph.D.*
Forest Resources (Forestry): *B.S., M.F.*
General Agriculture: *B.S., M.S., M.Ag.*
Plant Pathology: *B.S., M.S., M.Ag., Ph.D.*
Poultry Science: *B.S., M.S., M.Ag.*
Veterinary Medicine: *D.V.M.*

University of Southern Mississippi
Hattiesburg, Mississippi 39401
Aquatic Biology: *M.S., Ph.D.*
Biology: *B.S., M.S., Ph.D.*
Environmental Science: *B.S.*
Fisheries Biology: *M.S., Ph.D.*
Marine Biology: *M.S., Ph.D.*

Resources Management and Outdoor Education:
   B.S., M.S.
   Wildlife Biology: *M.S., Ph.D.*

Missouri

Avila College
   Kansas City, Missouri 64145
   Biology: *B.S.*
   Microbiology: *B.S.*

Central Missouri State University
   Warrensburg, Missouri 64003
   Recreation (Camping and Outdoor Education): *B.S.*
   Agriculture Technology: *M.S.*
   Biology: *B.S., M.S., M.S.E.*
   Biology (Wildlife Biology): *B.S.*
   Biology (Forestry): *B.S.*
   Pre-Veterinary Medicine: *Non-Degree*

Crowder Junior College
   Neosho, Missouri 64850
   Agri-Business Technology: *A.A.S.*

Culver - Stockton College
   Canton, Missouri 63435
   Biology: *B.A., B.S.*
   Medical Laboratory Technology: *A.S.*

Department of Agriculture
   Kansas City, Missouri 63501
   Animal Technology: *Certificate*

Lincoln University
   Jefferson City, Missouri 65102
   Biology: *B.S.*
   Medical Technology: *B.S.*

Maple Woods Community College
   Kansas City, Missouri 64156
   Animal Health Technology: *A.A.S.*

Northeast Missouri State University
   Kirksville, Missouri 63501
   Biology: *B.S., B.S.E., M.S.*
   Earth Science: *B.S.*
   Environmental Science: *B.S.*
   Recreation: *B.S.*
   Zoology: *B.S.*

St. Louis University
   St. Louis, Missouri 63103
   Biology: *A.B.*
   Earth and Atmospheric Science: *A.B.*
   Geology: *A.B.*

School of the Ozarks
   Point Lookout, Missouri 65726
   Agriculture: *B.S.*
   Biology: *B.S., B.A.*

Southeast Missouri State University
   Cape Girardeau, Missouri 63701
   Agriculture: *B.S.*
   Biology: *B.A., B.S.*
   Botany: *B.S.*
   Earth Science: *B.A., B.S.*
   Wildlife: *Non-Degree*
   Zoology: *B.A., B.S.*

Southwest Missouri State University
   Springfield, Missouri 65802
   Agriculture: *B.S., B.S.E.*
   Animal Science: *Non-Degree, B.S.*
   Biology: *B.A., B.S.*
   Pre-Veterinary Medicine: *Non-Degree*
   Wildlife Conservation and Management: *B.S.*

Stephens College
   Columbia, Missouri 65201
   Biology: *A.A., B.A.*
   Equestrian Science: *A.A., B.A.*
   Geology: *A.A., B.A.*
   Natural Science: *A.A., B.A.*
   Recreation: *A.A., B.A.*

University of Missouri
   Columbia, Missouri 65201
   Animal Biochemistry and Nutrition: *M.S., Ph.D.*
   Animal Husbandry: *B.S., M.S., Ph.D.*
   Biochemistry: *M.S., Ph.D.*
   Biological Sciences: *M.A., Ph.D.*
   Entomology: *M.S., Ph.D.*
   Fisheries and Wildlife: *B.S., M.S., Ph.D.*
   Forestry: *B.S., M.S., Ph.D.*
   Laboratory Animal Medicine: *M.S.*
   Microbiology: *Ph.D.*
   Nutrition: *M.S., Ph.D.*
   Pathology: *Ph.D.*
   Physiology: *M.S., Ph.D.*
   Psychology: *Ph.D.*
   Recreation and Park Administration: *M.S.*
   Veterinary Anatomy: *M.S.*
   Veterinary Medicine: *D.V.M.*
   Veterinary Medicine and Surgery: *M.S.*
   Veterinary Microbiology: *M.S.V.M., Ph.D.*
   Veterinary Pathology: *M.S., Ph.D.*
   Veterinary Pharmacology: *M.S., Ph.D.*
   Veterinary Pharmacology: *M.S., Ph.D.*
   Veterinary Physiology: *M.S., Ph.D.*
   Zoology: *B.S., M.S., Ph.D.*

Montana

Montana State University
   Bozeman, Montana 50717
   Agriculture-Business: *B.S.*
   Agriculture Education: *B.S.*
   Agricultural Production (Agronomy): *B.S., M.A., M.S.*
   Agricultural Production (Animal Science): *B.S.*
   Agricultural Production (Plant Science): *B.S.*
   Agricultural Production (Range Science): *B.S.*
   Agricultural Production (Recreational Areas
      Management): *B.S.*
   Agricultural Science (Animal Science): *B.S.*
   Agricultural Science (Crops): *B.S.*
   Agricultural Science (Plant Protection): *B.S.*
   Agricultural Science (Range Science): *B.S.*
   Agricultural Sceince (Recreational Areas Manage-
      ment): *B.S.*
   Agricultural Science (Soils): *B.S.*
   Animal Science: *M.A., M.S.*
   Botany: *B.S., M.A., M.S., Ph.D.*
   Crop & Soil: *Ph.D.*
   Earth Science: *B.S., M.A., M.S.*
   Entomology: *M.A., M.S., Ph.D.*

Fish & Wildlife Management: *B.S., M.A., M.S., Ph.D.*
Microbiology: *B.S., M.A., M.S., Ph.D.*
Plant Pathology: *M.A., M.S., Ph.D.*
Range Science: *M.A., M.S.*
Soils: *M.A., M.S.*
Veterinary Science: *M.A., Ph.D.*
Zoology: *B.S., M.A., M.S., Ph.D.*

Northern Montana College
   Havre, Montana 59501
   Conservation & Wildlife Management: *Non-Degree*
   Fish & Wildlife Management: *Non-Degree*

University of Montana
   Missoula, Montana 58911
   Biology: *B.A.*
   Biology (Environmental): *B.A.*
   Botany: *B.A.*
   Forestry: *B.S., B.S., M.F., Ph.D.*
   Geology: *B.A.*
   Microbiology: *B.A., M.S., Ph.D.*
   Recreation: *B.A.*
   Resource Administration: *M.S.*
   Resource Conservation: *B.S., M.S.*
   Wildlife Biology: *B.S., M.S.*
   Zoology: *B.A., M.S., Ph.D.*

Nebraska

Chadron State College
   Chadron, Nebraska 69337
   Agriculture: *A.A., B.A.*
   Biology: *B.A., B.S.Ed.*
   Earth Science: *B.A., B.S.Ed., M.S.Ed.*
   Pre-Veterinary: *Non-Degree*
   Recreation: *B.A.*

Hastings College
   Hastings, Nebraska 68901
   Biology: *B.A.*

Kearny State College
   Kearny, Nebraska 68847
   Biology (Environmental Studies): *B.A., B.S.*
   Biology (Wildlife): *B.A., B.S.*
   Pre-Veterinary Medicine: *Non-Degree*

Nebraska Wesleyan University
   Lincoln, Nebraska 68504
   Biology: *B.A., B.S.*

Nebraska Western College
   Scottsbluff, Nebraska 69361
   Agriculture: *A.A., A.S.*
   Agriculture - Business Production: *Non-Degree*
   Biology & Ecology: *A.A., A.S.*
   Farm & Ranch Management: *Non-Degree*
   Forestry & Wildlife Management: *A.A., A.S.*
   Pre-Veterinary Medicine: *A.A., A.S.*

Union College
   Lincoln, Nebraska 68506
   Biology: *B.S.*

University of Nebraska
   Curtis, Nebraska 69025
   Animal Technology: *A.T.A.*
   Production Agriculture Technology: *A.T.A.*

University of Nebraska
   Lincoln, Nebraska 68508
   Agronomy: *B.S., M.S., Ph.D.*
   Animal Science: *B.S., M.S., Ph.D.*
   Biology: *B.A., B.S.*
   Botany: *B.A., B.S., M.S., Ph.D.*
   Entomology: *B.S., M.S., Ph.D.*
   Horticulture & Forestry: *B.S., M.S., Ph.D.*
   Life Sciences: *B.A., B.S., M.A., M.S., Ph.D.*
   Natural Resources: *B.S.*
   Plant Pathology: *B.S.*
   Poultry & Wildlife Sciences: *B.S., M.S.*
   Recreation: *B.A.*
   Soil Science: *B.S.*
   Veterinary Medicine: *M.S.*
   Zoology: *B.A., B.S., M.A., M.S., Ph.D.*

University of Nebraska at Omaha
   Omaha, Nebraska 68101
   Biology: *B.A., B.S.*
   Recreation/Leisure Studies: *B.S.*

Nevada

University of Nevada
   Reno, Nevada 89557
   Agriculture: *A.S., B.S.*
   Animal Science: *B.S., M.S.*
   Biology: *B.S., M.S., Ph.D.*
   Biology (Botany): *B.S., M.S., Ph.D.*
   Biology (Ecology): *B.S., M.S., Ph.D.*
   Biology (Zoology): *B.S., M.S., Ph.D.*
   Earth Science: *B.S.*
   Farm & Range Management: *A.S.*
   Forestry: *B.S., M.S.*
   Geology: *B.S.*
   Park & Turf Management: *A.S.*
   Plant Science: *B.*
   Range Management: *B.S., M.S.*
   Recreation Management: *B.S., M.S.*
   Soil Science: *B.*
   Veterinary Medicine (Pre-Professional): *Non-Degree*
   Veterinary Science: *B.S.*
   Wildlife Conservation: *B.S., M.S.*

University of Nevada - Las Vegas
   Las Vegas, Nevada 89154
   Biology: *B.S.*
   Earth Science: *B.S.*
   Geology: *B.S.*

New Hampshire

Darthmouth College
   Hanover, New Hampshire 03755
   Biological Science: *M.A., Ph.D.* *
   Earth Science: *Ph.D.*

New Hampshire Vocational - Technical College
   Berlin, New Hampshire 03570
   Natural Resources Management: *Diploma, A.A.S.*

Rivier College
   Nashua, New Hampshire 03060
   Medical Technology: *A.S.*

University of New Hampshire
  Durham, New Hampshire 03824
  Animal Science: *B.S.*
  Applied Science: *A.A.S.*
  Applied Science (Animal Science): *A.A.S.*
  Applied Science (Plant Science): *A.A.S.*
  Biology: *B.S., M.S.*
  Botany & Plant Pathology: *B.A., Ph.D.*
  Entomology: *B.A., M.S.*
  Environmental Conservation Forestry: *B.S., M.S., Ph.D.*
  Forestry (Forest Management): *B.S., M.S., Ph.D.*
  Forestry (Forest Resources): *B.S., M.S., Ph.D.*
  Forestry (Forest Science): *B.S., M.S., Ph.D.*
  Forestry (Forest Technology): *B.S., M.S., Ph.D.*
  Plant Science: *B.S., M.S., Ph.D.*
  Pre-Veterinary Medicine: *B.S., M.S.*
  Recreation & Parks: *A.A., B.S.*
  Recreation & Parks (Recreation Administration): *B.S.*
  Recreation & Parks (Park Management): *B.S.*
  Soil Science: *B.S., M.S., Ph.D.*
  Wildlife Management: *B.S., M.S., Ph.D.*
  Zoology: *B.A., M.S., Ph.D.*

New Jersey

Camden County College
  Blackwood, New Jersey 08012
  Animal Science Technology: *A.A.S.*

Cook College, Rutgers, The State University of New Jersey
  New Brunswick, New Jersey 80903
  Animal Science: *B.S., M., Ph.D.*
  Biology: *M.S., Ph.D.*
  Ecology: *B., M., Ph.D.*
  Environmental Planning and Design: *B.S.*
  Environmental Studies: *B.S.*
  Forestry: *B.*
  Natural Resource Management: *B.S.*
  Zoology: *B.S., M.S., Ph.D.*

Douglass College, Rutgers, The State University of New Jersey
  New Brunswick, New Jersey 08903
  Biological Sciences: *B.*
  Microbiology: *B.*
  Physical Oceanography: *B.*

Drew University
  Madison, New Jersey 07940
  Behavioral Science: *B.A.*
  Biology: *B.A.*
  Botany: *B.A.*
  Psychobiology: *B.A.*
  Zoology: *B.A.*

Fairleigh Dickinson University
  Madison, New Jersey 07940
  Biological Sciences (Marine Biology): *B.S.*
  Earth Sciences: *B.A.*

Glassboro State College
  Glassboro, New Jersey 08028
  Biological Science: *B.A.*
  Conservation and Outdoor Education: *M.S.*

Jersey City State College
  Jersey City, New Jersey 07305
  Biology: *B.A., M.A.* *
  Leisure & Recreational Studies: *B.A., B.S.*

Montclair State College
  Upper Montclair, New Jersey 07043
  Biology: *B.A., M.A.*
  Environmental Studies: *B.S., M.A.*
  Recreation Professions (Outdoor Recreation): *B.*

Princeton University
  Princeton, New Jersey 08540
  Biochemical Sciences: *A.B., Ph.D.*
  Biology: *A.B., Ph.D.*
  Biology (Environmental Studies): *Ph.D.*
  Environmental Studies: *B.S.E.*

Rutgers University - The State University of New Jersey
  (New Brunswick Campus)
  New Brunswick, New Jersey 08903
  Animal Sciences: *M.S., Ph.D.*
  Biology: *M.S.T.*
  Botany: *M.S., Ph.D.*
  Ecology: *M.S., Ph.D.*
  Entomology: *M.S., Ph.D.*
  Environmental Science: *M.S., Ph.D.*
  Plant Pathology: *M.S., Ph.D.*
  Plant Physiology: *M.S., Ph.D.*
  Soil & Crops: *M.S., Ph.D.*
  Zoology: *M.S., Ph.D.*

Rutgers University - The State University of New Jersey
  (Newark Campus)
  Newark, New Jersey 07102
  Animal Behavior: *M.S.* *, *Ph.D.* *
  Zoology: *B., M., Ph.D.*

Stevens Institute of Technology
  Hoboken, New Jersey 07030
  Modern Biology: *B.S.*
  Ocean Engineering: *M.S., Ph.D.*

Stockton State College
  Pomona, New Jersey 08240
  Biology: *B.S.*
  Environmental Studies: *B.S., B.A.*
  Marine Science: *B.S.*

New Mexico

Eastern New Mexico University - Portales Campus
  Portales, New Mexico 88130
  Biology: *B.A., B.S., M.S.*
  Pre-Veterinary: *Non-Degree*
  Wildlife Management: *B.S.*

New Mexico State University
  Las Cruces, New Mexico 88001
  Agriculture: *B.S.*
  Agriculture (Forestry): *Non-Degree*
  Agriculture (Veterinary Medicine): *Non-Degree*
  Agricultural Biology: *B.S.*
  Agronomy: *B.S., M.S., Ph.D.*
  Agronomy (Recreational Areas Management): *B.S.*
  Agronomy (Soil Science): *B.S.*
  Animal Science: *B.S., M.S., Ph.D.*
  Biology: *B.S., M.S., Ph.D.*
  Farm & Range Management: *B.S., M.S.*
  Fishery Science: *B.S., M.S.*
  Range Science: *B.S., M.S., Ph.D.*
  Wildlife Science: *B.S., M.S.*

Western New Mexico University
Silver City, New Mexico 88061
Biology: *B.*
Botany: *B.*
Pre-Forestry: *Non-Degree*
Zoology: *B.*

New York

Adelphi University
Garden City, New York 11530
Biology: *M.S.* *
Psychology: *M.A.* *, *Ph.D.* *

Agricultural Technical College at Alfred (State University
of New York)
Alfred, New York 14802
Agricultural Technology (Agronomy & Environmental
Protection): *A.A.S.*
Agricultural Technology (Animal Husbandry): *A.A.S.*
Agricultural Technology (General Agriculture): *A.A.S.*
Agricultural Technology (Recreation Land Manage-
ment): *A.A.S.*

Agricultural & Technical College at Canton (State
University of New York)
Canton, New York 13617
Animal Husbandry: *A.A.S.*
Veterinary Science Technology: *A.A.S.*

Agricultural & Technical College at Cobleskill (State
University of New York)
Cobleskill, New York 12043
Animal Husbandry: *A.*
Conservation & Wildlife Technology: *A.*
Fisheries & Wildlife Technology: *A.*

Agricultural & Technical College at Delhi (State
University of New York)
Delhi, New York 13753
Animal Husbandry (Dairy Production): *A.A.S.*
Animal Husbandry (Horse Management): *A.A.S.*
Dairy & Food Science (Environmental Health): *A.A.S.*
General Agriculture: *A.A.S.*
Horticulture: *A.A.S.*
Parks & Recreation Management: *A.A.S.*
Veterinary Science Technology: *A.A.S.*

Agricultural & Technical College at Farmingdale (State
University of New York)
Farmingdale, New York 11735
Agronomy: *A.S., A.A., A.A.S.*
Animal Science: *A.A., A.S., A.A.S.*
Animal Technology: *A.A., A.S., A.A.S.*
Biological Technology: *A.A., A.S., A.A.S.*
Poultry Science: *A.A., A.S., A.A.S.*
Recreation Leadership: *A.A., A.S., A.A.S.*

Agricultural & Technical College at Morrisville (State
University of New York)
Morrisville, New york 13408
Agronomy: *A.*
Animal Husbandry (Dairy): *A.*
Animal Husbandry (Horse): *A.*
Natural Resource Conservation: *A.*

Barnard College (Columbia University)
New York, New York 10027
Environmental Conservation & Management: *A.B.*
Geology: *A.B.*

Cayuga County Community College
Auburn, New York 13021
Biology: *Non-Degree*
Forest Technology: *Non-Degree*
Recreation: *Non-Degree*

Cazenovia College
Cazenovia, New York 13035
Equine Studies: *A.A., A.S., A.A.S.*

City College (City University of New York)
New York, New York 10031
Animal Behavior - Biopsychology: *Ph.D.* *

Colgate University
Hamilton, New York 13346
Biology: *B.A.*
Geology: *B.A.*
Natural Science: *B.A., M.A.T.*
Natural Science (Marine Science): *B.A., M.A.T.*

College at Brockport (State University of New York)
Brockport, New York 14420
Earth Science: *B.*
Psychology: *M.A.* *
Recreation & Leisure: *B.*

College at Buffalo (State University of New York)
Buffalo, New York 14222
Biology: *B.A., B.S.Ed.*
Biology (Botany): *B.A.*
Biology (Conservation): *B.A.*
Biology (Ecology): *B.A.*
Forest Biology (Silvics): *B.S.*
Forest Biology (Wildlife Biology): *B.S.*
Forest Biology (Zoology): *B.S.*
Forest Technology: *A.A.S.*

Columbia University
New York, New York 10027
Ocean Engineering: *M.*
Parasitology: *M., Ph.D.*

Cornell University
Ithaca, New York 14850
Animal Breeding: *M.S., Ph.D.*
Animal Cytogenetics: *M.S., Ph.D.*
Animal Nutrition: *M.S., Ph.D.*
Animal Physiology: *M.S., Ph.D., D.Sc.V.M.*
Aquatic Science: *B.S., M.S., Ph.D.*
Avian Developmental Genetics: *M.S., Ph.D.*
Beef Husbandry: *M.S., Ph.D.*
Biochemistry: *M.S.* *, *Ph.D.* *
Dairy Husbandry: *M.S., Ph.D.*
Ecology & Evolution: *B., M.*
Ecology & Systematics: *Ph.D.* *
Fishery Science: *M.S., Ph.D.*
Immunology: *M.S., Ph.D., D.Sc.V.M.*
Livestock Breeding: *M.S., Ph.D.*
Natural Resources Conservation: *B.S., M.S., Ph.D.*
Neurobiology & Behavior: *M.S.* *, *Ph.D.* *
Parasitology: *M.S., Ph.D., D.Sc.V.M.*
Psychology: *Ph.D.* *
Reproductive Physiology: *M.S., Ph.D.*

Sheep Husbandry: *M.S., Ph.D.*
Statistical Genetics: *M.S., Ph.D.*
Swine Husbandry: *M.S., Ph.D.*
Theriogenology: *M.S., Ph.D.*
Veterinary Anatomy: *M.S., Ph.D., D.Sc.V.M.*
Veterinary Bacteriology: *M.S., Ph.D., D. Sc. V.M.*
Veterinary Medicine: *D.V.V./M.S., D.V.M./Ph.D.*
Veterinary Pathology: *M.S., Ph.D., D.Sc. V.M.*
Veterinary Pharmacology: *M.S., Ph.D., D.Sc.V.M.*
Veterinary Surgery: *M.S., Ph.D., D.Sc. V.M.*
Veterinary Virology: *M.S., Ph.D., D. Sc. V.M.*
Wildlife Science: *M.S., Ph.D.*
Zoology: *B.S., M.S., Ph.D.*

C.W. Post College (Long Island University)
Greenvale, New York 11548
Marine Science: *M.S.* *

Downstate Medical Center (State University of New York)
Brooklyn, New York 11203
Animal Technology: *B.S.*
Laboratory Animal Science: *B., Certificate*

Erie Community College City Campus
Buffalo, New York 14209
Recreation Leadership: *A.A.S.*

Herbert H. Lehman College (City University of New York)
Bronx, New York 14068
Pre-Veterinary Medicine: *B.A., B.S.*
Recreation Education: *B.S.*

Hunter College (City University of New York)
New York City, New York 10021
Zoology: *B.S.*

Maritime College at Fort Schuyler (State University of New York)
Bronx, New York 10465
Meteorology & Oceanography: *B.S.*

Paul Smith's College
Paul Smith's, New York 12970
Forestry: *A.A.S.*

Rensselaer Polytechnic Institute
Troy, New York 12181
Environmental Engineering: *B.S., M.Eng., Ph.D.*

State University at Albany (State University of New York)
Albany, New York 12222
Biological Sciences: *M.S.*, Ph.D.* *

State University at Binghamton (State University of New York)
Binghamton, New York 13901
Biological Sciences: *B.A., B.S.*
Geology: *B.A., B.S.*
Psychology: *M.A.*, Ph.D.* *

State University at Buffalo (State University of New York)
Buffalo, New York 14214
Biology: *B.A.*
Geology: *B.A.*

State University at Stony Brook (State University of New York)
Stony Brook, New York 11790
Biochemistry: *B.S., B.A.*
Biology: *B.A., B.S., M.A., Ph.D.*
Earth Science (Geology): *B.A., B.S.*
Earth & Space Sciences: *B.A., B.S., M.A., Ph.D.*
Ecology & Evolution: *B.A., B.S., M.A., Ph.D.*
Microbiology: *Ph.D.*
Psychology: *B.A., M.A., Ph.D.*

Teachers College (Columbia University)
New York, New York 10027
Recreation & Related Community Service: *M.A., M.S., M.Ed., D.Ed., Ph.D.*

University of Rochester
Rochester, New York 14627
Biology: *M.S.*, Ph.D.* *

Veterinary College at Cornell University (State University of New York)
Ithaca, New York 14850
Biochemistry: *M.S.*, Ph.D.* *
Pharmocology: *M.S.*, Ph.D.* *
Physiology: *M.S.*, Ph.D.* *
Veterinary Medicine: *D.V.M.*

North Carolina

Brevard College
Brevard, North Carolina 28712
Agricultural Sciences: *A.A., Diploma*
Biology: *A.A., Diploma*
Forestry: *A.A., Diploma*

Central Carolina Technical Institute
Sanford, North Carolina 27330
Agricultural Science: *A.A.S.*
Veterinary Medical Technology: *A.A.S.*

College of the Albermarle
Elizabeth City, North Carolina 27909
Pre-Agriculture: *A.S.*
Pre-Forestry: *A.S.*
Pre-Science: *A.S.*

Duke University
Durham, North Carolina 27706
Biology: *A.B., B.S.*
Botany: *M.A., M.S., Ph.D.*
Forestry & Environmental Studies: *B.A., B.S., M.A., M.S., Ph.D.*
Marine Sciences: *B., M., Ph.D.*
Marine Sciences (Marine Biology): *B., M., Ph.D.*
Marine Sciences (Oceanography): *B., M., Ph.D.*
Zoology: *A.B., B.S., Ph.D.*
Zoology (Animal Behavior): *A.B., B.S., Ph.D.*
Zoology (Ecology): *A.B., B.S., Ph.D.*

East Carolina University
Greenville, North Carolina 27834
Agriculture: *Non-Degree*
Biology: *B.A., B.S.* ·
Environmental Health: *B.S.*
Forestry: *Non-Degree*
Parks, Recreation & Conservation: *B.S.*

Haywood Technical Institute
   Clyde, North Carolina 28721
   Forest Management: *A.A.S.*
   Forest Products Technology: *A.A.S.*
   Forest Recreation: *A.A.S.*
   Horticulture: *A.A.S.*
   Wildlife Management: *A.A.S.*

James Sprunt Institute
   Kenansville, North Carolina 28349
   Agricultural Business Technician: *A.A.S.*
   Poultry & Livestock Technician: *A.A.S.*

Lenoir—Rhyne College
   Hickory, North Carolina 28601
   Biology: *A.B., B.S.*
   Earth Science: *B.S.*
   Environmental Studies: *A.B.*
   Pre-Environment Management Studies: *Non-Degree*
   Pre-Forestry: *Non-Degree*

Martin Community College
   Williamstown, North Carolina 27893
   Biological Science: *A.A.*
   Botany: *A.A.*
   Environmental Science Technician: *A.A.S.*
   Fish & Wildlife Management: *A.*
   Forest Management: *A.*
   Zoology: *A.A.*

Mount Olive College
   Mount Olive, North Carolina 28365
   Natural & Physical Sciences: *A.A., A.S.*

North Carolina Agricultural & Technical State University
   Greensboro, North Carolina 27411
   Animal Science: *B.*

North Carolina State University
   Raleigh, North Carolina 27607
   Agriculture (General): *A.A.S.*
   Agriculture Education: *M.S.*
   Agricultural Pest Control Management: *A.A.S.*
   Animal Science: *B.S., M.S., Ph.D.*
   Biological Engineering: *M.S., Ph.D.*
   Biological Science (Biochemistry): *B.S.*
   Biological Science (Microbiology): *B.S., M.S., Ph.D.*
   Botany: *B.S., M.S., Ph.D.*
   Conservation: *B.S.*
   Crop Science: *B.S., M.S., Ph.D.*
   Earth Science: *B.S.*
   Ecology: *M.S.*
   Entomology: *B.S., M.S., Ph.D.*
   Forestry: *B.S., M.S., Ph.D.*
   Genetics: *M.S., Ph.D.*
   Horticulture: *B.S., M.S., Ph.D.*
   Livestock Management & Technology (Dairy & Animal Husbandry): *A.A.S.*
   Marine Science: *M.S., Ph.D.*
   Pest Management & Crop Protection: *B.S.*
   Plant Pathology: *M.S., Ph.D.*
   Poultry Science: *B.S., M.S.*
   Pre-Veterinary Medicine: *B.S.*
   Recreational Resources Administration: *M.S.*
   Soil Science: *B.S., M.S., Ph.D.*
   Soil Technology: *A.A.S.*
   Turf Grass Management: *A.A.S.*

Veterinary Medicine: *Non-Degree*
Wildlife Biology: *B.S., M.S.*
Zoology: *B.S., M.S., Ph.D.*
Zoology (Marine Biology): *B.S.*

Shaw University
   Raleigh, North Carolina 27602
   Zoology: *B.S.*

University of North Carolina at Chapel Hill
   Chapel Hill, North Carolina 27514
   Bacteriology & Immunology: *M.S., Ph.D.*
   Biology: *A.B., B.S.*
   Botany: *B.S., M.A., M.S., Ph.D.*
   Ecology: *M.A., M.S., Ph.D.*
   Epidemiology: *M.S., M.S.P.H., Dr.P.H, Ph.D.*
   Environmental Sciences Engineering: *M.S., M.S.E.E., M.S.P.H., Ph.D.*
   Geology: *B.A., B.S., M.A., M.S., Ph.D.*
   Marine Science: *M.S., Ph.D.*
   Parasitology & Laboratory Practice: *M.S., M.S.P.H., Dr.P.H., Ph.D.*
   Recreation Administration: *M.S.*
   Zoology: *B.A., B.S., M.S., M.A., Ph.D.*

Wake Forest University
   Winston-Salem, North Carolina 27109
   Biology: *B.A.*
   Forestry: *Non-Degree*
   Microbiology: *B.S.*

Warren Wilson College
   Swannanoa, North Carolina 28778
   Biological Sciences (Zoology): *B.A.*
   Outdoor Recreation: *Non-Degree*

North Dakota

North Dakota State University-Bottineau Branch
   Bottineau, North Dakota 53818
   Park and Recreation Technology: *A.A.S., Diploma*
   Soil and Water Technology: *A.A.S.*
   Urban Forestry Technology: *A.A.S., Diploma*
   Wildlife and Fisheries Technology: *A.A.S.*

North Dakota State University
   Fargo, North Dakota 58102
   Agricultural Economics: *B.S., M.*
   Agricultural Education: *B.A., B.S., M.*
   Agricultural Entomology: *Ph.D.*
   Agronomy: *B.A., B.S., M., Ph.D.*
   Animal Health Technology: *A.S.*
   Animal Science: *B.A., B.S., M., Ph.D.*
   Bacteriology: *B.A., B.S., M.*
   Biology: *B.A., B.S.*
   Botany: *B.A., B.S.*
   Earth Science: *B.A., B.S.*
   Entomology: *B.A., B.S., M., Ph.D.*
   Horticulture: *B.A., B.S., M.*
   Plant Pathology: *B.A., B.S., M., Ph.D.*
   Plant Science: *Ph.D.*
   Psychology: *B.A.*, B.S.**
   Soils: *B.A., B.S., M., Ph.D.*
   Veterinary Science: *A.S., B.A., B.S., Non-Degree*
   Wildlife Fisheries: *B.A., B.S.*
   Zoology: *B.A., B.S.*

University of North Dakota
  Grand Forks, North Dakota 58202
  Biology: *B.A., M., Ph.D.*
  Botany: *B.A.*
  Earth Science: *B.A.*
  Fishery & Wildlife Management (Fisheries): *B.A.*
  Fishery & Wildlife Management (Game): *B.A.*
  Geology: *B.A., M., Ph.D.*
  Natural Science: *B.A.*
  Pre-Cytotechnology: *Non-Degree*
  Pre-Veterinary Medicine: *Non-Degree*
  Recreation: *B.A., B.S., M.*
  Recreational Leadership: *A.A.*
  Zoology: *B.A.*

University of North Dakota
  Williston, North Dakota 58801
  Agriculture: *Non-Degree*
  Agriculture (Agricultural Economics): *Non-Degree*
  Agriculture (Agricultural Education): *Non-Degree*
  Agriculture (Agricultural Engineering): *Non-Degree*
  Agriculture (Agronomy): *Non-Degree*
  Agriculture (Animal Science): *Non-Degree*
  Biology: *A.A., A.S., Non-Degree*
  Forestry: *A.A., A.S., Non-Degree*
  Pre-Fisheries & Wildlife Management: *A.A., A.S.,*
    Non-Degree

Ohio

Antioch University
  Yellow Springs, Ohio 45387
  Biology: *B.A., B.S.*
  Biology (Pre-Veterinary): *B.A., B.S.*
  Environmental Interpretation: *B.A., B.S.*
  Environmental Studies: *B.A., B.S.*

Bowling Green State University
  Bowling Green, Ohio 43403
  Biology: *Ph.D. ***
  Environmental Studies: *B.S.*
  Psychology: *Ph.D. ***

Columbus Technical Institute
  Columbus, Ohio 43215
  Animal Health Technology: *A.A.S.*

Kent State University
  Kent, Ohio 44242
  Biological Science: *B.S., B.A., M.S., M.A., Ph.D.*
  Conservation: *B.S.*
  Ecology: *B., M., Ph.D.*
  Fisheries and Wildlife Management: *B., M.*
  Zoology: *B.S., M.S., Ph.D.*

Marietta College
  Marietta, Ohio 45750
  Biology: *B.S.*

Miami University
  Oxford, Ohio 45056
  Biological Science Education: *B.S.Ed.*
  Botany: *B.A., M.A., M.S.*
  Environmental Science: *M.En.*
  Forestry: *Non-Degree*
  Microbiology: *B.A., M.A., M.S.*
  Zoology: *B.A., M.A., M.S.*

Montgomery County Joint Vocational Schools
  Clayton, Ohio 45315
  Animal Care Aide: *Certificate*

Mount Saint Joseph on the Ohio, College of Ohio
  Mount Saint Joseph, Ohio 45051
  Natural Science: *B.*

Ohio University
  Athens, Ohio 45701
  Cellular Biology: *B., M., Ph.D.*
  Ecology: *B., M., Ph.D.*
  Endocrinology: *B., M., Ph.D.*
  Entomology: *B., M., Ph.D.*
  Epidemiology: *B.*
  Invertebrate Zoology: *B., M., Ph.D.*
  Vertebrate Zoology: *B., M., Ph.D.*
  Zoology: *B.S., M.S. *, Ph.D. ***

Ohio State University
  Columbus, Ohio 43210
  Animal Science: *B., M., Ph.D.*
  Cooperative Fishery Unit: *M.S., Ph.D.*
  Cooperative Wildlfie Research Unit: *M.S., Ph.D.*
  Dairy Science: *B., M., Ph.D.*
  Entomology: *M.S. *, Ph.D. ***
  Environmental Education: *B.S., M.S.*
  Fisheries and Wildlife Management: *B.S., M.S.*
  Forestry: *B.S., M.S., Ph.D.*
  Landscape Architecture: *B.L.A.*
  Parks and Recreation Administration: *B.S., M.S.*
  Resource Development: *B.S., M.S.*
  Veterinary Anatomy: *M., Ph.D.*
  Veterinary Medicine: *D.V.M., M., Ph.D.*
  Veterinary Medicine and Radiology: *M., Ph.D.*
  Veterinary Parasitology: *M., Ph.D.*
  Veterinary Pathology: *M., Ph.D.*
  Veterinary Pharmacy: *M., Ph.D.*
  Veterinary Physiology: *M., Ph.D.*
  Zoology: *B.S., M.S., Ph.D.*

Raymond Walters General and Technical College of the
    University of Cincinnati at Blue Ash
    Blue Ash, Ohio 45236
  Animal Health Technology: *A.S.*
  Environmental Control/Protection Technology: *A.S.*
  Pre-Forestry/Wildlife Management: *A.S.*
  Science Technology: *A.S.*

University of Akron
  Akron, Ohio 44325
  Biology: *M.S. ***
  Psychology: *M.A. *, Ph.D.*

University of Cincinnati
  Cincinnati, Ohio 45221
  Anatomy: *Ph.D.*
  Biology (Botany): *B.S., M.S., Ph.D.*
  Biology (Zoology): *B.S., M.S., Ph.D.*
  Developmental Biology: *M.S., Ph.D.*
  Environmental Health Science: *M.S., Ph.D.*
  Geology: *B.S., M.S., Ph.D.*

University of Toledo
  Toledo, Ohio 43606
  Biology: *B.A., B.S.*
  Geology: *B.A., B.S.*
  Pre-Veterinary: *B.A., B.S.*

Xavier University
 Cincinnati, Ohio 45207
 Natural Science: *B.*

Oklahoma

Bethany Nazarene College
 Bethany, Oklahoma 73008
 Behavioral Sciences: *A.B., B.S.*
 Biological Sciences: *A.B., B.S.*
 Natural Science: *A.B., B.S.*
 Pre-Agriculture: *Non-Degree*

Cameron University
 Lawton, Oklahoma 73501
 Agriculture: *Non-Degree*
 Agriculture (Agricultural Education): *Non-Degree*
 Agriculture (Agronomy): *Non-Degree*
 Agriculture (Animal Science): *Non-Degree*
 Agriculture (Entomology): *Non-Degree*
 Agriculture (Forestry): *Non-Degree*
 Agriculture (Horticulture): *Non-Degree*
 Biology: *B.S.*
 Biology (Botany): *B.S.*
 Biology (Zoology): *B.S.*
 Natural Science: *B.S.*
 Pre-Veterinary Medicine: *Non-Degree*

Carl Albert Junior College
 Poteau, Oklahoma 74953
 Veterinary Science: *A.A., Non-Degree*

Central State University
 Edmond, Oklahoma 73034
 Biology: *B.S., B.S. Ed., M. Ed.*
 Natural Science: *M.Ed.*

Eastern Oklahoma State College
 Wilburton, Oklahoma 74578
 Agricultural Economics: *A.A.S.*
 Agricultural Education: *A.S.*
 Agronomy: *A.S.*
 Biological Science: *A.A.*
 Entomology and Wildlife Conservation: *A.A.*
 Environmental Technology: *A.A.S.*
 Forestry: *B.S., Non-Degree*
 Forestry Technology (Arboriculture): *A.A.S.*
 Forestry Technology (Parks Management): *A.A.S.*
 Pre-Veterinary Science: *A.S.*
 Ranch Operation Technician: *A.A.S.*
 Recreation: *A.A.*

Langston University
 Langston, Oklahoma 73050
 Animal Husbandry: *B.S.*
 Animal Science: *B.S.*
 Biology: *B.S.*

Northeastern Oklahoma A&M College
 Miami, Oklahoma 74354
 Agriculture: *Non-Degree, A.A.*
 Agronomy: *Non-Degree, A.A.*
 Animal Science: *Non-Degree, A.A.*
 Botany: *Non-Degree, A.A.*
 Dairy: *Non-Degree, A.A.*
 Earth Science: *Non-Degree, A.A.*
 Forestry: *Non-Degree, A.A.*
 Veterinary Medicine: *Non-Degree, A.A.*

Wildlife Conservation: *Non-Degree, A.A.*
 Zoology: *Non-Degree, A.A.*

Northwestern Oklahoma State University
 Alva, Oklahoma 73717
 Agriculture: *Non-Degree, B.S.*
 Agri-Business: *B.S.*
 Agricultural Ecology: *B.S.*
 Agronomy: *Non-Degree*
 Animal Science: *Non-Degree*
 Biology: *B.S.*
 Botany: *B.S.*
 Horticulture: *Non-Degree*
 Natural Science: *B.S. Ed.*
 Veterinary Medicine: *Non-Degree*
 Wildlife Ecology: *Non-Degree*
 Zoology: *B.S.*

Oklahoma Panhandle State University
 Goodwell, Oklahoma 73939
 Agronomy: *B.S.*
 Animal Science: *B.S.*
 Biology: *B.S.*
 Natural Science: *B.S.*
 Pre-Veterinary Medicine: *Non-Degree*

Oklahoma State University
 Stillwater, Oklahoma 74074
 Agronomy: *B.S., M.S.*
 Agronomy (Soil Science): *Ph.D.*
 Animal Science & Industry: *B.S.*
 Animal Science (Animal Breeding): *Ph.D.*
 Animal Science (Animal Nutrition): *Ph.D.*
 Animal Science & Industry (Animal Science): *M.S.*
 Animal Science & Industry (Dairy Science): *M.S.*
 Bioenvironmental Engineering: *M.S.*
 Biological Science: *B.S.*
 Botany: *B.S., M.S., Ph.D.*
 Entomology: *B.S., M.S., Ph.D.*
 Environmental Science: *M.S., Ph.D.*
 Forest Resources: *M.S.*
 Forestry: *B.S.*
 Horticulture: *B.S., M.S.*
 Microbiology: *B.S., M.S., Ph.D.*
 Natural Sciences: *B.S.*
 Plant Pathology: *B.S., M.S., Ph.D.*
 Pre-Veterinary Science: *B.S.*
 Veterinary Medicine: *D.V.M.*
 Veterinary Parasitology: *M.S., Ph.D.*
 Veterinary Pathology: *M.S., Ph.D.*
 Wildlife Ecology: *B.S., M.S., Ph.D.*
 Zoology: *B.S., B.A., M.S., M.A., Ph.D.*

Southeastern Oklahoma State University
 Durant, Oklahoma 74701
 Biology: *B.S., B.S.Ed.*
 Conservation: *B.S.*
 Pre-Veterinary Medicine: *Non-Degree*

Southwestern Oklahoma State University
 Weatherford, Oklahoma 73096
 Biological Sciences: *B.S., M.Ed.*
 Natural Science: *B.S.Ed., M.Ed.*
 Pre-Veterinary Medicine: *Non-Degree*

University of Oklahoma
Norman, Oklahoma 73019
Botany: *B.S., M.S., Ph.D.*
Environmental Science: *M.S., Ph.D.*
Microbiology: *B.S., M.S., Ph.D.*
Zoology: *B.S., M.S.*, Ph.D.**

University of Oklahoma - Health Sciences Center
Oklahoma City, Oklahoma 73190
Parasitology: *B., M.*

The University of Tulsa
Tulsa, Oklahoma 74104
Education (Humane Education): *M.Ed., Ed.D.*
Environmental Biology: *B.A., B.S.*
Geology: *B.A., B.S.*
Health Sciences (Pre-Veterinary): *B.A., B.S.*
Recreation: *B.S.*

Oregon

Blue Mountain Community College
Pendleton, Oregon 97801
Biology: *A.*
Pre-Forestry: *A.*
Pre-Veterinary: *A.*
Veterinary Technology: *Certificate, A.*
Wildlife Management: *A.*
Zoology: *A.*

Central Oregon Community College
Bend, Oregon 97701
Agriculture: *Non-Degree*
Biology: *Non-Degree*
Fisheries & Wildlife Science: *Non-Degree*
Forestry Technology (Forest Management): *A.S.*
Medical Records Technology: *Certificate, A.S.*
Pre-Forestry: *Non-Degree*
Pre-Professional (Veterinary): *Non-Degree*
Zoology: *A.S.*

Clackamas Community College
Oregon City, Oregon 97045
Agri-Business: *A.S.*
Biology: *Non-Degree*
Entomology: *Non-Degree*
Pre-Forestry: *Non-Degree*
Zoology: *Non-Degree*

Clatsop Community College
Astoria, Oregon 97103
Biology: *Non-Degree*
Entomology: *Non-Degree*
Forestry Technology: *A.S.*
Livestock Technology: *A.S.*
Microbiology: *Non-Degree*
Oceanographic Technology: *A.S.*
Zoology: *Non-Degree*

Lewis and Clark College
Portland, Oregon 97219
Biology: *B.S.*

Mount Hood Community College
Gresham, Oregon 97030
Biology: *A.S.*
Entomology: *A.S.*
Forestry Technology: *A.S.*
Medical Receptionist: *Certificate*
Microbiology: *A.S.*
Zoology: *A.S.*

Oregon State University
Corvallis, Oregon 97330
Agricultural & Resource Economics: *B.S., M.S., Ph.D.*
Animal Science: *B.S., M.S., Ph.D.*
Biology: *B.S.*
Entomology: *B.A., B.S., M.A., M.S., Ph.D.*
Forest Management: *B.S., M.F., M.S., Ph.D.*
Forest Science: *M.F., M.S., Ph.D.*
Microbiology: *B.A., B.S., M.A., M.S., Ph.D.*
Oceanography: *M.A., M.S., Ph.D.*
Rangeland Resources: *B.S., M.Agr., M.S., Ph.D.*
Resource Economics: *Ph.D.*
Resource Recreation Management: *B.S., B.A.*
Veterinary Medicine: *M.S.*
Wildlife Science: *B.S., Ag.M., M.S., Ph.D.*
Zoology: *B.S., B.A., M.S., M.A., Ph.D.*

Portland Community College
Portland, Oregon 97219
Biology: *Non-Degree*
Microbiology: *Non-Degree*
Recreation: *A.A.*
Veterinary Science Technology: *A.S.*
Zoology: *A.A.*

Southern Oregon State College
Ashland, Oregon 97520
Biology: *B.S., B.A.*
Entomology: *Non-Degree*
Forestry: *Non-Degree*
Outdoor Education: *M.S.*
Pre-Veterinary Medicine: *B.S.*
Range Management: *Non-Degree*
Wildlife Management: *Non-Degree*
Zoology: *Non-Degree*

Treasure Valley Community College
Ontario, Oregon 97914
Agriculture: *Certificate*
Agricultural Technology: *A.S.*
Biology: *Non-Degree*
Forestry: *Non-Degree*
Landscaping & Public Ground Management: *A.S.*
Veterinary Medicine: *Non-Degree*

University of Oregon
Eugene, Oregon 97403
Biology: *B.S., B.A., M.S., M.A., Ph.D.*
Ecology: *M.A., M.S., Ph.D.*
Marine Biology: *M.A., M.S., Ph.D.*
Microbiology: *M.A., M.S., Ph.D.*
Physiology: *M.A., M.S., Ph.D.*
Pre-Veterinary Medicine: *B.S.*
Recreational & Park Management: *B.S., B.A., M.A.,
    M.S., Ph.D.*
Zoology: *M.A., M.S., Ph.D.*

Pennsylvania

Allentown College of St. Francis de Sales
  Center Valley, Pennsylvania 18034
  Biology: *A.B., B.S.*

Bloomsburg State College
  Bloomsburg, Pennsylvania 17815
  Biology: *B.S.*
  Earth Sciences: *B.A.*
  Pre-Veterinary Medicine: *Non-Degree*

Bucknell University
  Lewisburg, Pennsylvania 17837
  Animal Behavior: *B.S., M.S.*
  Biology: *B.S., M.S.*
  Pre-Veterinary Medicine: *Non-Degree*

California State College
  California, Pennsylvania 15419
  Biological Sciences: *B.A.*
  Earth Science: *B.A.*
  Environmental Studies: *B.A.*
  Nature Conservation & Recreation: *B.A.*
  Outdoor Recreation & Conservation: *B.A.*
  Urban Recreation & Park Administration: *B.A.*

Delaware Valley College of Science and Agriculture
  Doylestown, Pennsylvania 18901
  Agronomy: *B.S.*
  Animal Husbandry: *B.S.*
  Biology: *B.S.*
  Dairy Husbandry: *B.S.*
  Horticulture: *B.S.*

Drexel University
  Philadelphia, Pennsylvania 19104
  Biological Sciences: *B.S., M.S., Ph.D.*
  Environmental Engineering: *M.S., Ph.D.*
  Environmental Science: *M.S., Ph.D.*
  Unified Science: *B.S.*
  Water Resources: *M.S.*

Duquesne University
  Pittsburgh, Pennsylvania 15219
  Biology: *B.*
  Botany: *M.*
  Zoology: *M.*

Gannon College
  Erie, Pennsylvania 16501
  Biology: *B.A., B.S.*
  Biology (Botany): *B.A., B.S.*
  Biology (Ecology): *B.A., B.S.*
  Biology (Microbiology): *B.A., B.S.*
  Biology (Zoology): *B.A., B.S.*
  Earth Science (Wildlife Management): *B.S.*
  Pre-Veterinary Science: *Non-Degree, B.A., B.S.*

Gettysburg College
  Gettysburg, Pennsylvania 17325
  Biology: *B.A.*
  Forestry: *Non-Degree*
  Pre-Veterinary Medicine: *Non-Degree*

Harcum Junior College
  Bryn Mawr, Pennsylvania 19010
  Animal Center Management: *A.S.*
  Animal Technician: *A.S.*

Harrisburg Area Community College
  Harrisburg, Pennsylvania 17110
  Biology: *A.A.*
  Recreational Leadership: *A.A.*

Kutztown State College
  Kutztown, Pennsylvania 19530
  Biological Science: *B.Ed.*
  Biology: *B.S.*
  Earth Science (Marine Science): *B.S.*
  Earth - Space Science: *B.Ed.*

Median School
  Pittsburgh, Pennsylvania 15222
  Animal Health Technology: *Certificate*

Pennsylvania State University
  University Park, Pennsylvania 16802
  Animal Bioscience: *B.S.*
  Animal Industries: *M.Agr., M.S., Ph.D.*
  Animal Nutrition: *M.S., Ph.D.*
  Animal Production: *B.S.*
  Biology: *M.S., Ph.D.*
  Ecology: *M.S., Ph.D.*
  Entomology: *B.S., M.Agr., M.S., Ph.D.*
  Environmental Pollution Control: *M.E.P.C., M.Eng., M.S.*
  Environmental Resource Management: *B.S.*
  Forest Products: *B.S.*
  Forest Resources: *B.S., M.S., M.F.R., Ph.D.*
  Forestry Science: *B.S.*
  Lab Animal Technician: *Assoc.*
  Poultry Science: *M.S., Ph.D.*
  Recreation & Parks: *B.S., M.S., M.Ed.*
  Recreation & Parks (Outdoor Recreation): *B.S., M.S., M.Ed.*
  Veterinary Science: *M.S., Ph.D.*
  Wildlife Technology: *Assoc.*
  Zoology: *M.S., Ph.D.*

Pennsylvania State University - Hershey Medical Center
  Hershey, Pennsylvania 17033
  Laboratory Animal Medicine: *M.*

Pennsylvania State University - Ogontz Campus
  Abington, Pennsylvania 19001
  Agriculture (General): *B.*
  Agronomy: *B.*
  Animal Industry: *B.*
  Animal Science: *B.*
  Biology: *B.*
  Earth Science: *B.*
  Environmental Resource Management: *B.*
  Forest Science: *B.*
  Horticulture: *B.*
  Man/Environmental Relations: *B.*
  Plant Science: *B.*
  Recreation & Parks: *B.*

Slippery Rock State College
  Slippery Rock, Pennsylvania 16057
  Biology: *B.A., M.Ed.*
  Biology (Biological Sciences): *B.A., M.Ed.*
  Biology (Botany): *B.A., M.Ed.*
  Biology (Cytotechnology): *Non-Degree*
  Biology (Zoology): *B.A., M.Ed.*
  Environmental Education: *M.Ed.*
  Environmental Studies: *B.S.*
  Marine Science: *B.S.*

Marine Science (Marine Biology): *B.S.*
Marine Science (Marine Ecology): *B.S.*
Marine Science (Marine Geology): *B.S.*
Marine Science (Geophysics): *B.S.*
Marine Science (Chemical & Physical Oceanography):
  B.S.
Recreation: *B.S., M.Ed.*

Susquehanna University
  Selinsgrove, Pennsylvania 17807
  Biology: *B.A.*
  Environmental Studies: *Certificate*

Swarthmore College
  Swarthmore, Pennsylvania 19081
  Biology: *B.A., B.S.*
  Biology (Botany): *B.A., B.S.*
  Biology (Cellular & Developmental Biology): *B.A., B.S.*
  Biology (Ecology): *B.A., B.S.*
  Biology (Ethology): *B.A., B.S.*
  Biology (Genetics & Evolution): *B.A., B.S.*
  Biology (Physiology): *B.A., B.S.*
  Biology (Zoology): *B.A., B.S.*

Temple University
  Philadelphia, Pennsylvania 19122
  Biology: *M.A.*, Ph.D.**
  Botany: *A.A.*
  Environmental Engineering Technology: *B.S.*
  Horticulture: *A.A.*
  Microbiology & Immunology: *M.S., Ph.D.*
  Physiology - Biophysics: *M.S., Ph.D.*
  Psychology: *M.A.*, Ph.D.**
  Recreation: *B.S., M.Ed., Ed.D.*

University of Pennsylvania
  Philadelphia, Pennsylvania 19104
  Animal Science: *B.*
  Anthropology: *Ph.D.**
  Biology: *Ph.D.**
  Landscape Architecture: *M.L.A.*
  Parasitology: *Ph.D.*
  Psychology: *Ph.D.**
  Regional Planning: *M.R.P.*
  Veterinary Medicine: *B., D.V.M.*

Rhode Island

Rhode Island School of Design
  Providence, Rhode Island 02903
  Landscape Architecture: *B.L.A.*

University of Rhode Island
  Kingston, Rhode Island 02880
  Agriculture & Resource Technology: *B.S.*
  Animal Pathology: *M., Ph.D.*
  Animal Science: *B.S., M.S.*
  Biological Sciences: *B.A., B.S., M.S., Ph.D.*
  Fisheries & Marine Technology: *A.S., B.S., M.S., Ph.D.*
  Natural Resources: *B.S.*
  Ocean Engineering: *M., Ph.D.*
  Oceanography: *B.S., M.S., Ph.D.*
  Oceanography (Chemical): *M., Ph.D.*
  Oceanography (Geological): *M., Ph.D.*
  Oceanography (Physical): *M., Ph.D.*
  Pre-Veterinary Studies: *B.S.*
  Zoology: *B.S., M.S.*, Ph.D.**

South Carolina

Clemson University
  Clemson, South Carolina 29631
  Agricultural Sciences (Animal Science): *B.S., M.Ag.*
  Agricultural Sciences (Dairy Science): *B.S., M.Ag.*
  Economic Biology (Economic Zoology): *B.S., M.Ag.*
  Economic Biology (Entomology): *B.S., M.Ag.*
  Environmental Systems Engineering: *M.Eng.,*
    M.S., Ph.D.
  Forest Management: *B.S.*
  Forestry: *M.S., M.F.*
  Microbiology: *B.S.*
  Pre-Veterinary Medicine: *B.S., Non-Degree*
  Recreation & Park Administration: *B.S., M.R.P.A.*
  Wildlife Biology: *M.S.*
  Zoology: *B.S., M.S.*, Ph.D.**

Orangeburg-Calhoun Technical College
  Orangeburg, South Carolina 29115
  Animal Science: *A.*

South Carolina State College
  Orangeburg, South Carolina 29115
  Pre-Agriculture (Animal Science): *Non-Degree*
  Veterinary Medicine: *B.S.*

Tri-County Technical College
  Pendleton, South Carolina 29670
  Animal Science: *A.A.S.*
  Dairy Science: *A.A.S.*
  Medical Laboratory Technician: *A.A.S.*
  Veterinary Assistant Technology: *A.A.T.*

South Dakota

Black Hills State College
  Spearfish, South Dakota 57783
  Biology: *B.S., B.A.*
  Outdoor Education: *B.S., B.A.*
  Pre-Professional (Veterinary Medicine): *Non-Degree*
  Pre-Professional (Wildlife Management): *Non-Degree*

South Dakota State University
  Brookings, South Dakota 57006
  Agricultural Education: *M.S.*
  Agronomy: *M.S., Ph.D.*
  Animal Science: *B.S., M.S., Ph.D.*
  Biology: *B.S., M.S.*
  Dairy Science: *M.S.*
  Entomology: *B.S., M.S.*
  Microbiology: *M.S.*
  Plant Pathology: *M.S.*
  Veterinary Science: *Non-Degree*
  Wildlife & Fisheries Science (Fisheries): *M.S.*
  Wildlife & Fisheries Science (Wildlife): *M.S.*

University of South Dakota at Springfield
  Springfield, South Dakota 57062
  Biology: *A.S., A.A.*
  Pre-Veterinarian: *B.S.*

University of South Dakota
  Vermillion, South Dakota 57069
  Biology: *B.S., B.A., M., Ph.D.*
  Earth Science: *B.A., B.S., M.N.S.*
  Pre-Veterinary Medicine: *Non-Degree*
  Recreation: *B.S.*

Tennessee

Columbia State Community College
  Columbia, Tennessee 38401
  Agri-Business: *A.S.*
  Agriculture: *A.S.*
  Biology: *A.S.*
  Biology: *A.S.*
  Biology (Entomology): *A.S.*
  Biology (Fisheries): *A.S.*
  Biology (Histology): *A.S.*
  Biology (Wildlife): *A.S.*
  Biology (Zoology): *A.S.*

East Tennessee State University
  Johnson City, Tennessee 37601
  Biology: *B.A., B.S., M.S.*
  Biomedical Science: *M.S., Ph.D.*
  Biomedical Science (Cellular Biophysics): *M.S., Ph.D.*
  Biomedical Science (Microbiology): *M.S., Ph.D.*
  Biomedical Science (Physiology): *M.S., Ph.D.*
  Environmental Health: *B.S.E.H., M.S.E.H.*
  General Science: *B.A., B.S.*
  General Science (Biology Emphasis): *B.A., B.S.*
  General Science (Earth & Space Science Emphasis): *B.A., B.S.*
  Pre-Veterinary Medicine: *B.A., B.S.*

Hiwassee College
  Madisonville, Tennessee 37354
  Agriculture: *A.A., Non-Degree*
  Forestry: *A.A., Non-Degree*
  Pre-Cytotechnology: *A.A., Non-Degree*
  Pre-Microbiology: *Non-Degree*
  Wildlife Management: *A.A., Non-Degree*

LeMoyne-Owen College
  Memphis, Tennessee 38126
  Biology: *B.S.*
  Natural Science: *B.S.*

Martin College
  Pulaski, Tennessee 38478
  Agriculture: *A.A.*
  Behavioral Science: *A.A.*
  Biology: *A.A.*
  Pre-Forestry: *A.A.*
  Pre-Veterinary Medicine: *A.A.*
  Recreation Leadership: *A.A.*
  Wildlife Management: *A.A.*

Memphis State University
  Memphis, Tennessee 38152
  Biology: *B.A., B.S.*
  Biology (Botany): *B.A., B.S.*
  Biology (Entomology): *B.A., B.S.*
  Biology (Invertebrate Zoology): *B.A., B.S.*
  Biology (Microbiology): *B.A., B.S.*
  Geology: *B.S.*
  Pre-Veterinary Medicine: *Non-Degree*
  Recreation & Park Administration: *B.S.Ed.*

Middle Tennessee State University
  Murfreesboro, Tennessee 37130
  Agri-Business: *A.S.*
  Agriculture: *B.S.*
  Agriculture (Agri-Business): *B.S.*
  Agriculture (Animal Science): *B.S.*
  Agriculture (Environmental Science & Technology): *B.S.*
  Agriculture (Plant & Soil Science): *B.S.*
  Biology: *M.S., M.S.T.*
  Earth Science (Geology): *B.A.*
  Geography (Park Service): *B.A.*
  Pre-Agricultural Engineering: *Non-Degree*
  Pre-Forestry: *Non-Degree*
  Pre-Forestry (Forest Resources Management): *Non-Degree*
  Pre-Forestry (Wildlife & Fisheries Science): *Non-Degree*

Tennessee State University
  Nashville, Tennessee 37203
  Agricultural Science: *M.S.*
  Animal Science: *B.S.*
  Biology: *B.A., B.S., M.A., M.S.*
  Plant Science: *B.S.*
  Recreation: *B.S., M.S.*

Tennessee Technological University
  Cookeville, Tennessee 38501
  Agriculture: *B.S.*
  Agriculture (Agricultural Natural Resources Management): *B.S.*
  Agriculture (Agricultural Science): *B.S.*
  Agriculture (Agronomy): *B.S.*
  Agriculture (Animal Husbandry): *B.S.*
  Agriculture (Dairy Husbandry): *B.S.*
  Agriculture (Horticulture): *B.S.*
  Agriculture (Pre-Forestry): *B.S.*
  Agriculture (Pre-Veterinary Medicine): *B.S.*
  Wildlife Management (Fishery Biology): *B.S.*

University of Tennessee
  Knoxville, Tennessee 37916
  Agricultural Biology: *M.S., Ph.D.*
  Agricultural Business: *B.S.*
  Agricultural Education: *B.S., M.S.*
  Animal Science: *B.S., M.S., Ph.D.*
  Biology: *B.A., M.A.C.T.*
  Botany: *B.A., M.S., Ph.D.*
  Ecology: *M.S., Ph.D.*
  Forestry: *B.S.F., M.S.*
  Microbiology: *B.A., M.S., Ph.D.*
  Plant & Soil Science: *B.S., M.S., Ph.D.*
  Pre-Veterinary Medicine: *B.S.*
  Psychology: *M.A.*, M.S.*, Ph.D.**
  Veterinary Medicine: *D.V.M.*
  Wildlife & Fisheries Science: *B.S., M.S.*
  Zoology: *B.A., M.S., Ph.D.*

University of Tennessee
  Martin, Tennessee 38238
  Agriculture: *B.S.*
  Agriculture (Agricultural Business): *B.S.*
  Agriculture (Agricultural Education): *B.S.*
  Agriculture (Animal Science): *B.S.*
  Agriculture (General Agriculture): *B.S.*
  Agriculture (Plant Science): *B.S.*

Biology: *B.A., B.S.*
Biology (Botany): *B.A., B.S.*
Biology (Microbiology): *B.A., B.S.*
Biology (Zoology): *B.A., B.S.*
Forestry: *Non-Degree*
Natural Resources Management: *B.S.*
Natural Resources Management (Park & Recreation Mgt.): *B.S.*
Natural Resources Management (Soil & Water Conservation): *B.S.*
Natural Resources Management (Wildlife Biology): *B.S.*
Psychology: *B.A., B.S.*
Veterinary Medicine: *Non-Degree*

University of Tennessee
Nashville, Tennessee 37203
Biology: *B.A., B.S.*
Environmental Engineering: *B.S.*
Geology: *B.A., B.S.*

University of the South
Sewanee, Tennessee 37375
Biology: *B.A., B.S.*
Forestry: *B.A., B.S.*
Psychology: *B.A.*, B.S.**

Vanderbilt University
Nashville, Tennessee 37235
Environmental & Water Resources Engineering: *B.E., B.S., M.E., M.S., Ph.D.*
Environmental Studies: *B.*
General Biology: *B., M., Ph.D.*
Geology: *B., M.*

Texas

Abilene Christian University
Abilene, Texas 79601
Agriculture: *B.S.*
Agriculture (Agronomy): *B.S.*
Agriculture (Animal Science): *B.S.*
Agriculture (General Agriculture): *B.S.*
Agriculture (Range Science): *B.S.*
Biology (General & Wildlife): *B.S., M.S.*
Geology: *B.S.*
Pre-Veterinary Medicine: *Non-Degree*
Recreation: *B.S.*

Angelo State University
San Angelo, Texas 76901
Agriculture (Animal Science): *B.A., B.S.*
Biology: *B.A., B.S., M.A.T., M.S.*
Physical Science: *B.A., B.S.*
Pre-Veterinary Medicine: *Non-Degree*

Bee County College
Beeville, Texas 78102
Agriculture: *A.A., A.S.*
Biology: *A.S., A.S.*
Geology: *A.A., A.S.*
Recreation: *A.A., A.S.*

Blinn College
Brenham, Texas 77833
Agriculture: *A.A., Non-Degree*
Agri-Business: *A.A., Non-Degree*
Pre-Forestry: *A.A., Non-Degree*
Pre-Veterinary Medicine: *A.A., Non-Degree*
Wildlife: *A.A., Non-Degree*

Central Texas College
Killeen, Texas 76541
Agriculture: *A.S.*
Animal Production: *Certificate*
Environmental Control: *A.A.S.*
Farm & Ranch Management: *A.A.S.*
Farm & Ranch Production: *Certificate*
Horse Management: *A.A.S.*
Plant Production: *Certificate*
Physical Education (Recreation Leadership): *Certificate*
Science (Biology): *A.A., A.S.*
Science (Geology): *A.A., A.S.*

Cooke County College
Gainesville, Texas 76240
Agriculture: *A.S.*
Biology: *A.S.*
Biology (Environmental Biology): *A.S.*
Biology (Wildlife Management): *A.S.*
Biology (Zoology): *A.S.*
Farm & Range Management: *A.A.S.*

East Texas State University
Commerce, Texas 75428
Pre-Veterinary Medicine: *Non-Degree*

Frank Phillips College
Borger, Texas 79007
Agriculture: *A.A., A.A.S., Non-Degree*
Agriculture Technology (Farm/Range Management): *A.A.S.*
Biology: *A.A., A.A.S., Non-Degree*
Pre-Veterinary Medicine: *A.A., A.A.S., Non-Degree*

Henderson County Junior College
Athens, Texas 75751
Agriculture: *A.A., A.S., Non-Degree*
Biology: *A.A., A.S., Non-Degree*
Ranch Management: *A.A.S.*

Houston Community College
Houston, Texas 77007
Veterinary Assistant: *Certificate*

Howard College at Big Spring
Big Spring, Texas 79720
Agriculture: *A.A., A.S.*
Agriculture (Agronomy): *Non-Degree*
Agriculture (Agri-Business): *Non-Degree*
Agriculture (Agricultural Economics): *Non-Degree*
Agriculture (Agricultural Engineering): *Non-Degree*
Agriculture (Animal Science): *Non-Degree*
Agriculture (Dairy Industry): *Non-Degree*
Agriculture (Entomology): *Non-Degree*
Agriculture (Farm Management): *Non-Degree*
Agriculture (Horticulture): *Non-Degree*
Agriculture (Park Administration): *Non-Degree*
Agriculture (Veterinary Medicine): *Non-Degree*
Biology: *A.A., A.S., Non-Degree*
Geology: *A.A., A.S., Non-Degree*

Lamar State University
   Beaumont, Texas 77710
   Biology: *B.A., B.S., M.S.*
   Environmental Science: *B.S.*
   Geology: *A.A., A.S., B.A., B.S.*
   Oceanography Technician: *B.S.*

Lubbock Christian College
   Lubbock, Texas 79407
   Agriculture: *B.S.*
   Biology: *B.S.*
   Pre-Veterinary Medicine: *Non-Degree*

Mary Hardin - Baylor College
   Belton, Texas 76513
   Behavioral Science: *B.S.*
   Biology: *B.S., B.S.Ed.*
   Recreation: *B.A.*

Midwestern State University
   Wichita Falls, Texas 76308
   Biology (Classical): *B.S., M.S.*
   Biology (Ecology): *B.S., M.S.*
   Biology (Mollecular-Cellular): *B.S., M.S.*
   Biology (Pre-Veterinary): *B.S., M.S.*
   Biology (Wildlife): *B.S., M.S.*
   Geology: *B.S.*
   Recreational Administration: *B.S.*

Mountain View College
   Dallas, Texas 75211
   Biology (Mammalian Physiology): *A.A., A.S.*

Navarro Junior College
   Corsicana, Texas 75110
   Agriculture: *A.A., A.S.*
   Biology: *A.A., A.S.*
   Pre-Veterinary Medicine: *A.A., A.S.*

North Texas State University
   Denton, Texas 76203
   Biological Sciences: *B.S., M.S., Ph.D.*
   Biology: *B.S.*
   Geology (Earth Science): *B.S.*
   Recreation: *B.A., B.S., M.S., M.Ed.*

Prairie View A&M College
   Prairie View, Texas 77445
   Agriculture: *B.S.*
   Agriculture (Agricultural Education): *B.S.*
   Agriculture (Agricultural Engineering): *B.S.*
   Agriculture (Agronomy): *B.S.*
   Agriculture (Animal Science - Dairy): *B.S.*
   Agriculture (Animal Science - General): *B.S.*
   Agriculture (Animal Science - Poultry Science): *B.S.*
   Agriculture (Plant Science): *B.S., M.S.*
   Agriculture (Soil Science): *B.S., M.S.*
   Agriculture (Entomology): *B.S.*
   Agriculture (Veterinary Science): *B.S.*
   Biology: *B.S., M.S.*
   Earth Sciences: *B.A., B.S.*
   Recreation: *B.S., M.S., M.Ed.*

Rice University
   Houston, Texas 77001
   Biology: *B.A., M.A., Ph.D.*
   Environmental Science & Engineering: *B.A., M.S., Ph.D.*
   Geology: *B.A., M.A., Ph.D.*

Sam Houston State University
   Huntsville, Texas 77341
   Agriculture (Agriculture - Business): *B.S.*
   Agriculture (Agriculture Education): *B.S.*
   Agriculture (Animal Science): *B.S.*
   Agriculture (General Agriculture): *B.S.*
   Agriculture (Horticulture & Crop Science): *B.S.*
   Biology: *B.A., B.S.*
   Environmental Science: *B.S.*

San Antonio College
   San Antonio, Texas 78284
   Pre-Veterinary Medicine: *A.A., A.S., A.A.S.*
   Recreation Leadership: *A.A., A.S., A.A.S.*

Southwest Texas Junior College
   Uvalde, Texas 78801
   Agriculture: *A.A., Non-Degree*
   Farm & Ranch Management: *A.A.S.*
   Pre-Veterinary: *Non-Degree*

Southwest Texas State University
   San Marcas, Texas 78666
   Agriculture (Animal Science): *B.S.*
   Agriculture (Horticulture): *B.S.*
   Agriculture (Plant & Soil Science): *B.S.*
   Agriculture (Range Management): *B.S.*
   Biology: *B.S.*
   Veterinary Medicine (Pre-Professional): *Non-Degree*
   Recreational Administration: *B.S.*

Stephen F. Austin State College
   Nacogdoches, Texas 75962
   Agriculture: *B.S.*
   Agricultural Technology: *B.A.A.*
   Biology: *B.S.*
   Biology (Botany): *B.S.*
   Biology (Zoology): *B.S.*
   Environmental Management: *B.S.F., M.S., M.S.F., D.F., Ph.D.*
   Forestry: *B.S.F., M.S., M.S.F., D.F., Ph.D.*
   Forest Engineering: *B.S.F., M.S., M.S.F., D.F., Ph.D.*
   Forest Game Management: *B.S.F., M.S., M.S.F., D.F., Ph.D.*
   Forest Management: *B.S.F., M.S., M.S.F., D.F., Ph.D.*
   Forest Range Management: *B.S.F., M.S., M.S.F., .D.F., Ph.D.*
   Forest Recreation Management: *B.S.F., M.S., M.S.F., D.F., Ph.D.*
   Municipal Forest Management: *B.S.F., M.S., M.S.F., D.F., Ph.D.*

Sul Rose State University
   Alpine, Texas 79830
   Animal Technology: *Certificate*
   Animal Technology (Horse Science): *Certificate*
   Animal Technology (Veterinary Science Technology): *Certificate*
   Biology: *B.S., M.S.*
   Forest Range Management: *Non-Degree*
   Pre-Forestry: *Non-Degree*
   Pre-Veterinary: *Non-Degree*
   Range Animal Science (Agricultural Business): *B.S., M.S.*
   Range Animal Science (Animal Health Management): *B.S., M.S.*
   Range Animal Science (Animal Science): *B.S., M.S.*

Range Animal Science (Horse Science): *B.S., M.S.*
Range Animal Science (Range Management):
  B.S., M.S.
Range Animal Science (Wildlife Management):
  B.S., M.S.

Texas A&I University
  Kingsville, Texas 78363
  Agriculture (General): *B.S., M.S.*
  Animal Science: *B.S., M.S.*
  Animal Science (Range Option): *B.S.*
  Animal Science (Range-Wildlife): *B.S.*
  Animal Science (Pre-Veterinary Medicine): *B.S., M.S.*
  Biology: *B.S., M.S.*
  Geology: *B.S.*
  Plant & Soil Science (Crops Option): *B.S.*
  Plant & Soil Science (Soil Option): *B.S.*

Texas A&M University
  College Station, Texas 77843
  Agricultural Economics (Farm & Ranch Management):
    M.Ag., M.S., Ph.D.
  Agricultural Education: *M.Ag., M.S., Ph.D.*
  Agricultural Journalism: *M.Ag., M.S., Ph.D.*
  Animal Science: *M.Ag., M.S., Ph.D.*
  Biochemistry: *M.Ag., M.S., Ph.D.*
  Bioenvironmental Science: *M.Ag., M.S., Ph.D.*
  Biology (General Biology): *B.A., B.S.*
  Botany: *B.S.*
  Dairy Science: *M.Ag., M.S., Ph.D.*
  Entomology: *M.Ag., M.S., Ph.D.*
  Forestry: *M.Ag., M.S., Ph.D.*
  General Agriculture: *M.Ag., M.S., Ph.D.*
  Geology: *B.S., M.S., Ph.D.*
  Horticulture: *M.Ag., M.S., Ph.D.*
  Marine Biology: *B.S.*
  Marine Sciences: *B.S.*
  Microbiology: *B.S.*
  Plant Science: *M.Ag., M.S., Ph.D.*
  Poultry Science: *M.Ag., M.*
  Range Science: *M.Ag., M.S., Ph.D.*
  Recreation & Parks: *B.Ag., M.S., Ph.D.*
  Soil & Crops: *M.Ag., M.S., Ph.D.*
  Veterinary Medicine: *B.S., D.V.M.*
  Veterinary Medicine (Biomedical Science): *B.S.*
  Wildlife & Fisheries: *M.Ag., M.S., Ph.D.*
  Zoology: *B.S.*

Texas Christian University
  Fort Worth, Texas 76129
  Biology: *B.A., B.S., M.A., M.S., M.A.T.*
  Environmental Sciences: *B.S., M.S.*
  Geology: *B.A., M.A., M.S.*

Texas State Technical Institute
  Waco, Texas 76705
  Animal Technology: *A.A.S.*
  Recreation Supervision: *A.*

Texas Tech University
  Lubbock, Texas 79409
  Agricultural Education: *B.S., M.S.*
  Agricultural Economics: *B.S., M.S.*
  Agriculture: *Ph.D.*
  Agriculture (Agronomy Option): *Ph.D.*
  Agriculture (Range Science Option): *Ph.D.*
  Animal Breeding: *M.S.*

Animal Business: *B.S.*
Animal Nutrition: *M.S.*
Animal Production: *B.S.*
Animal Science: *B.S., Ph.D.*
Biological Sciences (Biology): *Ph.D.*
Biological Sciences (Botany): *B.A., B.S., M.S., Ph.D.*
Biological Sciences (Microbiology): *B.A., B.S.,
  M.S., Ph.D.*
Crops: *B.S., M.S.*
Crops (Agronomy): *B.S., M.S.*
Entomology: *B.S., M.S.*
Horticulture: *B.S., M.S.*
Pre-Veterinary Medicine: *B.S.*
Range Management: *B.S.*
Range Science: *M.S.*
Park Administration: *B.S., M.S.*
Soils: *B.S., M.S.*
Wildlife Management: *B.S.*
Wildlife Science: *M.S.*
Zoology: *B.A., B.S., M.S., Ph.D.*

Texas Womans University
  Denton, Texas 76204
  Biology: *B.A., B.S., M.A., M.S., M.S. Sci. Ed., Ph.D.*
  Biology (Botany): *B.A., B.S., M.A., M.S., M.S. Sci. Ed.,
    Ph.D.*
  Biology (Microbiology): *B.A., B.S., M.A., M.S.,
    M.S. Sci. Ed., Ph.D.*
  Biology (Zoology): *B.A., B.S., M.A., M.S., M.S. Sci. Ed.,
    Ph.D.*
  Recreation Administration: *B.S., M.A., Ph.D.*

Tyler Junior College
  Tyler, Texas 75701
  Agriculture: *A.S., A.A.*
  Biology: *A.S., A.A.*

University of Houston
  Houston, Texas 77004
  Biology: *B.S., M.S., Ph.D.*
  Biology (Pre-Veterinary): *B.S.*
  Coastal Center (Research Station): *M.S., Ph.D.*
  Geology: *B.S., M.S., Ph.D.*
  Population Biology: *M.S., Ph.D.*

University of Texas
  Austin, Texas 78712
  Biology (Aquatic): *B.S.*
  Biology (Molecular): *B.S.*
  Botany: *B.S., M.A., Ph.D.*
  Community and Regional Planning: *M.S., C.R.P.*
  Environmental Health Engineering: *M.S. in Eng.*
  Geological Sciences: *B.S., M.A., Ph.D.*
  Marine Science Institute: *M.A., Ph.D.*
  Marine Studies: *B.S., M.S., Ph.D.*
  Microbiology: *B.S., M.A., Ph.D.*
  Pre-Veterinary Medicine: *B.S., Non-Degree*
  Zoology: *B.S., M.A., Ph.D.*

University of Texas At El Paso
  El Paso, Texas 79999
  Biology: *B.S.*
  Geology: *B.S.*

Victoria College
Victoria, Texas 77901
Agriculture: *A.A., A.A.S.*
Farm & Ranch Management: *A.A., A.A.S.*
Pre-Veterinary Medicine: *A.A., A.A.S.*

West Texas State University
Canyon, Texas 79016
Animal Science: *B.*

Western Texas College
Synder, Texas 79549
Agriculture: *A.A.*
Biology: *A.A.*
Farm & Ranch Management: *A.A.S.*

Utah

Brigham Young University
Provo, Utah 84602
Animal Science: *A., B.S., M.S.*
Botany (Ecology): *Ph.D.*
Microbiology: *B.S., M.S., Ph.D.*
Range Science: *B.S., M.S.*
Range Science (Wildlife Recreation): *B.S.*
Recreation Education: *B.S., M.A., M.R.Ed.*
Zoology: *B.S., M.S., Ph.D.*
Zoology (Entomology): *B.S., M.S., Ph.D.*
Zoology (Fisheries & Wildlife Biology): *B.S., M.S., Ph.D.*
Zoology (Marine & Freshwater Biology): *B.S., M.S., Ph.D.*
Zoology (Physiology): *B.S., M.S., Ph.D.*
Zoology (Pre-Professional - Veterinary Science): *B.S.*

College of Eastern Utah
Price, Utah 84501
Natural Science (Biology): *A.A., A.S.*
Natural Science (Botany): *A.A., A.S.*
Natural Science (Ecology): *A.A., A.S.*
Natural Science (Entomology): *A.A., A.S.*
Natural Science (Geology): *A.A., A.S.*
Natural Science (Physiology): *A.A., A.S.*
Natural Science (Zoology): *A.A., A.S.*
Pre-Veterinary Science: *Non-Degree*

Dixie College
St. George, Utah 84770
Biology: *A.*
Zoology (Pre-Veterinary Science): *A.*
Zoology (Wildlife Science): *A.*
Zoology: *A.*

Snow College
Ephraim, Utah 84627
Agri-Business: *A.S.*
Agri-Business Technology: *A.A.S.*
Animal Science: *Non-Degree*
Pre-Veterinary Medicine: *A.S.*

Southern Utah State College
Cedar City, Utah 84720
Agricultural/Science: *Non-Degree*
Behavioral Science: *B.A.*
Biological Science: *B.S.*
Botany: *B.S.*
Pre-Veterinary Science: *B.S.*
Zoology: *B.S.*

University of Utah
Salt Lake City, Utah 84112
Biology: *B.A., B.S., M.S., M.Phil., Ph.D.*
Geology: *B.S., M.S., Ph.D.*
Leisure Studies: *B.S., M.S.*
Microbiology: *Ph.D.*

Utah State University
Logan, Utah 84322
Animal Sciences: *B.S., M.S., Ph.D.*
Bio Ecology: *M.S., Ph.D.*
Biology (Applied): *B.S.*
Biology: *B.S., M.S., Ph.D.*
Biology (Entomology): *M.S., Ph.D.*
Biology (Herpetology): *M.S., Ph.D.*
Biology (Mammalogy): *M.S., Ph.D.*
Biology (Microbiology): *M.S., Ph.D.*
Biology (Ornithology): *M.S., Ph.D.*
Biology (Parasitology): *M.S., Ph.D.*
Biology (Plant Physiology): *M.S., Ph.D.*
Biology (Plant Psysiology): *M.S., Ph.D.*
Biology (Plant Taxonomy): *M.S., Ph.D.*
Environmental Studies: *B.S.*
Forest Ecology: *M.S., Ph.D.*
Forest Management: *M.F.*
Forest Science: *B.S., M.S., Ph.D.*
Outdoor Recreation: *B.S., M.S., Ph.D.*
Plant Science: *B.S., M.S., Ph.D.*
Plant Science Ecology: *M.S., Ph.D.*
Psychology: *M.S., Ph.D.*
Public Health (Pre-Veterinary): *B.S.*
Range Ecology: *M.S., Ph.D.*
Range Science: *B.S., M.S., Ph.D.*
Veterinary Science: *B.S.*
Watershed Science: *B.S., M.S., Ph.D.*
Wildlife Ecology: *M.S., Ph.D.*
Wildlife Science: *B.S., M.S., Ph.D.*

Weber State College
Ogden, Utah 84408
Microbiology: *B.*
Natural Science (Pre-Forestry): *Non-Degree*
Zoology: *B.*
Zoology (Pre-Veterinary Medicine): *B.*

Vermont

Goddard College
Plainfield, Vermont 05667
Ecology: *B., M.*

Marlboro College
Marlboro, Vermont 05344
Biology: *B.S.*

University of Vermont
Burlington, Vermont 05401
Animal Pathology: *M.S.*
Animal Sciences: *B.S., M.S., Ph.D.*
Biological Science: *B.S., B.A.*
Environmental Studies: *B.S.*
Forestry: *B.S., M.S.*
Medical Laboratory Technology: *A.S., B.S.*
Microbiology: *M.S., Ph.D.*
Natural Resource Planning: *M.S.*
Plant & Soil Science: *B.S., M.S., Ph.D.*
Recreation Management: *B.S.*

Resource Economics: *B.S.*
Wildlife Biology: *B.S.*
Zoology: *B.A., M.A., M.S., Ph.D.*

Virginia

Blue Ridge Community College
Weyers Cave, Virginia 24486
Animal Science: *A.A.S.*

Bridgewater College
Bridgewater, Virginia 22812
Biology: *B.A., B.S.*
Pre-Forestry: *Non-Degree*
Veterinary Medicine: *B.A., Non-Degree*

College of William and Mary in Virginia
Williamsburg, Virginia 23185
Biology: *A.B., B.S., M.A., M.S., Ph.D.*
Geology: *B.S.*
Marine Biology Major: *M.A., Ph.D.*
Marine Fisheries Biology Major: *M.A., Ph.D.*
Marine Science: *M.A., Ph.D.*
Oceanography Major: *M.A., Ph.D.*
Pre-Forestry: *B.S.*
Psychology: *Ph.D.* *

Dabney S. Lancaster Community College
Clifton Forge, Virginia 24422
Agricultural & Natural Resources Technology (Forest):
A.A.S.
Agricultural & Natural Resources Technology (Wildlife): *A.A.S.*
Agriculture: *A.S.*
Biology: *A.S.*
Forestry: *A.S.*

Ferrum College
Ferrum, Virginia 24088
Agriculture: *A.S.*
Agronomy: *A.S.*
Animal Science: *A.S.*
Biology: *B.S.*
Dairy Science: *A.S.*
Environmental Studies: *A.S., B.S.*
Forestry and Wildlife: *A.S.*
Horticulture: *A.S.*
Natural Science: *A.A.S.*
Leisure Studies: *B.S.*
Poultry Science: *A.S.*
Pre-Veterinary Science: *A.S.*

Lord Fairfax Community College
Middletown, Virginia 22645
Agriculture & Natural Resource Technology (Agri-Business): *A.A.S.*
Agriculture & Natural Resource Technology (Natural Resource Management & Security): *A.A.S.*
Animal Husbandry: *Diploma*
Horse & Livestock Management: *Certificate*
Science (Agriculture): *A.S.*
Science (Biochemistry): *A.S.*
Science (Biology): *A.S.*
Science (Botany): *A.S.*
Science (Dairy Science): *A.S.*
Science (Entomology): *A.S.*
Science (Environmental Science): *A.S.*
Science (Forestry): *A.S.*

Science (Pre-Veterinary): *A.S.*
Science (Zoology): *A.S.*

Lynchburg College
Lynchburg, Virginia 24501
Biology: *M.S.*

James Madison University
Harrisonburg, Virginia 22801
Biology (Animal Science): *B.A., B.S., M.S.*
Biology (Ecology): *B.A., B.S., M.S.*
Biology (Entomology): *B.A., B.S., M.S.*
Biology (Physiology): *B.A., B.S., M.S.*

Northern Virginia Community College - Loudoun Campus
Sterling, Virginia 22170
Animal Science Technology: *A.A.S.*
Recreation & Parks: *A.A.S.*

Old Dominion University
Norfolk, Virginia 23508
Biology: *B.S., M.S.*
Geology: *B.S., M.S.*
Oceanography: *Ph.D.*
Psychology: *B.S., M.S.*

Paul D. Camp Community College
Franklin, Virginia 23851
Agronomy: *A.A.S.*
Livestock: *A.A.S.*

Radford College
Radford, Virginia 24141
Biology: *B.A., B.S.*
Earth Science: *B.A., B.S.*
Environmental Science: *B.A., B.S., Non-Degree*
Geology: *B.A., B.S.*
Recreation Administration: *B.A., B.S.*

Southern Seminary Junior College
Buena Vista, Virginia 24416
Animal Science (Equine Medicine & Management):
A.S.
Equitation: *Certificate*

Sullins College
Bristol, Virginia 24201
Equitation: *Certificate*

Thomas Nelson Community College
Hampton, Virginia 23670
Science (Agriculture): *A.S.*
Science (Biology): *A.S.*
Science (Forestry): *A.S.*
Science (Marine Science): *A.S.*

Virginia Commonwealth University
Richmond, Virginia 23220
Biology: *B.S., M.S.*
Biology (Pre-Veterinary): *B.S., M.S.*
Recreation: *B.S.*

Virginia Intermont College
Bristol, Virginia 24201
Biology: *B.A.*
Biology (Pre-Veterinary Medicine): *B.A.*
Horsemanship: *A.A., B.A., Certificate*

Virginia Polytechnic Institute & State University
Blacksburg, Virginia 24061
Agricultural Economics: *M.S., Ph.D.*
Agronomy: *M.S., Ph.D.*
Animal Science: *M.S., Ph.D.*
Biochemistry & Nutrition: *B.S., M.S., Ph.D.*
Biology: *M.S., Ph.D.*
Biology (Botany): *M.S., Ph.D.*
Biology (Microbiology): *M.S., Ph.D.*
Biology (Zoology): *M.S., Ph.D.*
Dairy Science: *M.S., Ph.D.*
Entomology: *M.S., Ph.D.*
Fisheries & Wildlife Science: *M.S., Ph.D.*
Forestry & Forest Products: *M.S., M.F., Ph.D.*
Genetics (Behavioral Genetics): *Ph.D.*
Genetics (Cytology & Cytogenetics): *Ph.D.*
Genetics (Animal & Plant Breeding): *Ph.D.*
Geology: *M.S., Ph.D.*
Horticulture: *M.S., Ph.D.*
Plant Pathology: *M.S., Ph.D.*
Poultry Science: *M.S., Ph.D.*

Virginia State College
Petersburg, Virginia 23803
Agricultural Technology (Animal Science): *B.S.*
Agricultural Technology (Plant Science): *B.S.*
Agricultural Technology (Pre-Veterinary Medicine):
   B.S.
Earth Science: *M.A., M.S.*
Life Science (Biology): *B.S., M.S.*
Life Science (Microbiology): *B.S., M.S.*

Washington

Bellevue Community College
Bellevue, Washington 98004
Landscape/Environmental Management: *A.A.*

Big Bend Community College
Moses Lake, Washington 98837
Agricultural Science: *A.AgS.*

Central Washington University
Ellensburg, Washington 98926
Biology: *B.A.*
Ecology: *B.A.*
Medical Technology: *B.A.*
Microbiology: *B.A.*
Wildlife: *B.A.*
Zoology: *B.A.*

Eastern Washington University
Cheney, Washington 99004
Biology: *B.A., B.S.*
Environmental Studies: *B.A.*
Medical Technology: *B.S.M.T.*
Pre-Veterinary Medicine: *Non-Degree*

Everett Community College
Everett, Washington 98201
Agriculture: *A.A.S.*
Agriculture Education: *A.A.S.*
Agronomy & Soils: *A.A.S.*
Biology: *A.A.S.*
Earth Science: *A.A.S.*
Entomology: *A.A.S.*
Environmental Studies: *A.A.S.*
Environmental Technology: *Certificate*

Farm Management: *Certificate*
Fisheries: *A.A.S.*
Forestry: *A.T.A., A.A.S.*
Forestry Aide: *A.T.A.*
Forestry Technician: *A.T.A.*
Geology: *A.A.S.*
Horticulture: *A.A.S.*
Microbiology: *A.A.S.*
Oceanography: *A.A.S.*
Outdoor Recreation: *A.A.S.*
Range Management: *A.A.S.*
Recreation Assistant: *Certificate, A.A.S.*
Recreation Technology: *A.A.S.*
Veterinary Medicine: *A.A.S.*
Wildlife Biologist: *A.A.S.*
Wildlife Management: *A.A.S.*
Zoology: *A.A.S.*

Fort Steilacoom Community College
Tacoma, Washington 98499
Animal Technician: *A.A.T.*

Grays Habor College
Aberdeen, Washington 98520
Biology: *A.S.*
Environmental Sciences: *A.S.*
Fisheries-Game Management Technician: *A.S.*
Forestry Technician Program: *A.S.*
Oceanography: *A.S.*

Green River Community College
Auburn, Washington 98002
Biology: *A.A.S.*
Forestry Technology: *A.A.S.*
Pre-Forestry: *A.A.S.*

Lower Columbia College
Longview, Washington 98632
Biological Science (Pre-Veterinary Medicine): *A.A.*
Biological Science (Pre-Wildlife Management): *A.A.*
Biological Science (Zoology): *A.A.*

Northwest College
Seattle, Washington 98101
Veterinary Technician: *Certificate*

Olympic College
Bremerton, Washington 98310
Biology: *A.S.*
Marine Science: *A.S.*
Outdoor Education: *A.*
Zoology: *A.S.*

Pacific Luthern University
Tacoma, Washington 98447
Biology: *B.S.*
Environmental Studies: *Certificate*

Peninsula College
Port Angeles, Washington 98363
Agriculture (Animal Science): *A.A., A.A.A., Certificate*
Agriculture (Entomology): *A.A., A.A.A., Certificate*
Agriculture (Forestry and Range Management): *A.A.,
   A.A.A., Certificate*
Oceanography: *A.*
Biological Science (Zoology): *A.A., A.A.A.*

Seattle University
 Seattle, Washington 98122
 Allied Health Technology: *B.S.*
 Biology: *B.A., B.S., B.S.B.*

Shoreline Community College
 Seattle, Washington 98133
 Biological Technology: *A.A.A.S.*
 Environmental Technology: *A.A.A.S.*
 Forestry Technology: *A.A.A.S.*
 Marine Biology Technology: *A.A.A.S.*
 Oceanography Technology: *A.A.A.S.*

Skagit Valley College
 Mount Vernon, Washington 98273
 Agriculture: *A.A.*
 Biological Sciences: *A.A.*

Spokane Community College
 Spokane, Washington 99207
 Animal Sciences: *Appl. A., L.A.*
 Forestry: *L.A.*
 Natural Resources Management: *Appl. A., L.A.*
 Natural Resources Management (Wildlife): *Appl. A., L.A.*
 Natural Resources Management (Parks & Recreation): *Appl. A., L.A.*
 Production Agriculture (Animal Production): *Appl. A., L.A.*

Spokane Falls Community College
 Spokane, Washington 99204
 Natural Resource Management: *A.*

University of Puget Sound
 Tacoma, Washington 98416
 Biology: *B.S.*
 Environmental Science: *B.S.*
 Natural Science: *B.S.*

University of Washington
 Seattle, Washington 98195
 Animal Medicine: *M.S., Ph.D.*
 Biology: *M.S., Ph.D.*
 Biochemistry: *M.S., Ph.D.*
 Fisheries: *M.S., Ph.D.*
 Forest Resources: *B.S., M.S., M.F.R., Ph.D.*
 Forestry: *B.S., M.S., Ph.D.*
 Forestry Recreation: *B.S.*
 Genetics: *M.S., Ph.D.*
 Landscape Architecture: *B.L.A.*
 Microbiology: *M.S., Ph.D.*
 Oceanography: *B.S., M.S., Ph.D.*
 Outdoor Recreation: *B.*
 Pathology: *M.S., Ph.D.*
 Physiology: *M.S., Ph.D.*
 Psychology: *Ph.D.*
 Wildlife: *B.S.*
 Zoology: *B.S., M.S., Ph.D.*

Washington State University
 Pullman, Washington 99163
 Animal Sciences: *B.S., M.S., Ph.D.*
 Animal Sciences (Technology): *A.S.*
 Biology: *B.S., M.S.*
 Environmental Science: *B.S., M.S.*
 Entomology: *B.S., M.S., Ph.D.*
 Forest Management: *B.S.*

 Forest and Range Management: *M.S.*
 Range Management: *B.S.*
 Recreation and Park Administration: *B.A., M.A.*
 Veterinary Medicine: *D.V.M.*
 Veterinary Science: *B.S., M.S., Ph.D.*
 Wildlife Biology: *B.S., M.S.*
 Zoology: *B.S., M.S.*, Ph.D.**
 Zoophysiology: *Ph.D.*

Western Washington College
 Bellingham, Washington 98225
 Environmental Studies: *B.S., B.A.*
 Recreation & Leisure Studies (Park Management): *B.S.*

Whitman College
 Walla Walla, Washington 99362
 Biology: *B.A.*
 Environmental Studies: *B.A.*

Whitworth College
 Spokane, Washington 99251
 Biology: *B.*
 Environmental Education: *B.*
 Environmental Studies: *B.*

West Virginia

Davis and Elkins College
 Elkins, West Virginia 26241
 Biology: *B.S.*
 Ecology and Environmental Science: *B.S.*
 Forestry: *B.S.*

Fairmont State College
 Fairmont, West Virginia 26554
 Veterinary Assistant: *A.*

Marshall University
 Huntington, West Virginia 25701
 Biological Sciences: *M.A., M.S.*

Potomac State College of West Virginia University
 Keyser, West Virginia 26726
 Veterinary Technology: *A.*

Salem College
 Salem, West Virginia 26426
 Biology: *B.S.*
 Equestrian Studies: *B.S.*

Shepherd College
 Shepherdstown, West Virginia 25443
 Biology: *B.S.*
 Park Administration: *B.S.*
 Pre-Veterinary: *Non-Degree*
 Recreation: *B.S.*

West Virginia Northern Community College - Wheeling-Weirton
 Wheeling, West Virginia 26003
 Park and Recreation Technology: *A.*

West Virginia State College
 Institute, West Virginia 25112
 Biology: *B.S.*
 Environmental Studies: *B.S.*

West Virginia University
  Morgantown, West Virginia 26506
  Agricultural Biochemistry: *M.S., Ph.D.*
  Agriculture: *M.Ag.*
  Animal Science: *M.S.*
  Biology: *M.S., Ph.D.*
  Forestry: *M.S.*
  Forestry (Forest Resources Science): *Ph.D.*
  Forestry (Recreation): *M.S.*
  Forestry (Wildlife): *M.S.*
  Plant Science (Bacteriology): *M.S.*
  Plant Science (Crop Science): *M.S.*
  Plant Science (Plant Pathology): *M.S.*

Wheeling College
  Wheeling, West Virginia 26003
  Biology: *B.S.*
  Biology (General Science): *B.S.*

Wisconsin

Blackhawk Technical Institute
  Janesville, Wisconsin 53545
  Livestock Management: *A.D.*

Lakeland College
  Sheboygan, Wisconsin 53081
  Biology: *B.A.*

Madison Area Technical College
  Madison, Wisconsin 53703
  Animal Technology: *A.A.S.*

Milwaukee Area Technical College
  Milwaukee, Wisconsin 53203
  Natural Science: *A.A.*

Mount Senario College
  Ladysmith, Wisconsin 54848
  Biology: *B.S.*

Northland College
  Ashland, Wisconsin 54806
  Pre-Natural Resources: *B.A.*
  Pre-Natural Resources (Conservation): *B.A.*
  Pre-Natural Resources (Fisheries): *B.A.*
  Pre-Natural Resources (Forestry): *B.A.*
  Pre-Natural Resources (Interpretation): *B.A.*
  Pre-Natural Resources (Wildlife Management): *B.A.*
  Pre-Veterinary Medicine: *Non-Degree*

Silver Lake College of the Holy Family
  Manitowoc, Wisconsin 54220
  Biology: *B.S.*
  Natural Science: *B.S.*
  Veterinary Medical Technology: *A.A.*

University of Wisconsin
  Madison, Wisconsin 53706
  Conservation Education: *M.S., Ph.D.*
  Dairy Science: *B.S., M.S., Ph.D.*
  Endocrinology: *Ph.D.*
  Entomology: *B.S., M.S., Ph.D.*
  Forestry: *B.S., M.S., Ph.D.*
  Genetics: *M.S., Ph.D.*
  Landscape Architecture: *B.S.*
  Meat and Animal Science: *B.S., M.S., Ph.D.*
  Natural Resources: *B.*
  Natural Science: *B.*
  Oceanography and Limnology: *Ph.D.*

Park Resource Management: *B.S.*
  Psychology and Primate Center: *Ph.D.* *
  Recreation Resource Management: *B.S.*
  Veterinary Science: *B.S., M.S., Ph.D.*
  Wildlife Ecology: *B.S., M.S., Ph.D.*
  Zoology: *M.A.* *, *M.S., Ph.D.* *

University of Wisconsin - Green Bay
  Green Bay, Wisconsin 54302
  Biology: *B.S.*
  Environmental Administration: *M.E.A.S.*
  Environmental Sciences: *B.A., B.S.*
  Global Ecology: *M.E.A.S.*
  Pre-Veterinary Medicine: *B.*
  Resource Management and Administration: *B.S.*
  Science Communication and Interpretation: *B.S.*

University of Wisconsin - La Crosse
  La Crosse, Wisconsin 54601
  Pre-Forestry: *Non-Degree*
  Recreation and Parks Administration: *B.*

University of Wisconsin - Milwaukee
  Milwaukee, Wisconsin 53201
  Biological Aspects of Conservation: *B.A., B.S.*
  Pre-Forestry (Wildlife Management): *Non-Degree*

University of Wisconsin - Oshkosh
  Oshkosh, Wisconsin 54901
  Biology: *B.S., M.S.*
  Natural Resources: *B.S., M.*
  Natural Science: *B.S.*
  Pre-Forestry: *Non-Degree*
  Pre-Veterinary: *Non-Degree*

University of Wisconsin - Platteville
  Platteville, Wisconsin 53818
  Pre-Conservation: *B.S.*
  Pre-Forestry: *B.S.*
  Pre-Wildlife Management: *B.S.*
  Pre-Veterinary Medicine: *B.S.*

University of Wisconsin - River Falls
  River Falls, Wisconsin 54022
  Animal Science: *B.S.*
  Resource Management: *B.S.*
  Resource Management (Conservation): *B.S.*

University of Wisconsin - Stevens Point
  Stevens Point, Wisconsin 54481
  Biology: *B.S., M.S.*
  Biology (Pre-Veterinary): *B.S.*
  Forestry: *B.S., M.S.*
  Resource Management: *B.S., M.S.*
  Water Resources (Fishery): *B.S., M.S.*
  Wildlife: *B.S., M.S.*

University of Wisconsin - Whitewater
  Whitewater, Wisconsin 53190
  Biology: *B.S., B.A.*
  Environmental Studies: *Non-Degree*

Wyoming

Casper College
  Casper, Wyoming 82601
  Animal Science Technology: *A.S.*
  Biology: *A.S.*
  Environmental Biology: *A.S.*
  Pre-Forestry: *A.S.*
  Wildlife: *A.S.*

Central Wyoming College
   Riverton, Wyoming 82501
   Agricultural Business: *A.A.S.*
   Agriculture: *A.S.*
   Pre-Forestry: *A.S.*
   Pre-Veterinary: *A.S.*
   Recreation & Park Administration: *A.A.*
   Wildlife Conservation: *A.S.*
   Zoology & Physiology: *A.S.*

Eastern Wyoming College
   Torrington, Wyoming 82240
   Animal Health Technology: *A.A.S.* *
   Animal Science: *A.A.*
   Biology: *A.A.*
   Farm/Ranch Management: *A.A.S.*
   Forestry: *A.A.*
   Veterinary Science: *A.A.*
   Wildlife Conservation and Management: *A.A.*

Northwest Community College
   Powell, Wyoming 82435
   Pre-Veterinary Medicine: *A.*

Technical College of the Rockies - Wyoming School of
   Animal Technology
   Thermopolis, Wyoming 82443
   Animal Technician: *Diploma*

University of Wyoming
   Laramie, Wyoming 82071
   Agricultural Business: *B.S.*
   Agricultural Communications: *B.S.*
   Agronomy (Crop & Soil Science): *M.S., Ph.D.*
   Animal Science: *B.S., M.S., Ph.D.*
   Biochemistry: *B.S., M.S., Ph.D.*
   Biology: *B.A., B.S., M.S.*
   Botany: *B.A., B.S., M.A., M.S., Ph.D.*
   Crop Science: *B.S.*
   Entomology: *B.S., M.S., Ph.D.*
   Farm & Ranch Management: *B.S.*
   General Agriculture: *B.S.*
   Microbiology: *B.S., M.S.*
   Parasitology: *M.S.*
   Plant Pathology: *M.S., Ph.D.*
   Physiology: *M.A., M.S., Ph.D.*
   Pre-Veterinary Medicine: *Non-Degree*
   Range Management: *B.S., M.S., Ph.D.*
   Recreation & Park Administration: *B.A., B.S., M.S.*
   Soil Science: *B.S.*
   Vocational Agriculture: *B.S.*
   Water Resources: *M.S.*
   Zoology: *B.A., B.S., M.A., M.S., Ph.D.*

Canada

Centralia College of Agriculture Technology
   Ontario Department of Agriculture and Food
   Huron Park, Ontario, Canada
   Agriculture Technology: *Diploma*

Dalhousie University
   Halifax, Nova Scotia
   Psychology: *M.A.* *, *Ph.D.* *

McMaster University
   Hamilton, Ontario L8S 4K1
   Psychology: *Ph.D.* *

Queen's University
   Kingston, Ontario K7L 3N6
   Biology: *M.S.* *, *Ph.D.* *

St. Lawrence College
   Kingston, Ontario, Canada K7L 5A6
   Animal Care Technology: *Diploma*
   Engineering Technology: *Diploma*
   Environmental Resources: *Diploma*

The University of Alberta
   Edmonton, Canada T6G 2E3
   Animal Science: *B.S., M.Ag., M.Sc., Ph.D.*
   Zoology: *M.S.* *, *Ph.D.* *

University of Guelph
   Guelph, Ontario N1G 2W1
   Animal and Poultry Science: *B.Sc., M.Sc., Ph.D.*
   Biochemistry: *B.Sc.*
   Biological Engineering: *B.Sc.*
   Biological Science: *B.Sc.*
   Biomedical Sciences: *M.Sc., Ph.D.*
   Biophysics: *B.Sc., M.Sc., Ph.D.*
   Botany and Genetics: *M.Sc., Ph.D.*
   Clinical Studies: *M.Sc.*
   Dairy Science: *B.Sc.*
   Earth Science: *B.Sc.*
   Ecology: *B.Sc.*
   Entomology-Agriculture: *B.Sc.*
   Environmental Biology: *B.Sc., M.Sc., Ph.D.*
   Fisheries and Wildlife Biology: *B.Sc.*
   Genetics: *B.Sc.*
   Horticultural Science: *M.Sc., Ph.D.*
   Land Resource Science: *M.Sc., Ph.D.*
   Landscape Architecture: *B.L.A.*
   Marine Biology: *B.Sc.*
   Microbiology: *B.Sc., M.Sc., Ph.D.*
   Nutrition: *M.Sc., Ph.D.*
   Nutrition and Biochemistry: *B.Sc.*
   Parks and Recreation: *B.L.A.*
   Pathology: *M.Sc., Ph.D.*
   Pre-Veterinary Medicine: *B.Sc.*
   Resource Management: *B.Sc.*
   Veterinary Medicine: *D.V.M.*
   Veterinary Microbiology and Immunology: *M.Sc., Ph.D.*
   Water Resource Engineering: *B.Sc.*
   Zoology: *B.Sc., M.Sc. , Ph.D., Ph.D.*

Univesity of Manitoba
   Winnepeg, Manitoba R3T 2N2
   Psychology: *M.A.* *, *Ph.D.* *

University of New Brunswick
   Fredericton, New Brunswick E3B 5A3
   Biology: *M.S.* *, *Ph.D.* *

University of Toronto
   Toronto, Ontario M5S 1A1
   Zoology: *M.S.* *, *Ph.D.* *

University of Western Ontario
   London, Ontario N6A 3K7
   Psychology: *M.A.* *, *Ph.D.* *

Explanation of Degree Symbols

A.	Associate Degree		D.V.M./M.S.	Doctor of Veterinary Medicine/Master of Science
A.A.	Associate of Arts		D.V.M./Ph.D.	Doctor of Veterinary Medicine/Doctor of Philosophy
A.A.A.S.	Associate in Applied Arts and Sciences		Ed.D.	Doctor of Education
A.A.S.	Associate in Applied Science		Ed.S.	Specialist in Education (Masters level)
	Associate in Arts and Sciences		J.D.	Juris Doctor - Law
A.B.	Bachelor of Arts		L.A.	Bachelor of Liberal Arts
A.D.	Associate Degree		LL.M.	Master of Laws - Law
A.F.T.	Associate in Forest Technology		M.	Masters Degree
Ag.M.	Master of Agriculture		M.Ag.	Master in Agriculture
A.O.S.D.	Associate in Occupational Studies Degree		M.Agr.	Master of Agriculture
Appl. A.	Applied Arts		M.A.S.	Master of Applied Science
A.S.	Associate of Science		M.A.T.	Master of Arts in Teaching
Assoc.	Associate Degree		M.E.	Master in Engineering
A.S.V.T.	Associate of Science in Veterinary Technology		M.En.	Master in Environmental Studies
A.T.A.	Associate in Technical Arts		M.Eng.	Master of Science in Engineering
B.	Bachelor Degree		M.E.A.S.	Master of Environmental Arts and Sciences
B.A.	Bachelor of Arts		M.F.	Master of Forestry
B.A.A.	Bachelor of Applied Arts		M.F.R.	Master of Forest Resources
B.A.S.	Bachelor of Applied Science		M.F.R.C.	Master of Forest Resources and Conservation
B.A.T.	Bachelor of Arts in Teaching		M.L.A.	Master of Landscape Architecture
B.G.S.	Bachelor of General Studies		M.N.S.	Master of Natural Science
B.L.A.	Bachelor of Landscape Architecture		M.Phil.	Master of Philosophy
B.S.	Bachelor of Science		M.P.A.	Master of Public Administration
B.Sc.	Bachelor of Science		M.R.P.	Master of Regional Planning
B.S.A.	Bachelor of Science in Agriculture		M.S.	Master of Science
B.S.B.	Bachelor of Science in Biology		M.Sc.	Master of Science
B.S.E.	Bachelor of Science in Engineering		M.S.Ag.E.	Master of Science in Agricultural Engineering
B.S.ED.	Bachelor of Science in Education		M.S.Eng.	Master of Science in Engineering
B.S.E.H.	Bachelor of Science in Environmental Health		M.S.E.E.	Master of Science in Environmental Engineering
B.S.E.S.	Bachelor of Science in Environmental Studies		M.S.E.H.	Master of Science in Environmental Health
B.S.F.	Bachelor of Science in Forestry		M.S.F.	Master of Science in Forestry
B.S.F.R.C.	Bachelor of Science in Forest Resources and Conservation		M.S.P.H.	Master of Science in Public Health
B.S.T.	Bachelor of Science in Technology		M.S.Sc.Ed.	Master of Science in Science Education
B. Tech.	Bachelor of Technology		M.S.T.	Master of Science in Teaching
C. Phil.	Candidate in Philosophy		Ph.D.	Doctor of Philosophy
D.	Doctors Degree		Sc.D.	Doctor of Science
D.A.	Doctor of Arts		S.J.D.	Doctor of Juridical Science - Law
D.F.	Doctor of Forestry		V.M.A.	Veterinary Medical Assisting
Dr. P.H.	Doctor of Public Health		★	Graduate Program in Animal Behavior
D.Sc.V.M.	Doctor of Science in Veterinary Science			
D.V.M.	Doctor of Veterinary Medicine			

APPENDIX II
Student Financial Aid

Assistance in the payment of college tuition is available in the form of scholarships, grants-in-aid, fellowships, graduate assistantships, student loans, and work-study programs. Tuition assistance is awarded in consideration of scholastic achievement, financial need, and personal character. Some forms of tuition aid also consider place of permanent residence in awarding funds.

A majority of the available undergraduate financial aid programs are administered directly by the scholastic institution attended by the student seeking financial aid. Most forms of aid are available to students without regard to their programs of study. However, curriculum restricted scholarships are available only to students who are program placed within a particular field of study. In-course awards for scholastic achievement are awarded at the conclusion of the school year based upon class ranking. Students who require part-time employment to defray the cost of schooling may be eligible for employment at their academic institutions under a federally supported College Work-Study Program. Also available are two forms of Federal Educational Opportunity Grants.

Loans available to students include the Federally Insured Student Loan Program which is administered through credit unions, banks and other eligible lending institutions. Students are not required to begin repayment of loans until graduation.

Scholarship programs are also independently administered by foundations, trusts, associations, and business firms. This form of financial aid is usually curriculum restricted and available only to students who are program placed within a particular field of study. Private institutions also offer fellowships, and grants-in-aid for graduate students.

General information on tuition assistance is available from the Student Financial Aid Office of the academic institution to which a person has made application for admission. Generally, formal action on a request for financial assistance cannot be initiated until the student has been accepted for admission. Several publications also address the subject of tuition assistance including *Scholarships, Fellowships and Loans* by Norman Feingold; Arlington, Massachusetts; Bellman Publishing Company, 1977.

The are several scholarships which directly relate to careers working with animals.

The Dog Writers' Educational Trust provides partial college scholarships to students who demonstrate an interest in careers involving work with dogs. The trust is administered by The Dog Writers' Association of America, Inc. (see Appendix IV)

The 4-H Awards Program provides $1,000 scholarships for six national winners in each of eight applicable categories: Dairy, Dog Care and Training, Sheep, Agricultural, Conservation of Natural Resources, Forestry, Gardening, and Veterinary Science. There are also special national award scholarships in agriculture, animal science, and livestock judging. Current and former 4-H members are eligible for the scholarship competition. The program is sponsored by the National 4-H Council and is administered through state 4-H offices. Information is available from the National 4-H Council, 150 North Wacker Drive, Chicago, Illinois 60606.

The Army Scholarship Program for undergraduate and graduate students provides for a commission in the Army Reserve and a monthly stipend plus tuition for pre-veterinary and veterinary school students. Upon graduation the veterinarian is required to serve one year in the Army for each year of program participation. Information is available from the Commander, U.S. Army Health Services Command, Attn: HSC-PE-P, Fort Sam Houston, Texas 78234.

Wildlife Management Institute Grants provide fellowships, scholarships, and grants-in-aid for graduate projects in wildlife ecology, management, and related fields of biology. Grant awards range from $1,500 to $3,000 annually for a maximum period of three years. Inquiries should be addressed to the Vice President, Wildlife Management Institute, 1000 Vermont Avenue, N.W., 709 Wire Building, Washington, D.C. 20005.

Environmental Conservation Fellowships provide for grants of up to $4,000 for graduate study in fields relating to wildlife, natural resources management, and protection of environmental quality. This program is administered by the National Wildlife Federation (see Appendix IV).

APPENDIX III
Career Guidance Literature

VETERINARY MEDICINE

TODAY'S VETERINARIAN — a pamphlet distributed by the American Veterinary Medical Association, 930 North Meacham Road, Schaumburg, Illinois 60196. (Price — send self addressed, stamped, business envelope)

ANIMAL TECHNOLOGY — a pamphlet available from the American Veterinary Medical Association, 930 North Meacham Road, Schaumburg, Illinois 60196. (Price — complimentary)

CAREERS FOR VETERINARIANS — a pamphlet available from the Animal and Plant Health Inspection Service, U.S. Department of Agriculture, Washington, D.C. 20250. (Price — complimentary)

ANIMAL HOSPITAL ATTENDANTS AND ANIMAL TECHNICIANS (Occupational Brief 480)—a pamphlet distributed by Chronicle Guidance Publications, Inc., P.O. Box 271, Moravia, New York 13118. (Price — $1.00)

VETERINARIANS (Occupational Brief 83) — a pamphlet distributed by Chronicle Guidance Publications, Inc., P.O. Box 271, Moravia, New York 13118. (Price — $1.00)

VETERINARIAN (Career Brief B29) — a pamphlet available from Careers, Inc., P.O. Box 135, Largo, Florida 33540. (Price — $.50)

OPPORTUNITIES IN VETERINARY MEDICINE — a book by Robert Swope, 1973, National Textbook Co., 8259 Niles Center Road, Skokie, Illinois 60076. (Price — $5.50 clothcover, $3.95 pap.)

YOUR FUTURE IN VETERINARY MEDICINE — a book by Wayne H. Riser, D.V.M., 1976, Arco Publishing Company, 219 Park Avenue South, New York, New York 10003. (Price — $1.95)

MS. VETERINARIAN — a book by Mary Price Lee, 1976, Westminster Press, Witherspoon Building, Philadelphia, Pennsylvania 19101. (Price — $7.50)

ANIMAL DOCTORS: WHAT IT'S LIKE TO BE A VETERINARIAN AND HOW TO BECOME ONE — a book by Patricia Curtis, 1977, Delacorte Press, 1 Dag Hammarskjold Plaza, New York, New York 10017. (Price — $7.95)

THE CAREER AND JOB FOR YOU AS A DOCTOR OF VETERINARY MEDICINE — a booklet available from The Institute for Research, 610 Federal Street, Chicago, Illinois 60605. (Price — $2.00)

VETERINARIANS IN TODAY'S ARMY — a pamphlet available from the Department of the Army, Office of the Surgeon General, Washington, D.C. 20314. (Price — complimentary)

ZOOLOGICAL PARKS

ZOO & AQUARIUM CAREERS — a pamphlet available from The American Association of Zoological Parks and Aquariums, Oglebay Park, Wheeling, West Virginia 26003. (Price — $.10)

CAREERS IN ZOO KEEPING — a pamphlet available from the Brookfield Zoo Chapter, American Association of Zoo Keepers, Chicago Zoological Society, Brookfield Zoo, Brookfield, Illinois 60513. (Price — complimentary)

ZOO JOBS — a pamphlet available from the Office of Education-Information, National Zoological Park, Washington, D.C. 20009. (Price — complimentary)

ZOO CAREERS — a book by William Bridges, 1971, William Morrow and Company, 105 Madison Avenue, New York, New York 10016. (Price — $6.43)

CONSERVATION

A WILDLIFE CONSERVATION CAREER FOR YOU — a pamphlet available from The Wildlife Society, Suite 611, 7101 Wisconsin Avenue, Washington, D.C. 20014. (Price — $.25)

WILDLIFE MANAGEMENT — a pamphlet available from the Wisconsin Department of Natural Resources, Box 7921, Madison, Wisconsin 53707. (Price — complimentary)

CONSERVATION WARDEN — a pamphlet available from the Wisconsin Department of Natural Resources, Box 7921, Madison, Wisconsin 53707. (Price — complimentary)

FISH AND WILDLIFE CONSERVATION AND MANAGEMENT CAREERS — a booklet available from The Institute for Research, 610 Federal Street, Chicago, Illinois 60605. (Price — $2.00)

SERVICE TO HUMANITY: A CAREER IN PARKS, RECREATION AND LEISURE SERVICES—a pamphlet available from the National Recreation and Park Association, 1601 North Kent Street, Arlington, Virginia 22209. (Price — complimentary)

WHERE THE ACTION IS — a pamphlet available from the National Recreation and Park Association, 1601 North Kent Street, Arlington, Virginia 22209. (Price — $.50)

PARK SUPERINTENDENTS (Occupational Brief 470) — a pamphlet distributed by Chronicle Guidance Publications, Inc. P.O. Box 271, Moravia, New York 13118. (Price — $1.00)

PARK RANGERS (Occupational Brief 120) — a pamphlet distributed by Chronicle Guidance Publications, Inc., P.O. Box 271, Moravia, New York 13118. (Price — $1.00)

PARK RANGER (Career Summary S128)—a pamphlet distributed by Careers, Inc., P.O. Box 135, Largo, Florida 33540. (Price—$.35)

RECREATION/PARKS ADMINISTRATOR (Career Brief B11) — a pamphlet available from Careers, Inc., P.O. Box 135, Largo, Florida 33540. (Price — $.50)

CONSERVATION OFFICER (Occupational Brief 213) — a pamphlet distributed by Chronicle Guidance Publications, Inc., P.O. Box 271, Moravia, New York 13118. (Price — $1.00)

WILDLIFE SPECIALIST (Career Brief B107) — a pamphlet available from Careers, Inc., P.O. Box 135, Largo, Florida 33540. (Price — $.50)

CAREERS FOR THE '70s: CONSERVATION — a book by Ed Dodd, 1971, Crowell-Collier Press, Macmillan Publishing Company, 866 Third Avenue, New York, New York 10022. (Price — $4.95)

YOUR CAREER IN PARKS AND RECREATION — a book by Virginia and Joseph R. McCall, 1976, Julian Messner Publishers, 1 West 39th Street, New York, New York 10018. (Price — $6.29)

GUIDE TO CONSERVATION CAREERS — a pamphlet available from The National Association of Conservation Districts, Room 1105, 1025 Vermont Avenue, Washington, D.C. 20005. (Price — complimentary)

CONSERVATION CAREERS — a pamphlet available from the National Wildlife Federation, 1412 16th Street, N.W., Washington, D.C. 20036. (Price — complimentary)

CONSERVATION CAREERS — a collection of articles available from the Soil Conservation Society of America, 7515 N.E. Ankeny Road, Ankeny, Iowa 50021. (Price — $1.50)

OPPORTUNITY IN RESOURCE MANAGEMENT — a pamphlet available from the United States Department of the Interior, Bureau of Land Management, Washington, D.C. 20240. (Price — complimentary)

BIOLOGICAL SCIENCE

CAREERS IN ANIMAL BIOLOGY — a pamphlet available from The American Society of Zoologists, Box 2739, California Lutheran College, Thousand Oaks, California 91360. (Price — send self-addressed business envelope with $.15 postage)

A CAREER IN ANIMAL SCIENCES — a pamphlet available from the American Society of Animal Science, 39 Sheridan Avenue, Albany, New York 12210. (Price — complimentary)

ANIMAL PHYSIOLOGIST (Career Summary S353) — a pamphlet distributed by Careers, Inc., P.O. Box 135, Largo, Florida 33540. (Price — $.35)

CAREERS IN BIOLOGY — a pamphlet available from the Education Department, American Institute of Biological Sciences, 1410 Wilson Boulevard, Arlington, Virginia 22209. (Price — complimentary)

BIOLOGIST (Occupational Brief 344) — a pamphlet distributed by Chronicle Guidance Publications, Inc., P.O. Box 271, Moravia, New York 13118. (Price — $1.00)

BIOLOGIST (Career Brief B26) — a pamphlet available from Careers, Inc., P.O. Box 135, Largo, Florida 33540. (Price — $.50)

ZOOLOGIST (Career Summary S18) — a pamphlet distributed by Careers, Inc., P.O. Box 135, Largo, Florida 33540. (Price — $.35)

ZOOLOGISTS (Occupation Brief 237) — a pamphlet available from Chronicle Guidance Publications, Inc., P.O. Box 271, Moravia, New York 13118. (Price — $1.00)

FOR THE HERPETOLOGIST — a pamphlet available from the American Society of Ichthyologists and Herpetologists, Division of Reptiles and Amphibians, National Museum of Natural History, Washington, D.C. 20560. (Price — complimentary)

CAREER OPPORTUNITIES FOR THE ICHTHYOLOGIST — a pamphlet available from the American Society of Ichthyologists and Herpetologists, NMFS Systematics Laboratory, National Museum of Natural History, Washington, D.C. 20560. (Price — complimentary)

OPPORTUNITIES IN BIOLOGICAL SCIENCES — a book by Charles A. Winter, 1976, National Textbook Co., 8259 Niles Center Road, Skokie, Illinois 60076. (Price — $5.50 clothcover, $3.95 pap.)

CAREER OPPORTUNITIES IN ORNITHOLOGY — an article reprint available from The American Ornithologists' Union, c/o Dr. Glenn Woolfenden, Department of Biology, University of South Florida, Tampa, Florida 33620. (Price — complimentary)

THE SCIENCE OF MAMMALOGY — a pamphlet from The American Society of Mammalogists, Bryan P. Glass, Secretary-Treasurer, The Museum, Oklahoma State University, Stillwater, Oklahoma 74074. (Price — complimentary)

CAREERS IN BIOLOGICAL SYSTEMATICS — a pamphlet available from either the Society of Systematic Zoology, c/o Department of Entomology, National Museum of Natural History, Smithsonian Institution, Washington, D.C. 20560 or the American Society of Plant Taxonomists, c/o Department of Botany, National Museum of Natural History, Smithsonian Institution, Washington, D.C. 20560. (Price — complimentary)

MICROBIOLOGY — a pamphlet available from The American Society for Microbiology, 1913 I Street, N.W., Washington, D.C. 20006. (Price — complimentary)

MICROBIOLOGIST (Career Summary S189) — a pamphlet distributed by Careers, Inc., P.O. Box 135, Largo, Florida 33540. (Price — $.35)

MICROBIOLOGISTS (Occupational Brief 135) — a pamphlet distributed by Chronicle Guidance Publications, Inc., P.O. Box 271, Moravia, New York 13118. (Price — $1.00)

CAREERS IN INDUSTRIAL MICROBIOLOGY — a pamphlet available from The Society for Industrial Microbiology, 1401 Wilson Boulevard, Arlington, Virginia 22209. (Price — complimentary)

CAREERS IN PHYSIOLOGY — a booklet available from The American Physiological Society, Education Office, 9650 Rockville Pike, Bethesda, Maryland 20014. (Price — complimentary)

CAREERS IN PARASITOLOGY — a booklet available from the American Society of Parasitologists, P.O. Box 368, 1041 New Hampshire, Lawrence, Kansas 66044. (Price — complimentary)

ICHTHYOLOGIST (Career Summary S1)—a pamphlet distributed by Careers, Inc., P.O. Box 135, Largo, Florida 33540. (Price—$.35)

ENTOMOLOGY . . . AN EXCITING SCIENTIFIC CAREER — a pamphlet available from The Entomological Society of America, 4603 Calvert Road, Box AJ, College Park, Maryland 20470. (Price — complimentary)

ENTOMOLOGIST (Career Summary S45) — a pamphlet available from Careers, Inc., P.O. Box 135, Largo, Florida 33540. (Price — $.35)

PATHOLOGY: THE SCIENCE OF DISEASE — a pamphlet available from the Intersociety Committee on Pathology Information, 9650 Rockville Pike, Bethesda, Maryland 20014. (Price — complimentary)

PATHOLOGIST (Career Summary S116) — a pamphlet distributed by Careers, Inc., P.O. Box 135, Largo, Florida 33540. (Price — $.35)

PALEONTOLOGIST (Career Summary S299) — a pamphlet distributed by Careers Inc., P.O. Box 135, Largo, Florida 33540. (Price $.35)

THIS IS THE PROFESSION OF PHARMACOLOGY — a booklet available from the American Society for Pharmacology and Experimental Therapeutics, 9650 Rockville Pike, Bethesda, Maryland 20014. (Price — complimentary)

PHARMACOLOGIST (Occupational Brief 181) — a pamphlet distributed by Chronicle Guidance Publications, Inc., P.O. Box 271, Moravia, New York 13118. (Price — $1.00)

PHARMACOLOGIST (Career Summary S19) — a pamphlet distributed by Careers Inc., Box 135, Largo, Florida 33540. (Price — $.35)

GNOTOBIOLOGY — a pamphlet available from the Association for Gnotobiotics, c/o Dr. T. D. Luckey, Department of Biochemistry, Medical Center, University of Missouri, Columbia, Missouri 65201. (Price — complimentary)

A CAREER IN NEMATOLOGY — a pamphlet available from the Education Committee of the Society of Nematologists, c/o R. S. Hussey, Department of Plant Pathology and Plant Genetics, University of Georgia, Athens, Georgia 30602. (Price — complimentary)

THE SCIENCE OF PHOTOBIOLOGY — an article reprint available from the American Society for Photobiology, Office of the Executive Secretary, 4720 Montgomery Lane, Bethesda, Maryland 20014. (Price — complimentary)

CAREERS IN PROTOZOOLOGY — a pamphlet available from the Society of Protozoologists, c/o Dr. R. Barclay McGhee, Department of Zoology, University of Georgia, Athens, Georgia 30602. (Price — complimentary)

SOURCES OF INFORMATION ON CAREERS IN BIOLOGY, CONSERVATION, AND OCEANOGRAPHY — a pamphlet available from the Smithsonian Institution, Washington, D.C. 20560. (Price — complimentary)

ANIMAL SCIENTISTS IN THE AGRICULTURAL RESEARCH SERVICE — a pamphlet available from the Agricultural Research Service, U.S. Department of Agriculture, Washington, D.C. 20250. (Price — complimentary)

ENTOMOLOGISTS IN THE AGRICULTURAL RESEARCH SERVICE — a pamphlet available from the Agricultural Research Service, U.S. Department of Agriculture, Washington, D.C. 20250. (Price — complimentary)

LIFE SCIENCES: OPPORTUNITIES IN THE FEDERAL SERVICE, ANNOUNCEMENT 421 — a pamphlet available from community offices of the U.S. Civil Service Commission or write the United States Civil Service Commission, 1900 E Street, N.W., Washington, D.C. 20415. (Price — complimentary)

ANTHROPOLOGISTS (Occupational Brief 382) — a pamphlet distributed by Chronicle Guidance Publications, Inc., P.O. Box 271, Moravia, New York 13118. (Price — $1.00)

BIOCHEMIST (Occupational Brief 132) — a pamphlet distributed by Chronicle Guidance Publications, Inc., P.O. Box 271, Moravia, New York 13118. (Price — $1.00)

BIOCHEMIST (Career Brief B101) — a pamphlet available from Careers, Inc., P.O. Box 135, Largo, Florida 33540. (Price — $.50)

ANTHROPOLOGIST (Career Summary S101) — a pamphlet available from Careers, Inc., P.O. Box 135, Largo, Florida 33540. (Price — $.35)

WHAT IS ANTHROPOLOGY? — a pamphlet available from the American Anthropological Association, 1703 New Hampshire Avenue, N.W., Washington, D.C. 20009. (Price — complimentary)

BIOPHYSICIST (Career Summary S298)—a pamphlet available from Careers, Inc., P.O. Box 135, Largo, Florida 33540. (Price $.35)

ENVIRONMENTAL SCIENCE

YOUR CAREER IN ECOLOGY — a pamphlet available from the Ecological Society of America, Department of Biology, Rutgers University, Camden, N.J. 08102. (Price — complimentary)

CAREER CHOICES — WORKING TOWARD A BETTER ENVIRONMENT — a booklet available from the U.S. Environmental Protection Agency, Washington, D.C. 20460. (Price — complimentary)

THE ENVIRONMENTALIST — a pamphlet available from the National Environmental Health Association, 1600 Pennsylvania, Denver, Colorado 80203. (Price $.50 plus self-addressed, stamped envelope)

OPPORTUNITIES IN ENVIRONMENTAL CAREERS — a book by Odom Fanning, 1975, National Textbook Company, 8259 Niles Center Road, Skokie, Illinois 60076. (Price — $6.50 clothcover, $4.75 pap.)

CAREERS IN ENVIRONMENTAL PROTECTION — a book by Reed Millard, 1974, Julian Messner Publications, 1 West 39th Street, New York, New York 10018. (Price — $5.79)

CAREERS IN WATER POLLUTION CONTROL — a pamphlet available from the Water Pollution Control Federation, 2626 Pennsylvania Avenue, N.W., Washington, D.C. 20037. (Price — complimentary)

ENVIRONMENT (Occupational Cluster Packet 506EV)—a collection of 7 occupational briefs distributed by Chronicle Guidance Publications, P.O. Box 271, Moravia, New York 13118. (Price — $2.50)

FORESTRY & AGRICULTURE

ASK ANY FORESTER — a pamphlet available from the Society of American Foresters, 5400 Grosvenor Lane, Washington, D.C. 20014. (Price — complimentary)

THE FORESTER IN YOUR LIFE — a pamphlet available from the Society of American Foresters, 5400 Grosvenor Lane, Washington, D.C. 20014. (Price — complimentary)

FOREST MANAGEMENT — a pamphlet available from the Wisconsin Department of Natural Resources, Box 7921, Madison, Wisconsin 53707. (Price — complimentary)

A JOB WITH THE FOREST SERVICE — a booklet available from The Forest Service, U.S. Department of Agriculture, Washington, D.C. 20025. (Price — $.35)

FOREST SERVICE CAREER GUIDE — a booklet available from The Forest Service, U.S. Department of Agriculture, Washington, D.C. 20025. (Price — complimentary)

WHAT THE FOREST SERVICE DOES — a pamphlet available from The Forest Service, U.S. Department of Agriculture, Washington, D.C. 20025. (Price — complimentary)

FORESTER (Career Brief B52) — a pamphlet available from Careers, Inc., P.O. Box 135, Largo, Florida 33540. (Price — $.50)

FORESTERS (Occupational Brief 88) — a pamphlet distributed by Chronicle Guidance Publications, P.O. Box 271, Moravia, New York 13118. (Price — $1.00)

FOREST TECHNICIAN (Career Summary S24) — a pamphlet distributed by Careers, Inc., P.O. Box 135, Largo, Florida 33540. (Price — $.35)

OPPORTUNITIES IN FORESTRY CAREERS — a book by E.L. Demmon, 1975, National Textbook Company, 8259 Niles Center Road, Skokie, Illinois 60076. (Price — $5.00 clothcover, $3.75 pap.)

YOUR FUTURE IN FORESTRY — a book by David H. Hanaburgh, 1974, Arco Publishing Company, 219 Park Avenue South, New York, New York 10003. (Price — $1.95)

CAREER PROFILES IN FORESTRY, CONSERVATION, ECOLOGY, AND ENVIRONMENTAL MANAGEMENT (F.S. 308) — The Forest Service, United States Department of Agriculture, Washington, D.C. 20025. (Price — $.20)

AGRIBUSINESS AND NATURAL RESOURCES (Occupational Cluster Packet 506AN) — a collection of 48 occupational briefs available from Chronicle Guidance Publications, Inc., P.O. Box 271, Moravia, New York 13118. (Price — $17.00)

EARTH SCIENCE

THE OCEANS AND YOU — CAREER PROSPECTS IN OCEANOGRAPHY — a booklet available from the Marine Technology Society, 1730 M Street, N.W., Washington, D.C. 20036. (Price — $3.00)

OPPORTUNITIES IN OCEANOGRAPHY (SIP 4537) — a booklet available from Smithsonian Institution Press, Publications Distribution Section, 1111 North Capitol Street, Washington, D.C. 20002. (Price — $1.25)

TRAINING AND CAREERS IN MARINE SCIENCE — a pamphlet available from The International Oceanographic Foundation, 3979 Rickenbacker Causeway, Virginia Key, Miami, Florida 33149. (Price — $.50)

SO YOU WANT TO BE A MARINE SCIENTIST? — a booklet available from the Wometco Miami Seaquarium, Rickenbacker Causeway, Miami, Florida 33149. (Price — $.35)

CAREERS IN THE EARTH SCIENCES — a book by Reed Millard, 1975, Julian Messner Publishers, 1 West 39th Street, New York, New York 10018. (Price — $7.29)

YOUR FUTURE IN OCEANOGRAPHY — a book by Norman H. Gaber, 1976, Arco Publishing Company, 219 Park Avenue South, New York, New York 10003. (Price — $1.95)

OCEANOGRAPHER (Occupational Brief 200) — a pamphlet distributed by Chronical Guidance Publications, Inc., P.O. Box 271, Moravia, New York 13118. (Price — $1.00)

OCEANOGRAPHER (Career Brief B187)—a pamphlet available from Careers, Inc., P.O. Box 135, Largo, Florida 33540. (Price—$.50)

MARINE SCIENCE (Occupational Cluster Packet 506MS) — a collection of 10 occupational briefs distributed by Chronicle Guidance Publications, Inc., P.O. Box 271, Moravia, New York 13118. (Price — $3.50)

FUTURE OF THE OCEANOGRAPHIC TECHNICIAN (Occupational Reprint R198) — a pamphlet available from Chronicle Guidance Publications, Inc., P.O. Box 271, Moravia, New York 13118. (Price — $1.00)

GEOLOGY: SCIENCE AND PROFESSION — a booklet available from the American Geological Institute, 5205 Leesburg Pike, Falls Church, Virginia 22041. (Price — $1.00)

GEOLOGIST (Career Summary S3) — a pamphlet distributed by Careers, Inc., P.O. Box 135, Largo, Florida 33540. (Price — $.35)

MARINE GEOLOGY — a pamphlet available from the United States Geological Survey, Department of the Interior, National Center, Reston, Virginia 22092. (Price — complimentary)

GEOLOGISTS (Occupational Brief 129) — a pamphlet distributed by Chronicle Guidance Publications, Inc., P.O. Box 271, Moravia, New York 13118. (Price — $1.00)

CAREERS IN GEOGRAPHY — a booklet available from the Association of American Geographers, 1710 Sixteenth Street, N.W., Washington, D.C. 20009 (Price — complimentary)

GEOPHYSICS, THE EARTH IN SPACE — a pamphlet available from the American Geophysical Union, 1909 K Street, N.W., Washington, D.C. 20006. (Price — complimentary)

GEOPHYSICISTS (Occupational Brief 148) — a pamphlet distributed by Chronicle Guidance Publications, Inc., P.O. Box 271, Moravia, New York 13118. (Price — $1.00)

THE CHALLENGE OF METEOROLOGY — a booklet available from the American Meteorological Society, 45 Beacon Street, Boston, Massachusetts 02108. (Price — complimentary)

PLANT AND SOIL SCIENCES

CAREERS IN AGRONOMY, CROP SCIENCE, SOIL SCIENCE — a booklet available from the American Society of Agronomy, 677 South Segoe Road, Madison, Wisconsin 53711. (Price — complimentary)

CAREERS IN RANGE SCIENCE AND RANGE MANAGEMENT — a pamphlet available from the Society for Range Management, 2760 West Fifth Avenue, Denver, Colorado 80204. (Price — complimentary)

BOTANY AS A PROFESSION — a pamphlet available from the Office of the Secretary, Botanical Society of America, New York Botanical Garden, Bronx, New York 10458. (Price — complimentary)

CAREERS IN PLANT PHYSIOLOGY — a pamphlet available from the American Society of Plant Physiologists, 9650 Rockville Pike, Bethesda, Maryland 20014. (Price — complimentary)

HORTICULTURE: A SATISFYING PROFESSION — a pamphlet available from the American Society for Horticulture Science, National Center for American Horticulture, Mount Vernon, Virginia 22121. (Price — complimentary)

HORTICULTURIST (Career Summary S132) — a pamphlet distributed by Careers, Inc., P.O. Box 135, Largo, Florida 33540. (Price — $.35)

HORTICULTURISTS (Occupational Brief 203) — a pamphlet distributed by Chronicle Guidance Publications, Inc., P.O. Box 271, Moravia, New York 13118. (Price — $1.00)

CAREERS IN HORTICULTURAL SCIENCES — a book by Dorothy and Joseph Dowdell, 1975, Julian Messner Publishers, 1 West 39th Street, New York, New York 10018. (Price — $6.29)

PLANT PATHOLOGY: A SCIENTIFIC CAREER FOR YOU — a pamphlet available from The American Phytopathological Society, 3340 Pilot Knob Road, St. Paul, Minnesota 55121. (Price — complimentary)

CAREERS IN MYCOLOGY — a pamphlet available from the Mycological Society of America, c/o Dr. Melvin S. Fuller, Department of Botany, University of Georgia, Athens, Georgia 30602. (Price — complimentary)

MYCOLOGIST (Career Summary S337)—a pamphlet distributed by Careers, Inc., P.O. Box 135, Largo, Florida 33540. (Price—$.35)

SOIL CONSERVATIONIST (Career Summary S181) — a pamphlet available from Careers, Inc., P.O. Box 135, Largo, Florida 33540. (Price — $.35)

SOIL SCIENTIST (Occupational Brief 276) — a pamphlet distributed by Chronicle Guidance Publications, Inc., P.O. Box 271, Moravia, New York 13118. (Price — $1.00)

SOIL CONSERVATIONISTS (Occupational Brief 201) — a pamphlet distributed by Chronicle Guidance Publications, Inc., P.O. Box 271, Moravia, New York 13118. (Price — $1.00)

CAREERS IN SOIL CONSERVATION SERVICE — a pamphlet available from the Soil Conservation Service, U.S. Department of Agriculture, Washington, D.C. 20025. (Price — complimentary)

PLANT SCIENTISTS IN THE AGRICULTURAL RESEARCH SERVICE — a pamphlet available from the Agricultural Research Service, U.S. Department of Agriculture, Washington, D.C. 20250. (Price — complimentary)

BOTANIST (Career Brief B112) — a pamphlet available from Careers, Inc., P.O. Box 135, Largo, Florida 33540. (Price — $.50)

AGRONOMIST (Career Summary S59) — a pamphlet available from Careers, Inc., P.O. Box 135, Largo, Florida 33540. (Price — $.35)

AGRONOMIST (Occupational Brief 179) — pamphlet distributed by Chronicle Guidance Publications, Inc., P.O. Box 271, Moravia, New York 13118. (Price — $1.00)

OTHER PUBLICATIONS

YOU AS OWNER-MANAGER OF A PET SHOP-STORE — a booklet available from The Institute for Research, 610 Federal Street, Chicago, Illinois 60605. (Price — $2.00)

SOME CAREER SUGGESTIONS FOR YOUNG PEOPLE INTERESTED IN WORKING IN THE HORSE INDUSTRY — a pamphlet available from the American Horse Council, Inc., 1700 K Street, N.W., Washington, D.C. 20006. (Price — complimentary)

ANIMAL CARE OCCUPATIONS (Occupational Brief 319) — a pamphlet distributed by Chronicle Guidance Publications, Inc., P.O. Box 271, Moravia, New York 13118. (Price $1.00)

ANIMAL KEEPER (Career Job Guide G16) — a pamphlet distributed by Careers, Inc., P.O. Box 135, Largo, Florida 33540. (Price — $.35)

BEEKEEPER (Career Summary S205) — a pamphlet available from Careers, Inc., P.O. Box 135, Largo, Florida 33540. (Price — $.35)

BEEKEEPERS (Occupational Brief 518) — a pamphlet distributed by Chronicle Guidance Publications, Inc., P.O. Box 271, Moravia, New York 13118 (Price — $1.00)

CURATORS (Occupational Brief 393) — a pamphlet distributed by Chronicle Guidance Publications, Inc., P.O. Box 271, Moravia, New York 13118. (Price — $1.00)

FISH MANAGEMENT — a pamphlet available from the Wisconsin Department of Natural Resources, Box 7921, Madison, Wisconsin 53707. (Price — complimentary)

CAREER GUIDE 2000 — a booklet relating to jobs in fishery, forestry and wildlife management distributed by the American Fisheries Society, 5410 Grosvenor Lane, Bethesda, Maryland 20014. (Price — $3.00)

FISHERIES AS A PROFESSION — a pamphlet available from the American Fisheries Society, 5410 Grosvenor Lane, Bethesda, Maryland 20014. (Price — $.25)

FISHERIES SCIENTISTS (Occupational Brief 190) — a pamphlet distributed by Chronicle Guidance Publications, P.O. Box 271, Moravia, New York 13118. (Price — $1.00)

ANSWERS TO YOUR QUESTIONS ABOUT AN EXCITING CAREER IN MEDICAL TECHNOLOGY — a pamphlet available from American Medical Technologists, 710 Higgins Road, Park Ridge, Illinois 60068. (Price — complimentary)

THE CHALLENGE OF URBAN PLANNING — a pamphlet available from the American Institute of Planners, 1776 Massachusetts Avenue, N.W., Washington, D.C. 20036. (Price — complimentary)

LANDSCAPE ARCHITECTURE, A CAREER . . . . — a pamphlet available from The American Society of Landscape Architects, 1750 Old Meadow Road, McLean, Virginia 22101. (Price — complimentary)

WOMEN IN LANDSCAPE ARCHITECTURE — a pamphlet available from The American Society of Landscape Architects, 1750 Old Meadow Road, McLean, Virginia 22101. (Price — complimentary)

URBAN PLANNER (Career Summary S118) — a pamphlet distributed by Careers, Inc., P.O. Box 135, Largo, Florida 33540. (Price — $.35)

MEDICAL ILLUSTRATOR (Career Summary S153) — a pamphlet distributed by Careers, Inc., P.O. Box 135, Largo, Florida 33540. (Price — $.35)

CAREERS IN THE U.S. DEPARTMENT OF AGRICULTURE — a pamphlet available from the Office of Personnel, U.S. Department of Agriculture, Washington, D.C. 20250. (Price — complimentary)

AGRICULTURAL RESEARCH CAREERS (Career Brief B120) — a pamphlet available from Careers, Inc., P.O. Box 135, Largo, Florida 33540. (Price — $.50)

AGRICULTURAL ENGINEERS CHANGE THE WORLD — a pamphlet available from the American Society of Agricultural Engineers, 2950 Niles Road, St. Joseph, Michigan 49085. (Price — complimentary)

ENGINEERS IN THE AGRICULTURE RESEARCH SERVICE — a pamphlet available from the Agricultural Research Service, U.S. Department of Agriculture, Washington, D.C. 20250. (Price — complimentary)

CAREER OPPORTUNITIES IN AGRICULTURAL ENGINEERING — a pamphlet available from the American Society of Agricultural Engineers, 2950 Niles Road, St. Joseph, Michigan 49085. (Price — complimentary)

PARAPROFESSIONALS: CAREERS OF THE FUTURE AND THE PRESENT — a book by Sarah Splaver, 1972, Julian Messner Publishers, 1 West 39th Street, New York, New York 10018. (Price — $5.29)

YOUR CAREER IF YOU'RE NOT GOING TO COLLEGE — a book by Sarah Splaver, 1971, Julian Messner Publishers, 1 West 39th Street, New York, New York 10018 (Price — $5.79)

NONTRADITIONAL COLLEGE ROUTES TO CAREERS — a book by Sarah Splaver, 1975, Julian Messner Publishers, 1 West 39th Street, New York, New York 10018 (Price — $7.29)

APPENDIX IV
Sources for Career Guidance

ANIMAL PROTECTION ORGANIZATIONS

The Humane Society of the United States, 2100 L Street, N.W., Washington, D. C. 20037.

Massachusetts SPCA, 350 South Huntington Avenue, Boston, Massachusetts 02130.

PROFESSIONAL ASSOCIATIONS

American Anthropological Association, 1703 New Hampshire Avenue, N.W., Washington, D. C. 20009.

American Association of Avian Pathologists, Dr. C. Hall, Secretary-Treasurer, Department of Veterinary Microbiology, Texas A&M University, College Station, Texas 77843.

American Association of Bovine Practitioners, Dr. Harold E. Amstutz, Secretary-Treasurer, P.O. Box 2319, W. Lafayette, Indiana 47906.

American Association of Equine Practitioners, Brig. Gen. Wayne O. Kester, Executive Director, Route 5, 22363 Hillcrest Circle, Golden, Colorado 80401.

American Association of Extension Veterinarians, Dr. H.G. Geyer, Secretary-Treasurer, Director, Environmental Programs, Extension Service, U.S. Department of Agriculture, Washington, D. C. 20250.

American Association of Feline Practitioners, Dr. Barbara Stein, President, 5301 West Devon Avenue, Chicago, Illinois 60646.

American Association of Industrial Veterinarians, Dr. Patrick C. Matchette, Secretary, 401 Greenwood, Waukegan, Illinois 60085.

The American Association of Pathologists and Bacteriologists, 9650 Rockville Pike, Bethesda, Maryland 20014.

American Association of Sheep and Goat Practitioners, Dr. Robert Pierson, President, Colorado State University, Fort Collins, Colorado 80651.

American Association of Swine Practitioners, Dr. F.D. Wertman, Jr., Executive Secretary, 826 Fleming Building, Des Moines, Iowa 50309.

American Association of Veterinary Anatomists, Dr. John E. Stump, President, Department of Anatomy, School of Veterinary Medicine, Purdue University, West Lafayette, Indiana 47907.

American Association of Veterinary Clinicians, Dr. Philip W. Murdick, Secretary-Treasurer, Ohio State University, Veterinary Hospital, 1935 Coffey Road, Columbus, Ohio 43210.

American Association of Veterinary Laboratory Diagnosticians, Dr. W.C. Lyle, Secretary-Treasurer, 6101 Mineral Point Road, Madison, Wisconsin 53705.

American Association of Veterinary Nutritionists, Dr. Harry E. Stoliker, Secretary-Treasurer, Allen Products Co., Inc., P.O. Box 2187, RD #3, Allentown, Pennsylvania 18001.

American Association of Veterinary Parasitologists, Dr. R.R. Bell, Secretary-Treasurer, Department of Veterinary Parasitology, Texas A&M University, College Station, Texas 77843.

American Association of Zoo Keepers, Dennis Grimm, President, Chicago Zoological Society, Brookfield Zoo, Brookfield, Illinois 60513.

American Association of Zoo Veterinarians, Dr. Wilbur B. Amand, Treasurer, Philadelphia Zoological Garden, Philadelphia, Pennsylvania 19104.

American Fisheries Society, 5410 Grosvenor Lane, Bethesda, Maryland 20014.

American Institute of Biological Sciences, Inc. 1401 Wilson Boulevard, Arlington, Virginia 22209.

American Institute of Planners, 1776 Massachusetts Avenue, N.W., Washington, D. C. 20036.

American Meteorological Society, 45 Beacon Street, Boston, Massachusetts 02108.

The American Ornithologist's Union, Inc., National Museum of Natural History, Smithsonian Institution, Washington, D. C. 20560.

The American Physiological Society, 9650 Rockville Pike, Bethesda, Maryland 20014.

The American Phytopathological Society, 3340 Pilot Knob Road, St. Paul, Minnesota 55121.

American Society of Agricultural Engineers, 2950 Niles Road, St. Joseph, Michigan 49085.

American Society of Ichthyologists and Herpetologists, Secretary: Dr. Bruce B. Collette, National Marine Fisheries Service, Systematics Laboratory, U.S. National Museum, Washington, D. C. 20560.

The American Society of Landscape Architects, 1900 M Street, N.W., Suite 750, Washington, D.C. 20036.

The American Society of Mammalogists, Secretary-Treasurer: Duane A. Schlitter, Section of Mammals, Carnegie Museum of Natural History, 4400 Forbes Avenue, Pittsburgh, Pennsylvania 15213.

American Society of Parasitologists, P. O. Box 368, 1041 New Hampshire, Lawrence, Kansas 66044.

American Society of Plant Physiologists, 9650 Rockville Pike, Bethesda, Maryland 20014.

American Society of Plant Taxonomists, Department of Botany, National Museum of Natural History, Smithsonian Institution, Washington, D. C. 20560.

The American Society of Zoologists, Box 2739, California Lutheran College, Thousand Oaks, California 91360.

American Veterinary Medical Association, 930 North Meacham Road, Schaumburg, Illinois 60196.

The Animal Behavior Society, c/o Dr. V.J. De Ghett, Department of Psychology, State University of New York, Potsdam, New York 13676.

Association of American Geographers, 1710 16th Street, N.W., Washington, D. C. 20009.

Association of Conservation Engineers, Aaron J. Lane, Secretary-Treasurer, Forestry, Fish & Game Commission, Route 2, Box 54A, Pratt, Kansas 67124.

Association for Gnotobiotics, c/o Dr. T.D. Luckey, Department of Biochemistry, Medical Center, University of Missouri, Columbia, Missouri 65201.

Association of Interpretive Naturalists, Inc., 6700 Needwood Road, Derwood, Maryland 20855.

The Dog Writers' Association of America, Inc., Sara Futh, Secretary-Treasurer, Kinney Hill Road, Washington Depot, Connecticut 06794.

The Mychological Society of America, c/o Dr. Melvin S. Fuller, Department of Botany, University of Georgia, Athens, Georgia 30602.

National Association of Biology Teachers, 11250 Roger Bacon Drive, Reston, Virginia 22090.

National Association of Dog Obedience Instructors, c/o Mrs. Mid Rothrock, Corresponding Secretary, 8439 Elphick Road, Sebastopol, California 95472.

National Association of Environmental Professionals, 1901 North Moore Street, Suite 805, Arlington, Virginia 22209.

National Association of State Foresters, Secretary-Treasurer: James Verville, Division of Forestry, Department of Game, Fish, and Parks, Sigurd Anderson Building, Pierre, South Dakota 57501.

National Association of State Park Directors, Secretary-Treasurer: George T. Hamilton, Director, Division of Parks, Department of Resources & Economic Development, State House Annex, Concord, New Hampshire 03301.

Conservation Education Association, Box 450, Madison, Wisconsin 53711.

Ecological Society of America, Department of Biology, Rutgers University, Camden, New Jersey 08102.

The Entomological Society of America, Box AJ, 4603 Calvert Road, College Park, Maryland 20470.

The Environmental Law Institute, Suite 620, 1346 Connecticut Avenue, Washington, D. C. 20036.

The Institute for Research, 610 Federal Street, Chicago, Illinois 60605.

The International Oceanographic Foundation, 3979 Rickenbacker Causeway, Virginia Key, Miami, Florida 33149.

International Society of Arboriculture, P. O. Box 71, 3 Lincoln Square, Urbana, Illinois 61801.

Intersociety Committee on Pathology Information, 9650 Rockville Pike, Bethesda, Maryland 20014.

Marine Technology Society, 1730 M Street, N.W., Washington, D. C. 20036.

The National Association of Conservation Districts, Room 1105, 1025 Vermont Avenue, N.W., Washington, D.C. 20005.

National Audubon Society, 950 Third Avenue, New York, New York 10022.

National Recreation and Park Association, 1601 North Kent Street, Arlington, Virginia 22209.

American Nature Study Society, R.D. 1, Homer, New York 13077.

National Environmental Health Association, 1600 Pennsylvania, Denver, Colorado 80203.

National Wildlife Federation, 1412 16th Street, N.W., Washington, D. C. 20036.

Sierra Club, 1050 Mills Tower, San Francisco, California 94104.

The Society for Industrial Microbiology, 1401 Wilson Boulevard, Arlington, Virginia 22209.

Society for Range Management, 2760 West Fifth Avenue, Denver, Colorado 80201.

Soil Conservation Society of America, 7515 N.E. Ankeny Road, Ankeny, Iowa 50021.

Water Pollution Control Federation, 2626 Pennsylvania Avenue, N.W., Washington, D. C. 20037.

Outdoor Writers Association of America, Inc., 4141 West Bradley Road, Milwaukee, Wisconsin 53209.

The Professional (Dog) Handlers' Association, c/o Clinton J. Callahan, Executive Vice-President, P.O. Box 207, Huntington, New York 11743.

Society of American Foresters, 5400 Grosvenor Lane, Washington, D. C. 20014.

Society of Nematologists, c/o R.S. Hussey, Department of Plant Pathology & Plant Genetics, University of Georgia, Athens, Georgia 30602.

Society of Protozoologists, Dr. R. Barclay McGhee, Department of Zoology, Society of Systematic Zoology, Department of Entomology, National Museum of Natural History, Smithsonian Institution, Washington, D. C. 20560.

Society of Systematic Zoology, Department of Entomology, National Museum of Natural History, Smithsonian Institution, Washington, D.C. 20560.

Western Interpreters Association, P. O. Box 1441, Crestline, California 92325.

The Wildlife Society, Suite 611, 7101 Wisconsin Avenue, N.W., Washington, D. C. 20014.

SPECIAL INTEREST ORGANIZATIONS

African Wildlife Leadership Foundation, Inc., 1717 Massachusetts Avenue, N.W., Washington, D. C. 20036.

Air Pollution Control Association, 4400 Fifth Avenue, Pittsburgh, Pennsylvania 15213.

American Association for Laboratory Animal Science, 2317 W. Jefferson, Suite 208, Joliet, Illinois 60435.

The American Association of Zoological Parks and Aquariums, Oglebay Park, Wheeling, West Virginia 26003.

American Forestry Association, 1319 18th Street, N.W., Washington, D. C. 20036.

American Geological Institute, 5205 Leesburg Pike, Falls Church, Virginia 22041.

American Geophysical Union, 1909 K Street, N.W., Washington, D. C. 20006.

American Horse Council, Inc., 1700 K Street, N.W., Washington, D. C. 20006.

American Medical Technologists, 710 Higgins Road, Park Ridge, Illinois 60068.

American Society of Agronomy, 677 South Segoe Road, Madison, Wisconsin 53711.

American Society of Animal Science, 39 Sheridan Ave., Albany, New York 12210.

American Society for Horticultural Science, National Center for American Horticulture, Mount Vernon, Virginia 22121.

The American Society for Microbiology, 1913 I Street, N.W., Washington, D. C. 20006.

The American Society for Pharmacology and Experimental Therapeutics, 9650 Rockville Pike, Bethesda, Maryland 20014.

American Society for Photobiology, 4720 Montgomery Lane, Bethesda, Maryland 20014.

Association of Consulting Foresters, Box 6, Wake, Virginia 23176.

Botanical Society of America, New York Botanical Garden, Bronx, New York 10458.

Conservation Education Association, Box 450, Madison, Wisconsin 53711.

Ecological Society of America, Department of Biology, Rutgers University, Camden, New Jersey 08102.

The Entomological Society of America, Box AJ, 4603 Calvert Road, College Park, Maryland 20470.

The Environmental Law Institute, Suite 620, 1346 Connecticut Avenue, Washington, D. C. 20036.

The Institute for Research, 610 Federal Street, Chicago, Illinois 60605.

The International Oceanographic Foundation, 3979 Rickenbacker Causeway, Virginia Key, Miami, Florida 33149.

International Society of Arboriculture, P. O. Box 71, 3 Lincoln Square, Urbana, Illinois 61801.

Intersociety Committee on Pathology Information, 9650 Rockville Pike, Bethesda, Maryland 20014.

Marine Technology Society, 1730 M Street, N.W., Washington, D. C. 20036.

The National Association of Conservation Districts, Room 1105, 1025 Vermont Avenue, N.W., Washington, D. C. 20005.

National Audubon Society, 950 Third Avenue, New York, New York 10022.

National Recreation and Park Association, 1601 North Kent Street, Arlington, Virginia 22209.

American Nature Study Society, R.D. 1, Homer, New York 13077.

National Environmental Health Association, 1600 Pennsylvania, Denver, Colorado 80203.

National Wildlife Federation, 1412 16th Street, N.W., Washington, D. C. 20036.

Sierra Club, 1050 Mills Tower, San Francisco, California 94104.

The Society for Industrial Microbiology, 1401 Wilson Boulevard, Arlington, Virginia 22209.

Society for Range Management, 2760 West Fifth Avenue, Denver, Colorado 80204.

Soil Conservation Society of America, 7515 N.E. Ankeny Road, Ankeny, Iowa 50021.

Water Pollution Control Federation, 2626 Pennsylvania Avenue, N.W., Washington, D. C. 20037.

APPENDIX V
Job Opportunities Announcements

Special interest journals, newsletters, and magazines have classified ad sections containing announcements of job openings in animal welfare and allied professions. These periodicals also accept for advertising, positions wanted by job seekers.

The classified ad section can be a valuable aid to the individual who is job hunting. Ads for available positions alert the job seeker to employers which are currently hiring. They also provide insight into current salaries, benefits, and working conditions. It is hoped the job seeker will discover available positions suited to his or her interests and experience.

The job seeker can inexpensively publicize his or her own availability through a classified ad. The ad provides an opportunity to be considered for a position not being advertised or otherwise publicly announced. Of course, classified ads should not be used exclusively in looking for a job. Moreover, a small number of available positions are advertised in periodicals and few employers rely upon such ads as a source of personnel.

There are substantial variations regarding the availability of periodicals featuring job opportunities announcements. Some associations mandate membership as a condition for subscribing to their periodicals. In some instances advertisement space is provided free of charge. Other publishers charge a fee for advertisements. Some publishers require that persons subscribe on an annual basis while other publishers permit the purchase of single issues.

SELECTED PERIODICALS WHICH PUBLISH ANIMAL-RELATED CAREER CLASSIFIEDS

AAZPA NEWSLETTER — A monthly newsletter which contains a classified advertisement section relating to occupational opportunities with zoos, aquariums, wildlife foundations, and wildlife preserves. Published by the American Association of Zoological Parks and Aquariums, Oglebay Park, Wheeling, West Virginia 26003. Subscriptions are available only to members. The associate member fee is $20.00 per year. Classified advertisement listings are free to members and are unavailable to non-members.

JOURNAL OF THE AMERICAN VETERINARY MEDICAL ASSOCIATION — A twice monthly journal which contains a classified personnel advertisement section relating to employment opportunities in veterinary medicine. Published by the American Veterinary Medical Association, 930 N. Meacham Road, Schaumburg, Illinois 60196. The annual subscription price is $15.00 for members and $36.00 for non-members. Single issues may be purchased at $2.50 per copy. The classified advertisement charge is $10.00 for the first 25 words and $.10 for each additional word.

HUMANE EDUCATION — A quarterly journal containing a classified personnel advertisement section relating to employment opportunities in humane education. Published by The National Association for the Advancement of Humane Education, P.O. Box 98, East Haddam, Connecticut 06423. The annual subscription price is $10.00. The classified advertisement charge is $5.00.

MODERN VETERINARY PRACTICE — A monthly magazine which contains a classified personnel advertisement section relating to employment opportunities in veterinary medicine. Published by American Veterinary Publications, P.O. Drawer KK, Santa Barbara, California 93102. The annual subscription price is $20.00. The classified advertisement charge is $1.50 per line with a $6.00 minimum fee.

OPPORTUNITIES — A bi-monthly bulletin featuring personnel announcements relating to occupational opportunities with nature centers, museums, parks, and natural science centers. Published by the Natural Science for Youth Foundation, 763 Silvermine Road, New Canaan, Connecticut 06840. Subscriptions are without charge to members and $15.00 to non-members. Classified advertisement listings are free to members and $3.00 to non-members.

AIN EMPLOYMENT OPPORTUNITIES LISTINGS — A monthly bulletin featuring personnel announcements relating to occupational opportunities with nature centers, museums, parks, and universities. Published by the Association of Interpretive Naturalists, 6700 Needwood Road, Derwood, Maryland 20855. Subscriptions are free to members and $10.00 to non-members. Situation wanted advertisements are not accepted.

VETERINARY MEDICINE/SMALL ANIMAL CLINICIAN — A monthly magazine which contains a classified personnel advertisement section relating to employment opportunities in veterinary medicine. Published by the Veterinary Medicine Publishing Company, 144 N. Nettleton, Bonner Springs, Kansas 66012. The annual subscription price is $20.00. Classified advertisement listings are free to subscribers and $.20 per word to other individuals.

SHELTER SENSE — A bi-monthly bulletin which contains a classified personnel advertisement section relating to occupational opportunities with animal shelters, animal welfare organizations, and animal control agencies. Published by The National Humane Education Center, 2100 L Street, N.W., Washington, D. C. 20037. The annual subscription price is $5.00. The classified advertisement charge is $5.00 for thirty words plus address.

ZOO REVIEW — A bi-monthly bulletin which contains a classified personnel advertisement section relating to employment opportunities in zoological park management and wildlife conservation. Published by Ralph Curtis Publishing, 2633 Adams Street, Hollywood, Florida 33020. The annual subscription price is $2.50. The classified advertisement charge is $.05 per word with a minimum fee of $1.00.

THE WILDLIFER — A bi-monthly newsletter which contains a classified personnel advertisement section relating to employment opportunities in wildlife management, forestry, and fisheries. Published by The Wildlife Society, 7101 Wisconsin Avenue, N.W., Suite 611, Washington, D. C. 20014. Subscriptions are available only to members. The annual membership fee is $12.00. Students may enroll as members for $6.00. Situation wanted advertisements are not accepted.

ANIMAL KEEPER'S FORUM — A monthly magazine which contains a classified personnel advertisement section relating to employment opportunities for zoo keepers. Published by the American Association of Zoo Keepers, National Headquarters, National Zoo, Washington, D. C. 20008. Subscriptions are available only to members. The annual membership fee is $10.00. Situation wanted advertisements are not accepted.

APPENDIX VI
Directories of Employers

Directories are in print which facilitate the task of communicating with potential employers. These directories contain comprehensive listings of nature centers, zoological parks, aquariums, animal welfare agencies, conservation organizations, and other applicable employers.

CONSERVATION DIRECTORY — A list of organizations, agencies, and officials concerned with the conservation of natural resources and wildlife. Published by The National Wildlife Federation, 1412 Sixteenth St., N.W., Washington, D. C. 20036. Price: $3.00.

DIRECTORY OF NATURAL SCIENCE CENTERS — A list of natural science centers, nature centers, museums, and other facilities which feature nature education programs. Published by the Natural Science for Youth Foundation, 763 Silvermine Road, New Canaan, Connecticut 06840. Price: $5.00.

HORSE INDUSTRY DIRECTORY — A list of horse industry organizations. Published by the American Horse Council, 1700 K Street, N.W., Washington, D. C. 20006. Price: complimentary to members and $2.00 to non-members.

DIRECTORY OF THE AMERICAN VETERINARY MEDICAL ASSOCIATION — A list of veterinarians, veterinary associations, and related interest groups. Published by the American Veterinary Medical Association, 930 North Meacham Rd., Schaumburg, Illinois 60196. Price: $11.00 to members and $25.00 to non-members.

THE AMERICAN HUMANE AGENCY DIRECTORY — A list of animal welfare agencies. Published by The American Humane Association, 5351 S. Roslyn, Englewood, Colorado 80110. Price: $35.00.

ZOOLOGICAL PARKS & AQUARIUMS IN THE AMERICAS — A listing of zoos and aquariums. Published by the American Association of Zoological Parks and Aquariums, Oglebay Park, Wheeling, West Virginia 26003. Price: $8.00 to members and $50.00 to non-members.

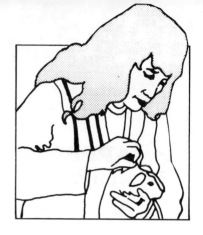

APPENDIX VII
Offices of U.S. Government Agencies

FISH AND WILDLIFE SERVICE REGIONAL OFFICES

Pacific
1500 Plaza Bldg., 1500 N.E. Irving St., Portland, Or. 97208

Southwest
Federal Bldg., U.S. Post Office and Court House, 500 Gold Ave., S.W., Albuquerque, N.M. 87103

North Central
Federal Bldg., Fort Snelling, Twin Cities, Mn. 55111

Southeast
17 Executive Park Dr., Atlanta, Ga. 30329

Northeast
1 Gateway Center, Newton, Ma. 02159

Alaska
813 D St., Anchorage, Ak. 99501

Denver
P.O. Box 25484, Denver Fed. Center, Denver Co. 80225

NATIONAL PARK SERVICE REGIONAL OFFICES

Mid-Atlantic
143 S. Third St., Philadelphia, Pa. 19106

North Atlantic
150 Causeway St., Boston, Ma. 02114

Southeast
1895 Phoenix Blvd., Atlanta, Ga. 30337

Midwest
1709 Jackson St., Omaha, Ne. 68102

Southwest
Old Santa Fe Trail, P.O. Box 728, Santa Fe, N.M. 87501

Rocky Mountain
P.O. Box 25287, Denver, Co. 80225

Western
450 Golden Gate Ave., P.O. Box 36036, San Francisco, Ca. 94102

Pacific Northwest
Rm. 931, 1424, 1424 Fouth Ave., Seattle, Wa. 98101

National Capital Parks
1100 Ohio Dr., S.W., Washington, D.C. 20242

FOREST SERVICE REGIONAL OFFICES

Northern
Federal Bldg., Missoula, Mt. 59801

Rocky Mountain
11177 W. 8th Ave., Box 25127, Lakewood, Co. 80225

Southwestern
517 Gold Ave., S.W., Albuquerque, N.M. 87101

Intermountain
Federal Office Bldg., 324 25th St., Ogden, Ut. 84401

California
630 Sansome St., San Francisco, Ca. 94111

Pacific Northwest
319 S.W. Pine St., Box 3623, Portland, Or. 97208

Southern
Suite 800, 1720 Peachtree Rd., N.W., Atlanta, Ga. 30309

Eastern
Clark Bldg., 633 W. Wisconsin Ave., Milwaukee, Wi. 53203

Alaska
Federal Office Bldg., Box 1628, Juneau, Ak. 99801

BUREAU OF OUTDOOR RECREATION REGIONAL OFFICES

Northeast
Federal Office Bldg., 7th Floor, 600 Arch St., Philadelphia, Pa. 19106

Southeast
148 Cain St., Atlanta, Ga. 30303

Lake Central
3853 Research Park Dr., Ann Arbor, Mi. 48104

Mid-Continent
Bldg. 41, P.O. Box 25387, Denver Federal Center, Denver, Co. 80225

Northwest
915 Second Ave., Seattle, Wa. 98174

Pacific Southwest
450 Golden Gate Ave., San Francisco, Ca. 94102

South Central
5000 Marble Ave., N.E., Albuquerque, N.M. 87110

BUREAU OF LABOR STATISTICS REGIONAL OFFICES

1603 Federal Office Building, Boston, Massachusetts 02203

1515 Broadway, Suite 3400, New York, N.Y. 10036

P.O. Box 13309, Philadelphia, Pennsylvania 19101

1371 Peachtree Street, N.E., Atlanta, Georgia 30309

230 South Dearborn Street, Chicago, Illinois 60604

911 Walnut Street, Kansas City, Missouri 64106

555 Griffin Square Building, Dallas, Texas 75202

450 Golden Gate Avenue, Box 36017, San Francisco, California 94102.

NATIONAL HEADQUARTERS

Agricultural Research Service, U.S. Department of Agriculture, Washington, D. C. 20250.

The Animal and Plant Health Inspection Service, United States Department of Agriculture, Hyattsville, Maryland 20782.

Bureau of Commercial Fisheries, United States Department of Interior, Washington, D. C. 20240.

Bureau of Health Manpower Education - Public Health Service, National Institute of Health, Bethesda, Maryland 20014.

Bureau of Land Management, U.S. Department of Interior, Washington, D. C. 20240.

Bureau of Outdoor Recreation, United States Department of Interior, Washington, D. C. 20240.

Bureau of Sport Fisheries and Wildlife, United States Department of Interior, Washington, D. C. 20240.

U.S. Civil Service Commission, 1900 E Street, Washington, D. C. 20415.

Department of the Army, Office of the Surgeon General, Washington, D. C. 20314.

U. S. Environmental Protection Agency, Office of Information, Washington, D. C. 20460.

The Forest Service, United States Department of Agriculture, Washington, D. C. 20250.

U. S. Geological Survey, Department of the Interior, National Center, Reston, Virginia 22092.

National Park Service, United States Department of Interior, Washington, D. C. 20240.

Soil Conservation Service, U. S. Department of Agriculture, Washington, D. C. 20025.

APPENDIX VIII
Suggested Readings

Carson, Gerald, *Men, Beasts, and Gods,* Charles Scribner's Sons, New York, N.Y., 1972. An accounting of Western man's attitudes toward animals including a review of the origins and development of U.S. animal welfare programs.

Morse, Mel, *Ordeal of the Animals,* Prentice-Hall, Englewood Cliffs, N.J., 1968. The author chronicles atrocities against animals.

Grahan, Ada and Frank J., *Wildlife Rescue,* Cowles Book Company, New York, N.Y., 1970. A biography of four persons who dedicated their lives to the protection of threatened wildlife.

Walsh, John, *Time is Short and The Water Rises,* E.P. Dutton & Company, New York, N.Y., 1968. The story of Operation Gwamba. The author, an agent for the International Society for the Protection of Animals, spent 18 months in South America coordinating the rescue of more than 10,000 animals threatened by the rising waters of a dam.

Scheffer, Victor, *A Voice for Wildlife,* Charles Scribner's Sons, New York, N.Y., 1974. An analysis of wildlife management policies and the issues confronting conservation workers.

Hediger, Heini, *Man and Animal in the Zoo,* Seymour Lawrence/Delacorte Press, New York, N.Y., 1969. An exploration of zoological park management and the relationship between zoo stock and their keepers.

Livingston, Bernard, *Zoos: Animals, People, Places,* Arbor House, New York, N.Y., 1974. An exploration of United States zoos, zoo exhibits, and daily life in a typical zoo.

Buchenholz, Bruce, *Doctor in the Zoo,* Studio Books, The Viking Press, New York, N.Y., 1974. Reviews a week in the life of the Bronx Zoo's veterinarian in residence.

Herriot, James, *All Creatures Great and Small,* St. Martin's Press, Inc., New York, N.Y., 1972. The author tells of his life as a veterinarian in rural England.

Collett, Rosemary K., *My Orphans of the Wild,* J.B. Lippincott Company, Philadelphia, Pa., 1974. Details the work of a family which established its own foundation and refuge for orphaned and injured wildlife.

Smithcors, J.F., *The Veterinarian in America 1625-1975,* American Veterinary Publications, Santa Barbara, Ca., 1975. A history of the practice of veterinary medicine.

NOTES

NOTES

NOTES